WARFIELD PRESS

PRESCOTT, ARIZONA

BEIRUT ARIZONA

Operation Fast and Furious

The Gunwalker Scandal:

Connecting Mexican Drugs, Gun Control and Islamic Terrorism

CHARLY GULLETT

BEIRUT ARIZONA: *Operation Fast and Furious*

The Gunwalker Scandal: Connecting Mexican Drugs, Gun Control and Islamic Terrorism

Copyright © 2011 by Charly Gullett

WARFIELD ACTIVIST SERIES: First Edition

Published in the United States by
Warfield Press LLC,
PO Box 12110, Prescott, Arizona 86304-2110

www.warfieldpress.com

10 9 8 7 6 5 4 3 2 1

ISBN-10   **0-9841559-4-5**
ISBN-13   **9780984155941**

Cover Art by Warfield Press Design Services: US Border Patrol Agent Brian Terry. Photographer unknown.

BEIRUT ARIZONA:
Operation Fast and Furious

The Gunwalker Scandal: Connecting Mexican Drugs,
Gun Control and Islamic Terrorism

"...I do not fear death for I have been close enough to it on enough occasions that it no longer concerns me. But I do fear the loss of my honor and would rather die fighting than to have it said that I was without courage. So I will fight you, no matter how insurmountable it may seem, to the death if need be, in order that it may never be said of me that I was not a warrior..."

Brian Terry

Table of Contents

Introduction

"...this is the perfect storm of idiocy."
–Carlos Canino, Acting ATF Attaché in Mexico

You don't hear it so much anymore, but there is an old, well-worn platitude in firearms activism: *"When guns are outlawed, only outlaws will have guns."* This has never been more poignant than in modern Mexico where private ownership of firearms for self-defense by honest citizens has been regulated into virtual non-existence, much to the chagrin of the Mexican families victimized by well-armed drug cartels and other narco-terrorists in Chihuahua, Sinaloa and pretty much anywhere near the southwestern US border.

Of course, the largely socialist Mexican government, corrupt police departments and the drug cartels seem to have an unlimited supply of weapons of every imaginable description (including military-grade weapons and munitions not available in American gun stores); weapons which they have used to murder each other and slaughter literally tens of thousands of Mexican citizens over the last few years; estimates suggest nearly 40,000 murders.

Some of them were innocent, many were not.

While this is an enormous international humanitarian problem, the really pressing issue from where I live in Arizona is that the players in this diabolical affront to sovereignty and human rights are starting to kill Americans here as well.

Unfortunately, we are now finding out that part of this violent nightmare has been fueled by renegade agents of our own government in an illegal arms trafficking misadventure. Originally sold to our congress and to a trusting and unsuspecting public in both Mexico and the US, the inter-agency operation was a well-financed, high visibility law enforcement program funded as part of a financial umbrella called Project Gunrunner. It appears the primary nexus for this profound loss of judgment and public trust was a network of career law enforcement agents, lawyers and politicians located in the US Department of Justice (DOJ) and the Bureau of Alcohol, Tobacco, Firearms and Explosives (ATF) offices located in Arizona, Washington DC and Florida. Taxpayer dollars, personnel, materiel and other government resources were systematically corrupted and transformed into an illegal and tragically deadly covert conflagration now known as *Operation Fast and Furious.*

Testimony by agents and officials in the ATF to date suggests the government's defense of this covert activity was their intent to identify and arrest the 'kingpins' of the Mexican arms trafficking industry and halt the flow of illegal weapons; in the parlance of ATF it is referred to as "disrupt, dismantle and destroy." The legal aspects of the program were created as part of a much broader DOJ program called the Southwest Border Initiative which included methamphetamine investigations by the Drug Enforcement Administration (DEA), the considerable efforts of the Customs and Border Protection agency (CBP, a.k.a. Border Patrol), the Federal Bureau of Investigation's (FBI) national firearms tracing center and the Immigration and Customs Enforcement (ICE) operations of Homeland Security to manage human trafficking as regards the international issues of illegal immigration. There is evidence the FBI was actually complicit in some of the activity through the use of paid informants, illegal use of computer resources and taxpayer dollars.

Intentionally misguided by White House, DOJ and ATF press releases which were manufactured to cloak the real program—congress and the public were also duped by the government's lapdog news cabal which willingly provided the necessary 'intellectual' air cover on the internecine elements of arms trafficking, drugs and illegal immigration flooding the American-Mexican border.

For the record, I believe the reason most Mexican citizens are forced into transporting drugs while illegally immigrating into the US is to escape the desperate economic nightmare of the dehumanizing totalitarian government-sponsored Socialism and rampant drug-related violence in Mexico. From what we see on this side of the new Maginot Line* in Arizona, Mexican illegals are for the most part good, honest, hard-working people, who care about their families and take responsibility for their own lives. They typically display a high degree of productivity and pride in their work and if they were actually legal citizens—*we would probably describe them as good conservative capitalists.* This is also the way they will be described by liberals in this country if they ever make the mistake of alienating the main-stream media (e.g. by voting Republican).

History suggests law-abiding citizens become criminals by virtue of a desperate and nearly bankrupt economy controlled by a clearly failed and corrupt bureaucracy intent on tax slavery for those who work (and a vast welfare state for those who don't), nationalized industry, fraudulent government programs and legalized Marxist redistribution of wealth and health—all coercively leveraged against its own people in order to perpetuate a small but powerful and wealthy elite.

In Mexico the average citizen's lot in life (increasingly similar to our own) is exacerbated by the routine victimization of its citizens not only by an uncaring and corrupt government but by a brutal criminal conspiracy of drug trafficking organizations (DTO's) involved in international narco-terrorism, human bondage, cultural misogyny and weapons trafficking. Both here and in Mexico, literally tens of thousands of square miles on the border have been completely overtaken by DTO's which include violent street gangs such as Mara Salvatrucha (MS-13), MEChA, the New Mexican Mafia and others who operate with total impunity from the law as illicit distribution networks for drugs, guns and money.

Coerced criminality however does not excuse nor does it justify other illegal behavior, it does not minimize or even remotely

---

* **Maginot Line;** a defensive barrier named after French Minister of War André Maginot, was a line of concrete fortifications, tank obstacles, artillery casemates, machine gun posts, and other defenses, which France constructed along its borders to protect itself from NAZI Germany prior to WWII.

mitigate the highly visible criminal element in Mexico who also crosses the border, sells drugs to our children, joins criminal gangs, assists in illegal money laundering operations, fraud, terrorism and counterfeiting—nor does it excuse illegals who arrive here only to pop out anchor babies in order to pick up free welfare and healthcare with the intent to live on the Octo-Mom gravy-train. Neither does this let illegal alien dead-beats off the hook who get drunk or stoned (or both), climb unlicensed and uninsured behind the wheel of a car and kill innocent Americans on our streets and highways—all of which inevitably drives up our taxes, taxes our patience and in a general sort of way makes us want to set our hair on fire.

The growing realization that criminality perpetrated by drug cartels that have partnered with Islamic terrorists on our southwestern border communities is a harbinger of America's future on a much wider and more dangerous scale.

Much of the argument on this side of the border repeatedly focuses on the social and economic impact of illegal drugs and immigration (problems we clearly need solve) as well as the enormous appetite for drugs widely modeled in Hollywood, Washington DC beltway and New York cocktail parties (and we must figure out how to hold this behavior up to the ridicule it deserves). But we must also begin to realize that while these issues are ugly truths and terribly critical—relatively speaking, they are only the most sanguine symptoms of a much larger and more lethal threat to America.

> *"...today, a decade after September 11th, America still does not fully understand the nature of the enemy that most threatens its citizens."*
>
> **Dr. Sebastian L. v. Gorka***

That threat is Islamic terrorism which has partnered with the Mexican drug cartel's narco-terrorism and human trafficking industry to combine Middle Eastern international arms trafficking,

---

* **THE EVOLUTION OF THE TERRORIST THREAT,** Prepared Testimony for House Armed Services Committee, Subcommittee on Emerging Threats and Capabilities by Dr. Sebastian L. v. Gorka, June 22, 2011.

fraud, counterfeiting and money laundering operations—specifically for the purpose of turning the United States into the newest member of the modern Muslim caliphate.

While there is nothing new about the openly contentious agenda of radical Islamic Jihad, nor is illegal immigration coupled with the violence of drug cartel criminality a news flash, but not enough Americans I think are actually aware of the business connection between the Mexican drug syndicate and Islamic mosques and Muslim community centers right in our own neighborhoods here in the United States. Firearms' trafficking and the scandal of Project Gunrunner is only one of these connections, but it is the one explored in depth in this research.

The overarching danger of this unholy *ménage e' trois* between the Mexican drug syndicates, renegade agents in our own government, and mystically-based Islamic Jihadists in the Middle East is that the current White House, liberal political elements in the Socialist wing of the Democratic Party, vindictive mainstream journalists, political correctness and rampant incompetence in the American government are aiding and abetting the success of both Mexican narco-terrorism and Islamic terrorist business enterprises. Elected officials are supposed to be looking out *first and foremost* for American security, sovereignty and economic interests—not running Mad Hatter schemes that contribute to victimizing citizens in foreign countries and murdering our own citizens on the altruistic altar of political collectivist ideology.

The incident that began to expose the fraud that finally connected these disparate criminal organizations for me was the murder of Arizona Border Patrol agent Brian Terry. Two rifles were recovered from the scene of that crime; rifles that the ATF now admits they intentionally (and illegally) allowed to fall into the hands of criminals *who they knew* were trafficking arms with the Mexican drug cartels.

Their plan (if you can call it that) was supposed to track firearms from their final point of *legal* sale in US gun shops and follow their *illegal* straw sale[*] into Mexico and into the hands of Mexican drug cartel kingpins. The idea was to facilitate large numbers of high-value drug lord kingpin arrests, convictions and jail-time which would ultimately end gunrunner trafficking on the border and destroy Mexican drug cartels; an aggressive goal at best. In official Obama-speak it would deny drug cartel violence *"...the tools of the trade"*.

Regrettably, they did not follow through, firearms were not followed, nor were they frequently interdicted here or in Mexico and in some cases—when they *were* discovered—the agent was told to stand down and let the weapons proceed to Mexico. Their own agents told their superiors the plan was insane and dangerous; dissenting agents were ignored and berated into compliance. As a result thousands of firearms originally sold in the US have been "walked" into the hands of Mexican drug operatives and the numbers incrementally added not only to the fraudulent and contrived computer data used to support new gun control regulations, but are now part and parcel to the milieu of murder on the border and beyond.

While two of these weapons showed up at Border Patrol Agent Brian Terry's murder still another appeared at the ambush site where ICE Agent Victor Avila was horribly wounded and his partner Agent Jamie Zapata was murdered on the way to a meeting in Mexico. Hundreds of Mexican Police and an uncounted number of innocent Mexicanos have also died as a result of what we now know was a genuinely ill-conceived gamble of lives.

Thanks to the efforts an ATF agent who decided to become a whistle-blower, two America journalists took up the investigation; David Codrea of Gun Rights Examiner[†] and Mike Vanderboegh of the Sipsey Street Irregulars[‡] have dogged this story with little

---

[*] **Straw Sale:** straw buyers or straw man sale, a law enforcement term, always pejorative, describing one who legally purchases a product but then illegally resells the same product.
[†] David Codrea at Examiner.com, accessed at http://www.examiner.com/gun-rights-in-national/a-journalist-s-guide-to-project-gunwalker
[‡] Mike Vanderboegh at http://sipseystreetirregulars.blogspot.com/

credit from the mainstream media; a media routinely recalcitrant in picking up the importance of this scandal and its connections to upper echelons of ATF and DOJ and continue to be intractable regarding connections to the shadowy international players in the Middle East.

Throughout the first half of 2011 the American public watched as ATF and DOJ stonewalled, dodged and lied to congressional investigations led by Senator Charles Grassley (R-IA) and Representative Darrell Issa (R-CA), dedicated public servants who repeatedly looked into the allegations, investigated the agencies involved and held both public and private hearings (see the Committee on Oversight June 2011 Transcript, Appendix A, pg. 165 and the July Transcript in Appendix B, pg. 219; if you are completely new to this story, a review of these congressional documents provides an excellent background to Operation Fast and Furious).

Investigators as well subpoenaed many government documents— much of it to no avail as employees of those agencies were too often under direct orders from DOJ to confound and confuse the investigation. ATF Acting Director Melson testified to this during special testimony with congressional investigators on July 4, 2011.

Worse, substantial evidence against DOJ and DEA have been filed in a US court in Illinois to subpoena other documents alleging the Sinaloa drug cartel, the largest DTO in Mexico, had actually made a deal with the US government. The filing for discovery suggests DEA agreed to provide Sinaloa operatives with ATF Operation Fast and Furious firearms and an agreement not to investigate or prosecute Sinaloa operatives no matter what crimes they committed in the US in exchange for information regarding the activities of competing Mexican DTOs sought by DEA. In those stunning court documents (see Appendix C, pg. 281), a man named Humberto Loya-Castro is identified as a high ranking member of the Sinaloa cartel who had entered into this agreement with DEA. In part that record states,

> "...weapons received by Sinaloa Cartel members and its leaders in Operation "Fast & Furious" were provided under the agreement entered into between the United States

government and Mr. Loya-Castro on behalf of the Sinaloa Cartel that is the subject of his defense..."

US v. Vicente Jesus Zambada-Niebla

This would explain one reason why ATF agents were never able to arrest and prosecute kingpins in the Sinaloa cartels and further, why agents were repeatedly given direct orders to stand down on interdictions involving arms trafficking headed for Mexico as well as all the subsequent stonewalling by ATF and DOJ regarding investigations into this scandal. This would also explain why the Government of Mexico was repeatedly not informed on any part of the operation.

And why, I would ask, in a free society, economically burdened and desperately betting on yet another platitude of government transparency called *'hope and change we can believe in'*, why would this be the case? In what was supposed to be the most transparent government in modern history, Americans have stood dumbfounded at the heavy, ham-handed Chicago Mafia-style bought-and-paid-for bureaucratic obfuscation and criminality of political operatives in the "Obama-Nation" administration.

ATF and their handlers at the Department of Justice knew, and have known for some time the ugly truth; beyond the dark underbelly of government deals with drug cartels, Project Gunrunner was a political ruse, based on the failed ideology of an ever growing government juggernaut, ferociously intent on disarming the American public. An integral part of this fraud included a strategy to ignore DOJ evidence of Islamic gun trafficking and money laundering in partnership with the Mexican drug cartels in favor of targeting American gun stores and federal firearms dealers to promote gun control as an effective ideological tool in an ongoing agenda of disarming the American public.

To effectively gain the approval of a President and an Attorney General who historically have advocated gun-control, DOJ and ATF needed a scapegoat as well as irrefutable evidence the goat was a clear and present danger. The goats in this case were law-abiding American gun stores, repeatedly identified by Obama, his willing political accomplices on the socialist left and a dutifully sycophantic media as the culprits responsible for "...*fueling extraordinary violence*" in our neighborhoods—what Secretary of State Hillary Clinton has called "...*the purveyors of violence in our country.*"

Identifying the sacrificial goat was the easy part; the constitutionally protected right of American citizens to keep—and importantly—to bear arms has been the incessant whipping boy for the social collectivists, academic leftists and liberal elites for decades. Finding evidence was a more difficult but not insurmountable problem for political professionals adept at feigned reality and foggy propaganda; they inflated what little data they had, they manufactured excuses and when necessary they lied.

The enormous number of firearms necessary to arm hundreds of thousands of cartel thugs in Mexico and the US could *never* have been facilitated by US gun shops because, I will show, there aren't enough guns in all the gun shops in Arizona—indeed in the entire Southwest—to produce that many firearms through legal retail sales. The *only* exception to this were a few large retail arms sales specifically manipulated by ATF to facilitate a fraud regarding the number of arms illegally trafficking into Mexico.

In fact, government documents discussed in this research indicate that since at least the 1970's the ATF has been aware of the real sources of large-scale arms trafficking in Mexico and it is a two-headed monster that has little or nothing to do with US gun stores.

Complicit in this enormous black market inventory of weapons are the governments of the United States and the Soviet Union who dumped literally *tens of millions* of small arms weapons and literally billions of your tax dollars into deploying small arms and heavy military weaponry into Mexico as well as Central and South America during the revolutionary period of the Cold War. But, the violent posturing of government titans during the Cold War was only one of the monster's heads.

As well, Mexican drug cartels receive illegally trafficked firearms from Middle Eastern terrorists; international narco-criminals who are not only brokering the sale of older Cold War heavy weapons (i.e. rockets, grenades, and anti-tank weapons) but are trafficking their own Communist Block (Combloc) arms and Middle Eastern drugs.

Originally this unholy partnership was created by Middle Eastern operatives to maximize profits on Mexican cartel arms sales in order to financially support the radical agenda for violently re-establishing the new Islamic caliphate in the Middle East; today that program has expanded to include the psychotic vision of a world-wide caliphate under the mystically violent control of radical Islamic Imams (and their corrupt secular business partners).

This exceedingly lucrative illegal partnership continues with both parties experiencing growth markets in drugs, counterfeiting, fraud, money laundering and violence. Mexico gets lots of military grade Combloc automatic firearms, ammunition, grenades--and through their Middle Eastern contacts—access to the expanding European black market for illegal Mexican drugs and weapons. The terrorist organizations not only leverage enormous arms profits in order to kill "infidels" everywhere, but they also gain much needed international trail access into Arizona and other border states; trails they must use to move money-laundered cash out of US mosques and Islamic community centers to further the nightmarish plan for our mystically indentured future.

The insane ATF program exposed by the death of Brian Terry and Jamie Zapata was a fraud. It was a media event manufactured with data that President Obama, Eric Holder, Ken Melson, Felipe Calderón, Hillary Clinton and others knew in October 2009 was bogus and fantastically inflated firearms trace data on weapons confiscated in Mexico and I have copies of the cables from the American embassy in Mexico to prove it.

It was a program intentionally designed to vilify American gun shops, gun laws and by way of guilt by association—American gun owners. The propaganda was magnified by a willful mainstream media, soft on terrorism and all too willing to help create a political atmosphere ripe for the socialist Democrat's favorite self-delusion for re-election—sweeping new gun control; and as you will see, I have copies of the ATF emails to prove that as well.

As an institution, both the government and the media have failed their inherently fundamental responsibilities to protect America militarily and intellectually. Importantly they have failed to adequately inform us of the well-organized, international and strategically planned Middle Eastern threat to destroy America.

This tragedy of failed American values and ethics begins on a winter's night in the Tumácacori Highlands in Arizona—but be prepared; it follows a brutal and violent path in Mexico, travels along dark connections in the radical Islamic communities in Central and South America and it ends in the Middle East along with the fate of America and our children's future.

Hell's Gate

"The unwillingness of this Administration – most specifically the Bureau of Alcohol, Tobacco, and Firearms – to answer questions about this deadly serious matter is deeply troubling. Allegations surrounding this program are serious and the ability of the Justice Department to conduct an impartial investigation is in question."

Rep. Darrell Issa (R-CA)[*]

As children we are told the great struggle of humanity from the beginning of time is gladiated between good and evil. Evil we are told often hides behind a thinly manufactured veil of fraud, a magician's sleight of hand, a shell game that lulls us into thinking our virtues—the important actions we take to perpetuate patriotic American values—that these virtues are able to succeed in the face of evil's sin. In fact the success rate is not in our favor.

Reality periodically reminds us that in the end, it is all pretty much a crap shoot; that particularly in politics, there is no good versus evil; only degrees in the corruption of power and the eternal victimization of our innocence through the fog of media-induced self-denial and charade.

On December 14, 2010, Brian Terry got up, probably showered and shaved, maybe had a cup of coffee and then dressed for the day ahead. He and his wife were planning a Christmas trip home to Michigan in two weeks and they probably shared small talk about family, holiday gifts and juggling work schedules. At some point, he kissed his wife goodbye and went to work like good taxpaying Americans everywhere. Unlike most of us, he was wearing a government issued semi-automatic handgun; Brian Terry was a soldier in the war against international narco-terrorism.

---

[*] **Darrell Edward Issa** (b. November 1, 1953) is the U.S. Representative for California's 49th congressional district and is the Chairman of the US House of Representatives Committee on Oversight and Government Reform.

He was optimistic about his work; he was well-trained and well equipped, in fact, enthusiastic about being on the right side of the war and mentally prepared to do whatever was required. Like the optimism of every soldier going into every bloody conflict in history, it was a war he fully expected to win.

Today was not going to be his day.

Terry was a very proud member of the US Customs and Border Protection (CBP) bureau, commonly known as the Border Patrol. He had joined the organization in 2006 and had come up through the ranks, earning membership in the elite BORTAC (Border Tactical) law enforcement team* detailed out of the Naco, Arizona duty station. A big, muscular athletic type standing over six feet, Terry had survived four challenging years in the U.S. Marine Corps—including a combat tour in Iraq during Operation Desert Storm—he had gone on to college, and then served nine honorable years as a police officer in Lincoln Park, Michigan.

Although all large government organizations have incipient problems, the CBP itself has a long and honorable history. President George Washington, signed the Tariff Act of July 4, 1789, which authorized the collection of duties on imported goods; four weeks later, on July 31, no less than the fifth act of Congress established the Border Patrol's original organization, the United States Customs Service.

As over-reaching taxation was considered repugnant for early Americans, for the next 125 years the US Customs Service was the primary source of government funds and footed the bill for the lion's share of our nation's early growth as well as infrastructure. In March, 2003, and as a direct result of the September 11, 2001 Islamic terrorist attack on America, the Customs Service along with other elements of law enforcement was reorganized to become part of the U.S. Department of Homeland Security.

---

* **BORTAC** (Border Tactical) agents are a sort of force multiplier for the Border Patrol; they must not only be highly capable fighters, they must also intimately know and be able to operate for long periods in the brutal desert terrain used by cartels to hide their criminal activities.

The CBP cuts an incredibly wide swath when it comes to law enforcement; they have a workforce of more than 43,000 sworn federal agents and officers operating within a total workforce of over 61,000 employees, including management, officers, agriculture specialists, aircraft pilots, trade specialists, mission support staff, computer and information technology personnel, canine enforcement officers, farriers and enforcement agents.

U.S. Customs and Border Protection as an important arm of Homeland Security is currently charged with regulating and facilitating the rather large tasks of monitoring international trade, collecting import duties, and enforcing many U.S. regulations including protecting United States agricultural and economic interests from harmful pests and diseases, and protecting American businesses from intellectual property theft, fraud and illegal trade.

While its primary mission is preventing terrorists and terrorist weapons from entering the United States, CBP is also importantly responsible for apprehending individuals attempting to enter the United States illegally, stemming the flow of illegal drugs, money laundering, human trafficking and other contraband. They oversee nearly 300,000,000 people entering and exiting the United States each year.

Although it is not surprising given the task they are responsible for, it is not well-known that CBP is the largest law enforcement agency in the United States with an annual appropriation budget of $1.4 billion dollars.[1]

The night Terry was killed, he and several other CBP agents were dispatched to a very remote and mountainous area of southern Arizona called Peck Canyon (Figure 1); it is about 12 miles due north of the international border with Mexico. The major US/Mexico border crossing at Nogales is about 15 miles southeast of the canyon. The local area is called Rio Rico and is a well-known illegal drug trafficking and smuggling corridor that intersects with US Interstate 19 and then follows the old Santa Cruz river drainage north to where it connects with the *Tohono O'odham's* San Xavier reservation on the southwestern edge of the Tucson AZ city limits.

For the most part, the narco-terrorists do not use the well-watched and heavily inspected border crossing at Nogales unless they absolutely have to do so; they prefer the road less travelled and for this reason, illegal crossings in this backcountry area are more likely moving to the south across the *Pajarito Mountains* as their local entry point to the US market.

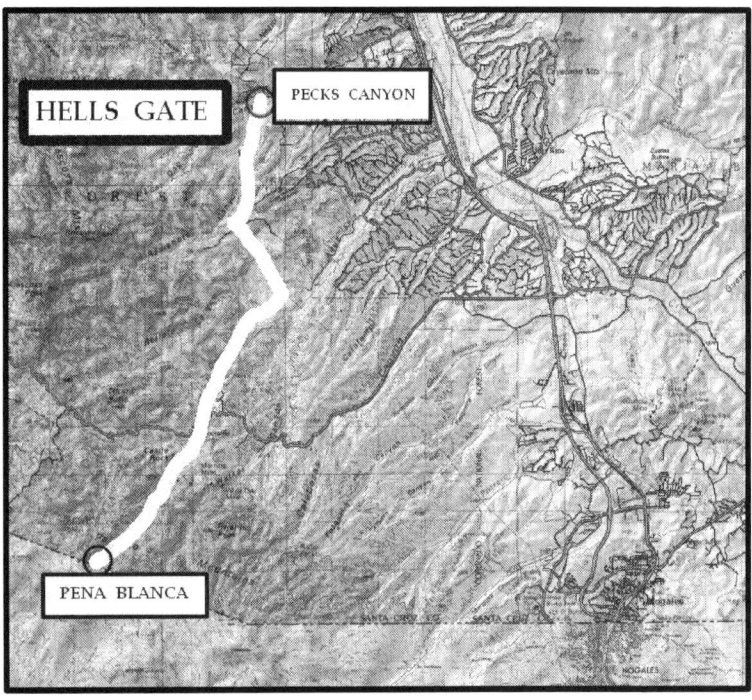

Figure 1: Hells Gate: the trail north from Pena Blanca to Pecks Canyon; about 12 miles. The international border at Nogales is at bottom right. Map Source: National Geographic TOPO!

The Pajarito Mountain terrain between Peña Blanca Canyon and Peck Canyon is exceedingly primitive with seasonal water drainages forming most of the canyons; at best, only four-wheel drive trails provide any kind of motorized access at all and in the area near the border there isn't even a dirt two-track in most places. In fact, the highest mountain in this primitive range is

Pajarito Peak* only a mile and half east of Peña Blanca canyon. This is not however an unknown route into the southwest from Mexico and has a long history of both legal and illegal activity.

This canyon and others like it are part of a complex system of trade routes that have existed in the southwestern US and Mexico for over 1000 years. They originally connected the ancient Mayan, Zapotec and Mimbres cultures to the Hohokam pueblos in Arizona; ancient stone ruins still mark these pre-historic trails which in this case begin in the *Sierra La Esmeralda* Mountains in Mexico's northern Sonora desert. Part of the *Sierra Madre Occidental,*[†] the entire geographic area from the international border at Sierra La Esmeralda extending north through the Pajarita to the *Atascosa Montañas*, Peck Canyon and the *Tumacácori Montañas* is known collectively as the Tumacácori Highlands.

Besides the usual collection of cactus and other sharp pointed vegetation, the highlands around Rio Rico where Terry was murdered are filled with both two and four legged predators. In Arizona the area is well-known for its *Cuatros Gatos* (the four cats) population of mountain lions, ocelot, bobcat, and (rarely) jaguar. The Tumacácori Highlands, the drug cartels, arms trafficking and illegal immigration all come together at the highest elevation of Peck's Canyon; it is called Hell's Gate.[‡]

The area also has a long pre-history of violence which began over 500 years ago between the aboriginal *O'odham* and invading northern Athabascan Apaches, and continued during the historical period with the 16th century Spanish entrada. Two major rebellions against the Spanish authority in the 1660s and 1750s, rivaled in

---

* **Pajarito Peak** at 5,236 feet (1,596 m)
† **Sierra Madre Occidental**, a geographic cordillera of coastal mountains that begins in South America and extends north through Central America into Guanajuato near the trans-Mexican volcanic belt (*Eje Volcánico* Transversal) in southern Mexico and then north to the Arizona border where it connects with American Rocky Mountains and other coastal ranges that reach all the way to Alaska. It is collectively known as the American cordillera and serves as the western geological infra-structure for all three continents.
‡ **Hell's Gate**: 31° 29.26 N, 111° 9.325 W

scale the bloody 1680 Pueblo Rebellion in northern New Mexico and Arizona (territory then claimed as New Spain).*

The armed resistance initially prevented increased incursions on a frontier area the Spanish called *Pimería Alta*. As the Spanish Empire attempted to expand its ideological hegemony into the edges of the American southwest, a string of Catholic missions were established to support their economic agenda for the change everyone would believe in (or else). The Catholic mission *San José de Tumacácori*† was established in 1691 by Father Eusebio Francisco Kino making it the site of the oldest Jesuit mission in southern Arizona. It was established at an ancient native *O'odham* settlement on the east side of the Santa Cruz River just a short distance north of where Terry was killed.

Although culturally inter-related, the various subgroups of the *O'odham* were not united at the time of the Spanish over-reach. However, after only a short period of time with the Spanish in charge of often brutal religious conversion, the *O'odham* decided to decline the spiritual opportunity for Spanish enlightenment and low levels of violence began escalating in 1684 with the Seri Revolt‡ in Sonora. Finally Luis Oacpicagigua (a.k.a. Luis of Sáric, one of the southwest's first community organizers) led the second violent *O'odham* uprising against the Spanish in 1751.§

---

* **Pueblo Revolt of 1680** was an uprising of the Pueblo people against Spanish colonization of the Americas in the New Spain province of New Mexico.

† **Mission San José de Tumacácori**; originally called *San Cayetano de Tumacácori.*

‡ **Seri Revolt** occurred during the 17th century when Jesuit missionaries attempted to confine the Seri to small areas around the Spanish missions in order to make farmers and convert them to Christianity. This was not acceptable to most Seris who were not inclined to agriculture. Those who attempted to leave the missions were pursued by Spanish military, returned, and severely punished. Whole families were arrested at various times and their women deported to Spanish colonies in Guatemala and forced into slavery and prostitution.

§ **Luis of Sáric**: a charismatic leader, Luis began the task of uniting the *O'odham* groups which at the time numbered greater than 10,000 indigenous inhabitants. The opening gamut of rebellion was the killing of 18 settlers lured to Oacpicagigua's home in Sáric. In the ensuing three months, Oacpicagigua and more than a hundred other men attacked the mission at Tubutama, and other Spanish settlements; in all more than a hundred settlers were killed. The rebellion lasted about one year.

Although it ultimately failed, the various tribal sub-groups of the *O'odham* on both sides of the present border became united in common dissent against what border anarchists now refer to as "artificial borders," political propaganda that has survived to this day and continues to fuel controversies associated with illegal border crossings.

For instance, one of the things Brian Terry watched with mixed emotions was the radical O'odham Solidarity Across Borders Collective (OSABC, Figure 2) who organized an activist sit-in demonstration on May 21, 2010. The event not only disrupted but actually shut down operations at CBP Border Control headquarters in Tucson in protest of what the anarchists call "militarization of indigenous lands".

The activists were charged with the standard law enforcement *tour d' force*; trespass and disorderly conduct. After lawyering up the OSABC defense team discovered the original trespassing charge had been incorrectly filed by the state prosecutor. The defense then filed a motion to dismiss the charge of criminal trespassing, which the court granted. The legal defense team, William G. Walker and Jeffrey J. Rogers, argued that the remaining charge of disorderly conduct did not apply because it did not meet any of the statutes of the charge. After less time than it took to acquit Casey Anthony, the Tucson judge found the six not guilty, acquitted on all charges and they were released (see Figure 2).

Figure 2: O'odham Solidarity Across Borders Collective (OSABC) photo-op.

"Today's not guilty verdict shows that we, as O'odham, are not the ones who are disorderly. It is the Border Patrol, the Department of Homeland Security, and the various levels of government that perpetrate the violence in our communities...When will the institutions, whose conduct continues for more than 500 years of trespassing, that terrorize indigenous and migrants communities, be held accountable?"

Alex Soto, OSABC border anarchist*

"No state entity can deny peoples' inherent right to freedom of movement...Borders are a colonial weapon used to continue the genocide of indigenous people and their culture...This results in the criminalization of those who defy borders through living their lives traditionally. You see the forced relocation of families from borders all around the world. Today we say no more to this criminalization of people."

Marisa Duarte, another OSABC border anarchist†

Perhaps you missed the words "corrupt Mexican government," "terrorism" and "drug cartel" in Soto's description of trespass and the perpetuation of violence; I know I did. It might also strike you as odd that Soto's charge of 500 years of *trespassing* does sort of require a border in order to be trespassed. It would appear only his borders are nescient. And can you imagine how Brian Terry felt when he read Duarte's comment about borders being a colonial weapon to continue genocide. This political diatribe is diagnostic of the indigenous hatred that Terry, Zapata and all members of US law enforcement are up against enforcing the rule of law on the border; a rule of law that protects the O'odham, Soto and Duarte's freedom of speech even when it promotes anarchy.

---

* **O'odham Solidarity Across Borders Collective** (OSABC) accessed on July 1, 2011 at: http://oodhamsolidarity.blogspot.com/
† **Ibid.**

So, with an unfamiliar name like O'odham and a radical anarchist agenda, who exactly are these guys and how do they figure into the equation of illegal drugs and terrorism?

First of all, they claim to be culturally descended from a group archaeologically known as the *Hohokam.** The *Akimel O'odham* (a.k.a. "River People" largely located along the Gila River area in Arizona and anthropologically and traditionally known as the *Pima*) are an important subgroup of the O'odham culture which also includes their *Onk Akimel O'odham* river cousins in the Salt River area and the officially unrecognized *Hia C-ed O'odham* ("People of the Sand") in western Arizona. And finally there are the *Tohono O'odham†* (or "People of the Desert") whose borders constitute no less than 4500 square miles neatly chopped out of the center of southern Arizona and northern Mexico. Tohono O'odham territory is the only Native American reservation to span the highly ventilated international border and runs deep into Mexico; it contains more ancient overland trade routes than any other single Native American territory in the southwest; a situation that has not escaped the attention of a wide variety of criminals.[2] This same pan-O'odham border is part of the disputed territory in a war between two major Mexican drug cartels that has killed 40,000 Mexicans in the last few years. It is also the violence of this war that ultimately killed Brian Terry and Jamie Zapata.

The Tohono O'odham Nation perceives the border not only as an impediment to their way of life, but restrictive to tribal freedoms.

---

* **Hohokam** is a derivative of the O'odham word "Huhugam" (pronounced hoo-hoo-gahm) which is literally translated as "those who have gone before" but meaning "the ancestors". Their ancestral claims, primarily used to leverage land holdings has been disputed; their own traditional history claims they came to the Arizona area 300 years ago, but the Hohokam were in the Phoenix valley nearly two-thousand years ago and their Sobaipuri descendants were in the area when the Spanish arrived. You'd think these guys could read a history book.

† **Tohono O'odham** have traditionally been called the *Papago* (meaning literally "tepary-bean eater") although this term has been despised by them for many years as it was applied to them by the conquistadores, who had heard them called this by tribal bands unfriendly to the Tohono O'odham. Locals often refer to these tribal members as the "TO's".

21

"...the U.S.-Mexico border has become 'an artificial barrier to the freedom of the Tohono O'odham.'"

Tohono O'odham Nation website*

No friend to the US Government, the Tohono O'odham Nation to this day considers their land illegally "occupied" by the United States government,[†] and their people do not recognize the US border as valid; a situation heavily leveraged by the Obama administration, the Mexican drug cartels and Islamic terrorists.

In fact, recent evidence indicates so much Mexican marijuana is moving through the Tohono O'odham reservation—located just south of Phoenix and Tucson—the DOJ found it necessary in their Executive Summary of the National Drug Threat Assessment [2010] to provide a good old Obama "shout-out" to the Tohono O'odham Nation amidst all those who support the narco-terrorist traffickers throughout the entire southwest border region.

> *"Marijuana production [has] increased in Mexico, resulting in increased flow of the drug across the Southwest Border, including through the Tohono O'odham Reservation in Arizona."*

National Center for Drug Intelligence (DOJ)[‡]

I intend to demonstrate in this research it is a dangerous fallacy to pretend Islamic terrorists do not exist in partnership with Mexican drug trafficking organizations who move contraband both ways across Tohono O'odham lands and through our borders. It is also dangerous to further assume that the drug cartels are merely feeding the casual entertainment habits of aging liberal hippies, leftist politicians and mainstream journalists who are smoking a few joints and staring lovingly at their antique lava lamps after work.

---

* **Tohono O'odam Nation** website, accessed June 22, 2011 at http://www.tonation-nsn.gov/history_culture.aspx
† **Ibid**
‡ **National Drug Threat Assessment** [2010, updated] accessed on June 24, 2010 at: http://www.justice.gov/ndic/pubs38/38661/38661p.pdf

According to a DOJ report, the clear drug of choice in the western states is Mexican-sourced Methamphetamine while the addicts in the eastern US still largely prefer to snort cocaine up their hose. Evidence suggests supplying the east coast habit with cocaine remains the single largest drug threat in America with nearly 40% of all illegal drugs moving across our borders destined specifically for the east coast.*

However, it is equally fallacious to ignore the fact that those who are soft on Islamic terrorism and their Mexican partners in the enormous marijuana and related drug industry south of the border—which is primarily supported by aging hippie liberals, street gangs, border anarchists and the Democratic Party—helped put a bullet into Brian Terry. Every latter-day 1960's freak that lights up a joint, snorts a line of cocaine or sticks a needle in his arm might just as well be pulling the trigger on an AK47 in support of the Mexican drug cartels and the radical Islamic Jihad against America.

Arizona Governor Jan Brewer (Figure 3) demanded that the Federal government do something about protecting Americans from the violence associated with this region. When Obama turned his large deaf ears to the problem, Brewer helped enact legislation (AZ SB1070) hoping to give local law enforcement the tools it needed to stem the flow of criminality into and out of Arizona. Both Senator John McCain and Governor Brewer asked for 3000 armed military troops to help enforce federal law; we got 500 *unarmed* National Guard on direct orders from the White House to supply technical support only. The President said he'd get back to them later with an update on his border policy.

The snowflake response from the "Chicago dipstick in charge" was to arrogantly and defiantly put up a road sign within 80 miles of the border and only 30 miles from Phoenix warning Americans that southern Arizona was too dangerous for any kind of travel. One of the signs warns residents and visitors alike that "smuggling and

---

* **National Drug Threat Assessment** [2010, updated] accessed on June 24, 2010 at: http://www.justice.gov/ndic/pubs38/38661/38661p.pdf

illegal immigration may be encountered in this area." Another says "travel not recommended" due to the presence of "active drug and human smuggling" routes.

Figure 3: Gov. Jan Brewer on Obama border solution. *"...does this look safe to you?"*

> *"Well, we finally got the message—these signs. These signs, calling our desert an active drug and human smuggling area. These signs warning people of danger and telling them to stay away. Washington says our border is as safe as it has ever been. Does this look safe to you?"*
>
> **Arizona Gov. Janet Brewer**

Then, in an unparalleled move to exacerbate an already untenable situation, Eric Holder's DOJ filed suit against Arizona for trying to protect its own citizens from syndicated criminal activity.

The two Arizona border officials carrying most of the water in place of the federal government are Sheriff Paul Babeu (Pinal County) and Sheriff Larry Dever (Cochise County); like Brian Terry they are both career law enforcement professionals. These two sheriffs are attempting to do with minimal economic backing and virtually no federal support what the federal government has repeatedly refused to do—protect Arizona citizens, enforce the rule law as defined in the US Constitution and defend American sovereignty.

Figure 4: Sheriff Paul Babeu at Yavapai Tea Party benefit for Border Sheriffs rally, Prescott Arizona March 3, 2011.

Understand this; the federal government has effectively ceded control and possession of southern Arizona to the drug cartels, human traffickers and other terrorists. Literally hundreds of square miles of the US are now off-limits to Americans but are free-travel zones for international criminals.

By the spring of 2011, it was clear that the border issue was becoming increasingly untenable in the American consciousness. On the same day Eric Holder testified that he didn't know anything about the illegal aspects of an ATF government program known as Project Gunrunner, Sheriff Babeu made the following comments at a Tea Party benefit in Prescott Arizona; the comments according to my notes were received by a stunned audience.

> "Our own government has become our enemy and is taking us to court at a time when we need help...If the president would do his job and secure the border; send 3,000 armed soldiers to the border, finish the fence and stop the illegal immigration and the drug smuggling and the violence, we wouldn't even be in this position...forcing us to take matters into our own hands. Instead the government has put up signs warning us about 'dangerous' immigrants.

"What's very troubling is the fact that at a time when we in law enforcement and our state need help from the federal government, instead of sending help they put up billboard-size signs warning our citizens to stay out of the desert in my county because of dangerous drug and human smuggling and weapons and bandits and all these other things and then, to make it worse than it already is they drag us into court. My question is "...why is the federal government putting up signs warning us to stay away from 'dangerous drug and human smuggling and weapons and bandits' instead of actively protecting us from those dangers? And, to top it all off, when some form of law enforcement tries to do just that our Department of Justice comes down on us with a lawsuit for overstepping our bounds. This is Asinine

"...and shame on the President of the United States for attacking us in law enforcement for trying to do our jobs...Never before in the history of the United States has the President come after law enforcement. We saw this in Cambridge Massachusetts when he accused the police of acting stupidly, he kicks law enforcement in the chops and he didn't even have the facts. He accuses us of having a history in law enforcement of disproportionately harassing blacks and Hispanics. Then he hammers us with this story of law enforcement harassing a father and his child walking down the street holding hands eating an ice cream cone...you can't get a more innocent image in your mind...this is unacceptable; but this isn't some drunk complaining to his friends in a bar about a speeding ticket, this is the leader of our country...to plant that distrust in the minds of the American people...How are we to raise our children to respect law enforcement if he's putting out these stories that we're the bad guys, Arizona is the bad guy—this is crazy."

Sheriff Paul Babeu*

---

* **Yavapai Tea Party Benefit for the Border Sheriffs**: March 3, 2011, Prescott AZ.

All of the American border patrol agents involved in the operation the night Terry was killed knew what they were up against both in terms of the political situation as well as the dangers of the terrain and the possibilities of a lethal encounter; like other elite law enforcement units, they were all mentally prepared and tough as a two dollar steak.

That night, a gang of five well-armed low-level thugs (known as rip-crews) were preying on their fellow Mexican émigrés by assaulting, raping and robbing both illegals and rival drug trains as they crossed the Arizona border along the Peck Canyon smuggling corridor northwest of Nogales. Each of the cartel criminals was carrying a military grade high power AK47 rifle. Law enforcement in border confrontations used to be a highly dangerous and risky activity *for the criminals;* not so much anymore.

Contemporary border patrol management, seeing themselves as sensitive to the complex issues of diversity and tolerance of minority criminals, anarchists and drug dealers, had ordered Terry and the rest of the BORTAC units to remove the leathal ammunition from their firearms and to use bean bag ammunition as a *less-lethal* deterrent against violent adversaries; criminal adversaries who actually don't value the use of beans outside of their traditional context. Bean bag loads in firearms do make a lot of noise and they hurt if you get hit with one—they may even cause a bad bruise—but they do very little in terms of real incapacitation against a well-armed, motivated and possibly drug-crazed or mystically inspired enemy who fully intends to kill you.

As you are about to see, this is the terrain that defines the dangerous stand-off liberal's now call the war on man-caused disasters. On one side you have the bad guys who get high-powered rifles courtesy of the US government; rifles as it turns out that were purchased with Obama bailout money at the expense of the American taxpayer. Islamic Hezbollah terrorists move freely across O'odham territory on our southern border transporting money to fund terrorism with cash donations made by American mosques. The President of the United States along with other border criminals actively pursues a politically motivated ideological agenda to denigrate the only people that stand between us, violent border chaos and American sovereignty, all the while finding nothing wrong with a new cash-cow mosque in New York City at Ground Zero.

Attorney General Eric Holder claims he doesn't know spit about any of this (a clear vote for the American people between incompetence and inchoate stupidity). ATF we now know for at least two years prior to Terry's murder was using paid informants of the FBI to help them move military style weapons into Mexico while Secretary of Homeland Security Janet Napolitano is out telling *everybody* our borders are safer than ever—and the good guys...what do they get?

They get *frijoles* to load bean bags into their firearms—oh yeah, and the best funeral Obama's political correctness and institutionalized ideology can buy for their families.

Trail of Tears

"Earlier this year, the Government Accountability Office issued a report that the Border Patrol has achieved operational control of 44 percent of the southern border. Of that, only 15 percent is under full control."

NPR, 2011

In 2009 President Barack Hussein Obama, Attorney General Eric Holder and Janet "Man-caused Disasters" Napolitano began to publically posit border violence as the fault of US gun dealers who were helping to illegally traffick firearms into the hands of Mexican criminal operatives. The increasingly inflated and often repeated statistic routinely parroted by Democratic Party apparatchiks, government officials and media lapdogs was this: *"...90% of all firearms captured in drug cartel operations and confiscations came from US firearms dealers."*[*]

An excellent example was this 2009 main stream media excerpt:

"The US Bureau of Alcohol, Tobacco, Firearms, and Explosives (ATF) reports that more than 90 percent of guns recovered in Mexico are traced back to the US. That includes thousands of semi-automatic rifles or other high-powered weaponry – typically purchased in stores or at guns shows legally in the US and smuggled over the border, usually in a pattern called "ant traffic" – so-named because they trickle in under car seats a few at a time."

Christian Science Monitor[†]

An eerily similar statement was offered from President Obama after a meeting with Mexican President Felipe Calderón reported in the Washington Post in April 2009.

---

[*]CNSNews,
http://www.cnsnews.com/news/article/us-embassy-cables-90-percent-most-lethal
[†] **US targets gun flows into Mexico in bid to stem drug violence,** by Sara Miller Llana, Staff writer Christian Science Monitor, April 2, 2009

"(President) Obama said more than 90 percent of weapons seized by Mexican authorities have come from the United States."

Scott Wilson*

The Attorney General was not shy in his interpretation of this statistic moving phony numbers into a metaphor of guilt while actually visiting Mexico City in the spring of 2009.

"There's no doubt that the vast majority of weapons seized in Mexico come from the United States. This is a reality we have to face in the United States..."

US Attorney General Eric Holder†

Soon after that article appeared early in 2009 it began to be repeatedly debunked; but incredibly, this statistic is still being reprinted in the summer of 2011. Like all well-formed Obama propaganda, lies take on a life of their own. Unfortunately, this bald-faced lie was specifically created as a hoax to dupe the American public.

In fact, Holder knew in 2009 at the time he made the above statement he did not have the data to back it up; he knew this because the ATF did not have access to the large number of confiscated weapons being held in Mexican warehouses and could not even make a rudimentary count let alone develop any statistically relevant analysis of the data.

I recently obtained access to a government cable labeled "CONFIDENTIAL" which exposes Holder's illusions. The document is a summary compiled by the American Embassy in Mexico of the meeting in April 2009 between Attorney General Eric Holder and Mexican President Felipe Calderón held immediately after a summit on arms trafficking attended by both Eric Holder and Janet

---

* **For Obama, Calderón, a Meeting of Minds,** by Scott Wilson, Washington Post Staff Writer, Friday, April 17, 2009

† **Top U.S. Officials Meet With Mexicans to Quell Growing Drug-Related Border Violence,** by Ginger Thompson and Elisabeth Malkin, New York Times, April 2, 2009, accessed from the NY Times website on June 28, 2011, at http://www.nytimes.com/2009/04/03/world/americas/03mexico.html

Napolitano. Holder by this time has already committed publically to the "...vast majority of weapons," hoax on April 2, but doesn't even request that data until April 14.

> *"...AG Holder noted that to support ongoing investigations of arms traffickers the U.S. needed to request ready access to weapons held by the Mexican army in warehouses, so those weapons could be traced."*
>
> **Confidential American Embassy Cable**
> **Detailed in Endnote** [3]

Holder made those comments knowing ATF had no access to the weapons, knowing that no count whatever had been made and yet by the end of the year the pundits in the media and other pusillanimous piss-ants for the White House were awash in parroting the 90% figure in spite of the complete lack of veracity in the data. In fact, Holder did not even get a response to his April request until October of 2009. Up until October Holder was only having illusions of grandeur about the data, after October it was legally a fraud.

The response was sent by the US Embassy in Mexico and addressed to a wide number of government agencies to be sure everyone *'got the memo'*. Recipients included all US consulates in Mexico, Secretary of State Hillary Clinton's office, Attorney General Eric Holder's DOJ, as well as the Department of Labor, Treasury and Commerce in addition to the Drug Enforcement Administration and Janet Napolitano's Department of Homeland Security; for some reason they forgot to copy the guy with the big ears in the White House, go figure.

The cable read in part:

> *(SBU) Comment. Claims by Mexican and U.S. officials that upwards of 90 percent of illegal recovered weapons can be traced back to the U.S. is based on an incomplete survey of confiscated weapons. In point of fact, without wider access to the weapons seized in Mexico, **we really have no way of verifying these numbers*** [ed. Note: emphasis added]"
>
> **US Embassy Cable, Mexico**
> **Detailed in Endnote** [4]

Between the time Holder personally requested the data from Mexico in the spring of 2009 and well into the fall, every single comment by the administration regarding the 90% figure was bogus. After Holder and everyone else received the official response, it was officially a legal compromise of the trust and integrity Americans place in their government and the officials who act in our behalf.

Even at the time Holder was initially hoisting the hoax up the flagpole, the veracity of this statistic was only faintly praised by cautious ATF spokespersons who, using the traditional Clinton deposition model, waffled on what the meaning of "*is—is*".

> *"While it is frequently reported that 90 percent of the guns used in drug-cartel violence in Mexico come from the United States, the federal Bureau of Alcohol, Tobacco, Firearms and Explosives told CNSNews.com that the number is defined in a very strict way, referring only to gun information relayed by Mexican authorities to the ATF."*

Edwin Mora, CNSNews.com, April 2009[*]

Even though ATF knew Holder was fabricating evidence, that story passed pretty much unnoticed in early 2009, but at that point no one knew it was the tell-tale sign of an enormous scandal.

To be sure, they had some data; information which was extracted from another significantly less well-known element of the Southwest Border Initiative, a computerized firearms tracing program called eTrace. As indicated, ATF does not personally inspect any of the weapons confiscated in Mexico which are used to populate the software fields in this weapons trace database; they don't even really know for sure how many total guns were confiscated, the number stolen by their own Mexican police and military for resale to cartels, or how many guns may not have been reported due to lack of serial numbers, ignorance, human error and/or other corruption. In reality, there are large federal warehouses in Mexico with tens of thousands of unreported guns (Figure 5) but there may have been twice that many or more that

---

[*] **CNSNews**, April 2, 2009, http://www.cnsnews.com/node/46080

corrupt officials in the government resold to the cartels; no one knows how many are recycled in this manner.

Figure 5: Seized weapons warehouse at the Secretary of the Defense headquarters in Mexico City. AP Photo, copyright Eduardo Verdugo.

According to a May 6, 2009, article written by the Associated Press only months after Obama took office, over 305,424 confiscated weapons are locked in vaults in Mexico;* and those numbers have likely increased in recent years. The ATF numbers used in the Holder's propaganda were actually based on a very small fraction of the total data; in fact, only about 11% of the total firearm confiscations in Mexico were used in the calculation (see Table 1).

Close examination of the actual eTrace database information indicates 8976 firearms were traced to what were originally legal firearm sales in US gun shops in 2009/2010 and would only comprise 23% of the firearms actually submitted for tracing and only a miniscule 0.02% of the 305, 424 warehoused weapons. Therefore the number does *not* include the enormous number of firearms in Mexican warehouses that went untraced. The real data

---

* **AP Impact: Mexico's Weapons Cache Stymies Tracing** by E. Eduardo Castillo, http://www.brownsvilleherald.com/common/printer/view.php?db=brownsville&id=97742 , published May 6, 2009; Accessed June 13, 2011

is hardly 90% of anything except Holder's ego-centric illusions in front of press cameras.

Table 1: Firearms Tracing Information for 2009 and 2010. Source ATF

Year	Submitted for Tracing	Firearms Traced to US dealers	Firearms NOT traced to US dealers
2009	26,813	5,800 (22%)	21,013 (78%)
2010	9,443	3,176 (34%)	6,267 (66%)

*"Clearly, the issue of U.S. guns being sent south of the border is a serious one, but...**the 90 percent figure appears to be a subsample of a sample**... Indeed, the percentage of U.S. arms appears to be far lower than 90 percent in specific classes of arms such as fully automatic assault rifles, machine guns, rifle grenades, fragmentation grenades and RPG-7s."*

STRATFOR.com[*]

Even Holder's Department of Justice (DOJ) became rudely aware the data lacked veracity when the Office of Inspector General (OIG) Evaluations and Inspections Division reviewed Project Gunrunner in 2010.

"ATF has been unable to expand gun tracing throughout Mexico...Further, most trace requests that are submitted to ATF from Mexico are considered "unsuccessful" [5] *because of missing or improperly entered gun data."*

OIG Report, Nov. 2010, Pg vii

"The poor quality of the tracing data and the resulting high rate of unsuccessful traces suggest that either the training is insufficient, training has been provided to the wrong people, or there are other unidentified problems with Mexican law enforcement's crime gun tracing. Most successful Mexican

---

[*] **STRAFOR Global Security and Intelligence Report**, *Mexico*, by Scott Stewart and Fred Burton, copyright July 9, 2009

crime gun trace requests were nonetheless untimely and of limited use for generating investigative leads...trace information they received from successful traces on Mexican crime guns was of limited use because the time-to-crime* interval was too long." [6]

OIG Report, Nov. 2010, Pg 77

ATF would soon learn not arguing with mainstream media and Mother Nature would be better for their budget which burgeoned dramatically as they continued to provide Obama and Holder inflated evidence faulting US firearms dealers in the southwestern United States.

"DTOs (Drug Trafficking Organizations) operating in Mexico rely on firearms suppliers to enforce and maintain their illicit narcotics operations. Intelligence indicates these criminal organizations have tasked their money-laundering, distribution and transportation infrastructures with reaching into the United States to acquire firearms and ammunition. These Mexican DTO infrastructures have become the leading gun-trafficking organizations operating in the southwest United States."

ATF website†

Although Project Gunrunner was originally initiated during the Bush administration, when the Obama administration entered the picture in 2009, the program's agenda fundamentally changed. Initiatives were publically redirected at weapons trafficking between American gun shops and Mexican drug cartels and the predominant activity became more about ATF empire building, political posturing and legislative wrangling than real crime fighting. The Mexican drug kingpins Holder was supposedly after never materialized into arrests let alone prosecutions, but the full court press was on to make a splash in the media as part of an

---

* **"Time to crime"** is a paralegal term used in prosecutions of illegal strawman firearms sales and refers to the length of time between a legal sale and the use of the firearm in a crime. In many cases, this period may exceed statutory limitations on prosecutions; see the endnote regarding Title 18, U.S.C. § 3282.

† http://www.atf.gov/publications/factsheets/factsheet-project-gunrunner.html

ongoing agenda to malign gun shops and use that political fodder to advance the ideological plank of liberal gun control.

Figure 6: Homeland Defense Secretary and all-around security ninny Janet Napolitano in Mexico City April 2009. Source FoxNews.com

Attorney General Eric Holder and Secretary of Homeland Defense Janet Napolitano made their first out of country visit to Mexico in April 2009 to announce American intentions to increase ATF budgets in support of the Southwest Border Initiative which included Project Gunrunner and eTrace software distribution systems.

Napolitano's presence at this announcement flies in the face of her statements that she knew nothing about the program; in fact she was in Mexico City publically bellying up a bundle of taxpayer dollars in support of the program as this article prior to her visit suggests,

> "Napolitano, who began her trip Wednesday in San Diego, announced plans to spend more than $400 million for the upgrading of entry ports and surveillance systems along the border."

The Christian Science Monitor*
April 2009

---

* **US targets gun flows into Mexico in bid to stem drug violence,** by Sara Miller Llana, Staff writer Christian Science Monitor, April 2, 2009

Similarly, Obama's feigned ignorance and Holder's nonchalance regarding knowledge of the program is in total contradiction to public statements and Holder's center-stage presence in Mexico making the original program announcement to Calderón and the Mexican people. In the spring 2011 hearings held by Rep. Darrell Issa, Holder testified he had only heard about Operation Fast and Furious "...a few weeks ago". Issa made public statements that he believed Holder was essentially lying through his teeth.

Then there was the issue of Deputy Attorney General David Ogden's statement in March 2009 which forever linked President Obama's name and taxpayer dollars to Project Gunrunner and all of its unfortunate results.

> *"The President has directed us to take action to fight these cartels and Attorney General Holder and I are taking several new and aggressive steps as part of the administration's comprehensive plan. Those steps include the following...the DOJ Bureau of Tobacco Alcohol Firearms and Explosives is increasing its efforts by adding 37 new employees in three new offices using $10 million dollars in recovery act funds and redeploying 100 personnel to the southwest border in the next forty-five days to fortify its Project Gunrunner which is aimed at disrupting arms trafficking between the United States and Mexico. ...ATF is doubling its presence in Mexico itself from five to nine personnel working with the Mexican's to facilitate gun tracing activity which specifically targets the illegal weapons and their sources in the United States."*

Deputy Attorney General David Ogden*
March 2009

---

* **David William Ogden** (b. Nov. 12, 1953), American attorney, known professionally as David W. Ogden, was the former Deputy Attorney General of the United States during the first year of the Obama administration.

Figure 7: David Ogden at the official launch of the program in Mexico

Of course, Ogden and others had no difficulty openly discussing Project Gunrunner; it was a very public program, funded on several occasions by congressional delegations that probably never read the bill.

> *"What good is reading the bill if it's a thousand pages and you don't have two days and two lawyers to find out what it means after you read the bill?"*

John Conyers (D-MI)*

On the other hand, its illegal counterpart, Operation Fast and Furious was a very 'below the radar' use of taxpayer bailout dollars and government personnel to leverage Project Gunrunner's legitimate operations into illegally trafficking guns out of the US. The corruption was fairly widespread; ATF's Operation Castaway

---

* **John Conyers, Jr.** (b. May 16, 1929, D-Mich.) U.S. Representative for the 14th congressional district, serving since 1965. He is currently the second longest-serving incumbent member of the House. Conyers often posts liberal diatribes at Daily Kos and Democratic Underground. Since May 2005, he's been a contributing blogger at The Huffington Post and his own blog. In late December 2006, Conyers "accepted responsibility" for possibly violating House rules. Also, in 1992, he was implicated in the House banking scandal. Not to be left out of frequent criminality associated with the liberal left politics of her husband, Conyers' wife, Monica, in June 2009 pleaded guilty to conspiring to commit bribery.

trafficking arms out of Florida into the Honduras was a similar redirection of funds and personnel. President Obama, Attorney General Holder and acting ATF director Ken Melson have all denied knowledge of the illegal activities involved with Operation Fast and Furious, yet all the while have publically initiated, directed, announced and taken credit for the much more public and vastly more legal side of Project Gunrunner.

Although I have heard individuals suggest that because congressional votes were used for financing Project Gunrunner budgets, that there is a quid pro quo as those votes represent 'official' knowledge and responsibility, I think trying to find culpability by connecting the dots at this level is a dry hole. Just because congress votes to finance a legal program and the funds are subsequently used illegally hardly suggests they knew about the illegality at the time of their vote.

However, it is incredibly difficult to believe the Attorney General of the United States and the Secretary of Homeland Security would make their first diplomatic junket to a foreign country in order to attend an international arms trafficking conference—specifically to announce the Southwest Border Initiative's Project Gunrunner—*knowing* the President of the United States himself had directed both the action, the taxpayer dollars and inevitably would be claiming the accolades and *not* request a complete briefing from their subordinates in ATF, ICE, DEA, DHS and the FBI on *exactly* what it was that they were stepping in front of the international media to announce.

Indeed, lack of the arm's length distance Holder claims to have had appears to be the very reason David Ogden would resign from DOJ only a year later. Former Clinton era Deputy Attorney General Jamie Gorelick and a partner at the same law firm as Ogden has stated her problem with the office was Attorney General Janet Reno's insistence on being involved in the day to day details of DOJ operations; Gorelick has publically stated Holder was in the weeds of DOJ operations from early on doing exactly the same thing to Ogden.

Further, I believe (and a great deal of testimony supports this)that everyone involved in ATF middle-management of Operation Fast and Furious actually believed in the righteousness of the program, was proud of what they were doing, thought it was the right thing to do and probably expected not only operational success but occupational promotion, financial compensation for a job well done, political power and even the eventual public recognition of their efforts. Under these circumstances, why would any inter-department briefing of such incredibly high expectations and importance not include a "*You're gonna' love this...*" section to the presentation?

Normally when a member of a large corporate or bureaucratic organization comes up with a really dumb idea to get promoted, more rational minds in the room diplomatically suggest, "...are you out of your freaking mind?"

While it appears that many ATF agents did exactly that and placed their careers on the line by expressing shock and disbelief in middle-management plans for Operation Fast and Furious, regrettably for Terry's family and hundreds of violence torn families in Mexico, many did not speak up and most simply followed orders.

The ATF/DOJ/DHS briefing that both Holder and Napolitano would have required of their subordinates prior to the Mexican arms conference, would have been delivered by one and only one person in ATF—Acting Director Kenneth E. Melson, who, like Holder, has been repeatedly shown was "in the weeds" with the daily operations of Project Gunrunner. Melson's information would undoubtedly have come up the chain from subordinates like Phoenix Field Division Special Agent in Charge William Newell, and specifically Group VII Strike Force case agent Hope MacAllister who was directly in charge of Operation Fast and Furious in Phoenix.

The seven-member team included Larry Alt, an 11-year ATF veteran with a law degree; Olindo Casa, a transfer from Chicago with 18 years under his belt; and the outspoken John Dodson, who had worked counternarcotics in the Army and the Loudoun County Sheriff's Office in Virginia before joining ATF around2004. Dodson would eventually become one of the two principal whistle-blowers who would out the information leading to this scandal. These individuals were up to their eyeballs in the illegal aspects of the gunrunner operation.

In fact, to suggest that a newly confirmed Attorney General, a career prosecutor with a penchant for detail and a nose for political advancement, a man who had prosecuted other politicians for cover-ups in the public eye* would have allowed himself to be at the center of an international media event making an announcement for a huge taxpayer funded program using millions of dollars of already controversial bailout money under his watch without knowing *exactly* what exposure and vulnerabilities were involved is only slightly more insulting than his high and mighty arrogance in denying it. Perhaps Deputy Ogden, who left the DOJ after the so-called 'management disagreements' with Attorney Holder could explain exactly what he meant in March 2009 by *"...several new and aggressive steps..."* when he announced DOJ's response to President Obama's direction for the entire inter-agency operation was going to include radically incremental Project Gunrunner enhancements.

Holder is also the likely architect of the expanding firearms pogrom against law-abiding citizens in support of his long-time gun-control advocacy in both the Clinton and Obama administrations. After the Mexico announcement, ATF reports and associated data increasingly began to trumpet the inflated number of weapons flowing into Mexico from the US. During the same month that Terry was murdered, ATF introduced yet another paper-tiger/paper-burden regulation on firearms dealers for new multiple-purchase tracking of rifles and shotguns, all of which I believe is to be entered into a suite of computer programs, which—when combined with internet portals—comprise an illegal firearms

---

* **Holder** joined the U.S. Justice Department's new Public Integrity Section during an interval lasting from 1976 to 1988. During his time there, he assisted in the prosecution of Congressman John Jenrette for bribery discovered in the Abscam sting operation. After his appointment by President William Jefferson Clinton to be United States Attorney he oversaw the conclusion of the corruption case against Dan Rostenkowski, part of the Congressional Post Office scandal.

registration mechanism they are not supposed to be keeping in the first place. This suite of programs which contains privacy information on law abiding citizens as well as criminals is now accessed, not only by ATF but by over thirty foreign governments through a digital magnifying glass called *Armas Cruzadas*. As part of Obama's socialist agenda for the redistribution of wealth in America (and in return for providing a scapegoat for Holder's anti-gun agenda) Congress subsequently awarded taxpayer bailout* money to ATF with overall FY2010 funding increased to $1.121 billion, including the requested increase for Project Gunrunner; an estimated expenditure of $61 million. An overall increase of $231 million for the Southwest Border Initiative (including funds for a Spanish language version of eTrace) was also requested and awarded in FY2010. The money was quickly spent.

> *"In 2009, ATF established several new offices dedicated to Project Gunrunner firearms trafficking investigations in McAllen, Texas, El Centro, California, and Las Cruces, New Mexico, including a satellite office in Roswell, New Mexico, in addition to new Gunrunner teams in Tucson, Arizona and El Paso, Texas. In September 2010, ATF announced plans to expand Project Gunrunner by opening additional Gunrunner offices in Sierra Vista, Arizona, and Brownsville, Texas. ...Additional expansion plans include the opening of three new offices located in U.S. Consulates in Mexico, as well as adding additional investigative and analytical staff to the ATF Country Office in Mexico City."*

ATF website†

---

* **Bailout** money came from the American Recovery and Reinvestment Act (ARRA) of 2009. $10 million in ARRA funding hired 37 new ATF employees to open, staff (via new hire and relocation of senior personnel,) equip, and operate new Project Gunrunner criminal enforcement teams in McAllen, TX; El Centro, CA; and Las Cruces, NM (which includes a subordinate satellite office in Roswell, NM.). Additionally, these funds support the assignment of two special agents to each of the U.S. consulates in Juarez and Tijuana, Mexico to provide direct support to Mexican officials on firearms-trafficking-related issues. Source: ATF website at: http://www.atf.gov/firearms/programs/project-gunrunner/
† **ATF Website**:
http://www.atf.gov/firearms

It is unclear how many out of work taxpayers with upside down mortgages would suddenly be offered jobs as ATF agents funded by shovel-ready bailout money, but we can rest assured that if they had a shovel they were a shoe-in for an interview.

> " [Laughing]...shovel ready was not as shovel ready as we expected..."

President Barack Hussein Obama
Jobs Conference, June 2011

eTrace

"Mexican officials said that in their meetings with Napolitano and Holder, the U.S. cabinet members pledged not only to try to stop weapons at the border, but also to help trace guns that are seized inside Mexico."

NPR's Jason Beaubien[*]

Using eTrace software, the AK47's used against Terry and his fellow agents were traced to a purchase on January 16, 2010 by a gunrunner named Jaime Avila during the height of Operation Fast and Furious. Avila was originally identified as a suspect in an ATF investigation on November 25, 2009. This occurred after he purchased weapons with a man named Uriel Patino, another straw buyer who had previously been identified as a cartel-associated suspect in October 2009. Over the next month and a half, Avila legally purchased with the blessings of FBI NICS background clearances, 13 more weapons, each dutifully recorded as a completely legal weapons transfer by the firearms dealer and under the jaded eyes of government employees with access to the digital eTrace firearms registration suite.

Incredibly, Avila bought the weapons recovered at the scene of Agent Terry's murder almost two months *after* government officials at ATF knew he was working with Patino and almost a year *before* the weapons were used in the Hell's Gate shootout that killed Brian Terry. This is one of the great sad realizations associated with this story; had it not been for the profoundly poor judgment of ATF management to instigate Operation Fast and Furious, Brian Terry might well be home with his family today; his murder was entirely preventable.

Avila's purchases would eventually total over fifty weapons under the willing and watchful eyes of ATF management voyeurs involved

[*] **U.S., Mexican Officials Meet On Border Security**, National Public Radio April 3, 2009, accessed on June 28, 2011 at NPR's website, http://www.npr.org/templates/story/story.php?storyId=102688596

in the planning and execution of Operation Fast and Furious. Patino's purchases would eventually exceed over 600 weapons. This sounds like a lot of weapons and for the average liberal who hates guns and would not own even one to protect their own family, indeed it appears to be a large number of firearms. However, hard research and data analysis presented here refutes these numbers as significant contributors to the volume of firearms which were made available to Mexican drug cartels by other operatives. As with all Fast and Furious retail purchases, gun shop owners—exercising the kind of due diligence one would expect from honest businesses and good Americans—voluntarily contacted ATF personnel and provided real time warnings of each and every preventable sale. In many cases ATF did not lift a finger to stop the weapon sales or prevent the weapons from illegally trafficking into Mexico. Shop owners were told, "...*No problem...make the sale, go home early*".

> "*On several occasions I personally requested to interdict or seize firearms in such a manner that would only further the investigation, but I was always ordered to stand down and not to seize the firearms,*"

ATF Group VII agent Olindo Casa

The day after Terry was murdered, anxious and apprehensive ATF agents who had originally complained about the dangers of the program frantically searched the eTrace database for the serial numbers reported in the crime. By late in the evening of December 15, their worst nightmares were fully realized. Weapons their management had told them to let walk into Mexico had, just as they had warned, walked right back into the United States and killed a fellow law enforcement officer. Only a few short months later, they would repeat this apprehensive exercise, hoping beyond hope the firearm used to blow the top of Rep. Gabrielle Giffords head off and to kill Federal Judge John Roll and several other Americans in Tucson was not one of the Fast and Furious weapons trafficked into and out of Mexico. It turned out the Tucson weapon was not part of the program, but it certainly was not for lack of trying on the part of ATF. Although most of the Fast and Furious weapons deals were small potatoes—most amounting to ten or twenty weapons—a few of the purchases were eye-popping. Although Operation Fast and Furious did not get into full swing until the Fall of 2009, by late February 2010 ATF had allowed over $600,000 of illegal weapons purchases and their serial numbers to be entered into eTrace. Although the congressional investigation does not detail which straw purchasers bought the weapons, one redacted entry lists one buyer purchasing $134,638 of weapons and another straw buyer allowed to purchase an incredible $204,110 in military style weapons. Since US law enforcement officers like Brian Terry are getting killed by the weapons ATF allowed to move into the hands of Mexican drug cartels, one can only guess how many Mexicans have also suffered the same fate and how many more on both sides of the border are going to die. It is probably a safe assumption most of the guns that went into Mexico stayed in Mexico and that's the real problem ATF has created for Mexican citizens. In the Socialist utopia of the Felipe Calderón administration, in a country torn apart by drug abuse, tax slavery, failed economics, arms trafficking and narco-terrorism, it is one additional burden the proud families of Mexico did not really need on their backs. Insanely, ATF did not even tell officials of the Mexican government about Operation Fast and Furious, let alone ask their permission to run guns across their sovereign international border. Some outrage has resulted from this diplomatic *faux pas* and some Mexican officials are now demanding ATF agents responsible for the operation be arrested and extradited for prosecution in Mexico. In a recent interview a high-ranking Mexican official stated,

> *"I obviously feel violated. I feel my country's sovereignty was violated. They should be tried in the United States and the Mexican government should also demand that they also be tried in Mexico since the incidents took place here. There should be trials in both places."*

Sen. Rene Arce Islas*

---

* **Sen. Rene Arce Islas:** chairman of Mexico's Commission for National Security; comments were made to FoxNews, *U.S. Officials Behind 'Fast and Furious' Gun Sales Should Be Tried in Mexico, Lawmaker Says*, by William La Jeunesse, July 05, 2011.

And Islas is not alone in this view of an operation that has ignited the ire of the Mexican people who have for a long while viewed the American government as corruptly complicit in Mexico's nationwide troubles with both drugs and guns.

> "I think we should at least try to prove that what happened in Mexico must be sanctioned by Mexican laws and under our sovereignty. What can't happen is that this now ends on an administrative sanction, or a resignation. No, no, no. Human lives were lost here. A decision was made to carry out an operation that brought very high risk to human lives."

Sen. Santiago Creel*

While extradition is unlikely, the idea that international sovereignty is suddenly an issue that Mexico has awakened to is like the proverbial pot calling the kettle black. In point of fact, American sovereignty on our southwestern border has been compromised by Mexico's abject abandonment of drug and immigration enforcement; a desertion of responsibility that has gone on for years. International criminals have been moving everything from opium, cocaine and marijuana to human smuggling and Islamic laundered cash across our sovereign border for decades—all of which has resulted in not only millions of addicted Americans and destroyed families, financial support of Islamic terrorist activities in the Middle East and the untold tragedies of tens of thousands of broken families of dead American soldiers. I just don't think Mexican outrage over sovereignty is an argument that will find much traction in the world community.

Still this does not let the US Government off the hook for ATF involvement in Mexican crime. In a recently released March 2010

---

* **Sen. Santiago Creel:** former Mexican Interior Minister Creel is considered to be a likely presidential nominee in 2012 to succeed Felipe Calderón.

memo,* ATF admits at the height of their program eTrace date indicated they allowed known gun smugglers to buy 359 guns and illegally move them into Mexico while 958 people died in that country during the same month. It is now estimated that 150 Mexican police officers alone have died so far as a result of this failed political strategy during Eric Holder's watch overseeing the enforcement of American justice and border sovereignty.

Neither were Mexican political leaders immune from this violence.

Late in 2010 Mexican police recovered two other AK-47 rifles in the course of their investigation of the kidnapping of Mario Gonzalez Rodriguez. We probably would not know of this one kidnapping among the thousands in Mexico except that Gonzales happened to be the brother of the now former Attorney General of Chihuahua, Patricia Gonzalez Rodriguez.

The Mexican news media dutifully provided enormous publicity on this celebrity kidnapping. Gonzalez was taken by six Sinaloa cartel gunmen and tortured for over two weeks. Three separate videos posted online show Gonzalez surrounded by hooded armed men with his hands and feet bound and apparently being electrocuted with electrical equipment attached to his feet. Gonzalez (obviously under duress) claims in the video that while her tenure as attorney general, his sister Patricia Gonzalez Rodriguez provided valuable political protection to members of a competing Juarez cartel. Confessions do not get you very far in Mexico; Gonzalez' dead body was later recovered, the kidnappers arrested and firearms in their possession were tracked by eTrace to Operation Fast and Furious.

And it appears the same fate as Terry's was awaiting yet another American law enforcement officer who was killed with one of the ATF gunrunner firearms while doing his job in Mexico. Immigration and Customs Enforcement (ICE) agent Jamie Zapata was murdered and his partner Victor Avila was seriously wounded during a car-jacking by Mexican thugs in February 2011, just as the American

---

* **Gunwalker Goes Pravda** by Bob Owens, PajamaMedia.com, published June 23, 2011 and accessed on the same date at: http://pajamasmedia.com/blog/gunwalker-goes-pravda-white-house-unleashes-msm

public began to be aware of the Operation Fast and Furious scandal.

Zapata was hit by five bullets in his chest and died en route to a hospital. He was killed by members of the Los Zetas cartel in a region controlled by cartel boss Jesus Enrique Rejon Aguilar.* Access to eTrace confirmed firearms used were connected to Fast and Furious.

Zapata's partner, Victor Avila, was wounded twice in the leg in the ambush on a major highway near the city of San Luis Potosi, about 250 miles north of Mexico City. The men, assigned to the U.S. Embassy in Mexico City, were returning to their office after a meeting with other U.S. personnel in San Luis Potosi. The shooting occurred when Zapata and Avila approached what they thought was a government checkpoint and rolled down the window to identify themselves. Unlike Terry, neither Zapata nor Avila had a chance to defend themselves from the drug cartel; like all Mexican citizens who have long ago lost the dignity of their own freedom and the right to defend themselves, US law enforcement officials are not allowed to possess firearms in Mexico.

And just when you thought it could not get any more insane, authorities in Mexico arrested a Los Zetas thug name Rejon Aguilar who was arrested along with Pedro Ortega Herrera identified as an active duty police official with the Ministry of Public Security in Mexico City. Almost unbelievably Ortega Herrera was responsible for providing official government security and support for Rejon Aguilar during travel to the state of Campeche. Corruption is systemic in Mexico where sources indicate half of all Mexican police cannot pass a background check.

"Some recent examples of Mexico's paramilitary abuses include the sexual assault and rape of dozens of female detainees by police in San Salvador Atenco, and the

---

* **Rejon Aguilar** was taken into custody July 3, 2011 in Atizapan, Mexico. He was one of Mexico's most-wanted men, and the U.S. Justice, State and Homeland Security departments had previously announced a reward of up to $5 million for his arrest and conviction.

*disappearances of dozens of teachers in the rebellious state
of Oaxaca in 2006, as well as the killings of seven innocent
bystanders, including the American journalist Brad Will by
off-duty policemen. Almost half of Mexican police officers
examined in 2008 have failed background and security tests,
a figure that rises to nearly 9 of 10 policemen in the border
state of Baja California."*

Merida Initiative*

Rejon Aguilar immediately spilled his guts on arms trafficking, at first blush his answers appeared to support Holder's contentions. When asked where the Zetas drug cartel obtained their weapons, he replied,

"...from the United States. All weapons come from the U.S."

Jesus Enrique Rejon Aguilar†

The adoring media made a lot out of the statement attempting to support Holder's aging claim that it was American gun stores at fault. But, reading the complete arrest interview Aguilar actually makes a much more damning accusation against both the US and Mexican governments who he claims were complicit in selling weapons to cartel buyers,

Interrogator: *How are they brought here?*

Rejón Aguilar: *Crossing the river. We used to bring them through the bridge, but it's become harder to do that.*

Interrogator: *Who purchases the weapons?*

Rejón Aguilar: *They are bought in the U.S. The buyers (on the U.S. side of the border) have said in the past that*

---

* http://en.wikipedia.org/wiki/Merida_Initiative
† **Mexican Police Transcript**: Captured Zeta Leader: We've purchased weapons from the "U.S. Government itself" By Mario Andrade DeadlineLive.info July 6, 2011, accessed at: http://deadlinelive.info/category/featured/

sometimes they would acquire them from the U.S. Government itself.

Interrogator: *And nowadays, who distributes them to you?*

Rejón Aguilar: *It's more difficult for us to acquire weapons nowadays, but we find ways. But it's easier for the Gulf Cartel to bring them across the border.*

Interrogator: *Why?*

Rejón Aguilar: *We don't know why, but they bring them (across the bridge) in the trunk of their cars without being checked (by Mexican Customs). One can only think that they must have reached a deal with the (Mexican) government.*

Straw buyers, the kind that purchase the "ant traffic" in gun stores—even with the aid and comfort of the ATF—do not purchase weapons directly from the US Government without another level of serious corruption that has previously been unidentified. Aguilar essentially affirms that there are entities of the government of the United States that are furnishing arms directly to the Mexican drug cartels and that the Mexican government is complicit in transferring those weapons across the border. According to the story Rejon Aguilar originally began moving guns across the Rio Grande when more traditional international border crossings (e.g. El Paso, Nogales, etc.) came under heavy scrutiny by law enforcement after the Sept 11, 2001 terrorist attack on the US.

Aguilar, like others in the violent Los Zetas enforcement unit is a former member of an elite Mexican paratroop and intelligence battalion known as the Special Air Mobile Force Group. The Zetas was founded by Mexican army Special Forces deserters (including Rejon Aguilar) in the 1990s who were initially hired as hit-men for the then powerful Gulf cartel. The group later split from their employers, organized their own operation sparking the bloody Mexican turf wars that have claimed thousands of lives. They are strongest in eastern Mexico and the northern border states of *Tamaulipas* and *Nuevo Leon*. The Los Zetas are expansionists. They are not content to operate only in their homeland on the Gulf Coast; they have steadily advanced south and west, increasing their presence in various regions, such as *San Luis Potosi, Coahuila, Jalisco,* and the ancient Yucatan Peninsula of the Maya. Data in the eTrace software suggests Fast and Furious weapons have reached into crimes committed as far away as 1700 miles from the US border.

However, there are important elements of arms trafficking that are not and cannot be reported by eTrace statistics. Los Zetas was reported as early as 2008 to be in possession of weapons that could not be explained by the so-called gun show loop-hole or the straw sales at American gun shops.

> *"Narco News, in a report in December 2008 examined the increasing militarization of narco-trafficking groups in Mexico and pointed out that U.S. military-issued ammunition popped up in an arms cache seized in Reynosa, Mexico, in November 2008 that was linked to the Zetas, a mercenary group that provides enforcement services to Mexican narco-trafficking organizations....The big battles in the drug war in Mexico are 'not being fought with Saturday night specials, hobby rifles and hunting shotguns,' Narco News reported in March 2009...at a time when the mainstream media was pushing a narrative that assigned the blame for the rising tide of weapons flowing into Mexico to U.S. gun stores and gun shows. Rather, we reported at the time, 'the drug trafficking organizations are now in possession of high-powered munitions in vast quantities that can't be explained by the gun-show loophole.' Those weapons, found in stashes seized by Mexican law enforcers and military over the past several years, include U.S.-military issued rifles, machine guns, grenade launchers and explosives."*

Narco News*

* **Pentagon Fingered as a Source of Narco-Firepower in Mexico,** by Bill Conroy – July 2, 2011 at Narco News, accessed at:

In the early spring of 2011, the Mexican military raided a Los Zetas camp near Falcon Lake, a tourist location spanning the international border and the location of a high profile murder in 2010 of American David Hartley. The military engaged in a heavy gun battle where a dozen Zetas died defending a narcotics and weapons cache, including what appeared to be US military M-60 and M-240 style heavy machine guns.

Mexican journalists with the newspaper *La Cronica de Hoy*[*] reported the weapons cache found at Falcon Lake also included anti-aircraft shoulder fired missiles. According to the same newspaper, several Mexican federal government entities have issued statements about similar weapons being found and confiscated in many other Mexican states and might've been used to assassinate PGR Prosecutor *José Luis Santiago Vasconcelos*, who died in a plane crash in 2008.

Anti-aircraft shoulder fired missiles and 7.62mm M-60 heavy machine guns (Figure 8) are just not the type of weapon you are going to routinely see on blue light special at the local K-Mart gun counter.

In retaliation for the raid against their island warehouse, Los Zetas captured the police commander in the Falcon Lake jurisdiction who was also investigating the Hartley murder, decapitated him and placed his head in a suitcase before placing it outside of a Mexican Army

Figure 8: M60 heavy machine gun in use during the Viet Nam war is still in use today. DINFOS photo.

http://narcosphere.narconews.com/notebook/bill-conroy/2011/02/pentagon-fingered-source-narco-firepower-mexico
[*] **La Cronica de Hoy**, May 2011, accessed at: http://ww.cronica.com.mx/

base.* Decapitation is popular with the cartels. A recent news story documented the cartel kidnapping of a fourteen year old American who was forced to decapitate political targets and prisoners. The depths of depravity witnessed in the drug wars is not to be underestimated.

Regardless, firearms linked to Operation Fast and Furious continue to turn up in eTrace searches and connected to Arizona crime scenes as this ABC news report documents.

> *"The ABC15 Investigators uncovered documents showing guns connected to at least two Glendale criminal cases and at least two Phoenix criminal cases also appear in the ATF's Suspect Gun Database, a sort-of watch list for suspicious gun sales."*

ABC15, Phoenix AZ†

The ATF Suspect Gun Database is yet another digital element in the computer suite of databases on ATF computer screens. Here ABC15 specifically refers to the Suspect Gun Database that is described as a data collection of suspicious firearms sales. One has to wonder exactly how all this trace information interacts with the legality of gun registration, a subject that will be discussed in another chapter.

Incredibly, another arms trafficking scheme called Operation Castaway‡ was being run during the same period by agents out of their ATF Florida headquarters where they were trafficking guns into Honduras with operational rules eerily similar to Operation Fast and Furious. The ultimate criminal end-user in this case was the violent gang organization known as *Mara Salvatrucha Trece* (a.k.a. MS-13).

---

* **Decapitation**: Boston Globe, May 13, 2011
† **Weapons linked to controversial ATF strategy found in Valley crimes,** Lori Jane Gliha, ABC15, Phoenix AZ. Posted June 30, 2011 and accessed at: http://www.abc15.com/dpp/news/local_news/investigations/weapons
‡ Operation Castaway: accessed at the ATF website:
http://www.atf.gov/press/releases/2010/09/092110-tam-major-international-trafficking-investigation-results.html

MS-13 is a trans-national criminal gang that originated in Los Angeles and has spread to other parts of the United States, Canada, Mexico, and Central America. The majority of the gang is ethnically composed of Central Americans and active in both urban and suburban areas. They are notorious for their use of violence and a sub-cultural moral code that consists of merciless revenge and brutal retributions. This excessive cruelty of the members earned them a path to be recruited by the Sinaloa Cartel battling Aguilar's highly militarized Los Zetas. Members of MS-13 distinguish themselves by tattoos covering the body and also often the face, as well as the use of their own sign language.

Virginia O'Brien, then Special Agent in Charge (SAC) of Operation Castaway, was previously the SAC of the Phoenix Field Division and was promoted to the Deputy Assistant Director of ATF to later

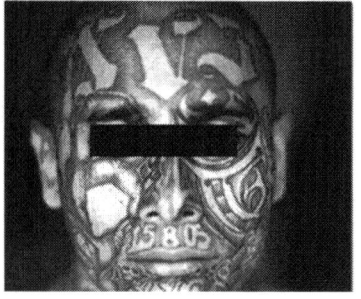

Figure 9: MS-13 gang member tattoos illustrate the violent nature of what has been called America's most dangerous gang.

accept the position as ATF's SAC in Tampa.

Mike Vanderboegh (Figure 10 Page 57), one of the first journalists who broke the story of Operation Fast and Furious at the Sipsey Street Irregulars website, has reported* there are emails in existence where O'Brien has advised those involved that Tampa ATF agents do not have to report their walked guns because Tampa operations are not a part of the Southwest Border Initiative or Project Gunrunner. Time will tell if O'Brien's alleged strategy for withholding arms trafficking information from congress previously modeled by Eric Holder, is a good career model for other ATF professionals.

---

* **Mike Vanderboegh**, http://sipseystreetirregulars.blogspot.com/ [posted 7/6/2011 7:27:41 PM]

While the total number of firearms ATF allowed to be trafficked into Mexico and other countries will probably never be fully known, what we do know is deeply disturbing. According to testimony by ATF agent John Dodson—and other whistle blowers—of the nearly 3000 weapons that ATF management hoped to trace to drug cartel kingpins in Mexico, very few have been recovered and over one thousand firearms are completely unaccounted for and still "walking".

> *"...So essentially in January 2010, or December when I got there, we knew Jaime Avila was a straw purchaser, had him identified as a known straw purchaser supplying weapons to the cartel. Shortly thereafter, we had previous weapons recovered from Mexico with very short time to crime rates purchased by Jaime Avila, as I recall. And then in May (2010) we had a recovery where Border Patrol encounters an armed group of bandits and recovered an AK variant rifle purchased by Jaime Avila...purchased during the time we were watching Jaime Avila, had him under surveillance, and we did nothing."*

ATF Agent John Dodson testimony

Figure 10: Mike Vanderboegh of the Sipsey Street Irregulars was one of the first journalists to break this story. Photo courtesy of FoxNew.com

A significant part of that surveillance involved access to eTrace and brings us to the subject of how ATF invades the privacy of American citizens under the guise of law enforcement. A less well understood, incredibly dangerous and dramatically under-reported aspect of the Southwest Border Initiative is the enormous ongoing investment in a software suite of state of the art computer programs of which eTrace is only one important element.

Along with the fate of tens of thousands in Mexico, Mario Gonzalez's body was found in November 2010 in a shallow unceremonious grave. As we indicated earlier, Gonzalez, one of many kidnapped victims in Mexico, was the brother of Attorney General Patricia Gonzalez Rodriguez. Officials eventually arrested the kidnappers and confiscated the two AK47 rifles in question, the serial numbers stamped on the weapons were quickly entered into a US taxpayer funded Spanish language version of eTrace. Almost immediately the program reported the two rifles were among the serial numbered weapons that had been trafficked into Mexico by ATF as part of Operation Fast and Furious.

The program itself contains digitized information (make, model, serial number, type of weapon and caliber) regarding firearms manufactured in or imported into the US. Weapons data for this program is entered by ATF personnel based on several sources of information (note: a complete list is included in Endnote[7]). Most firearms buyers will be familiar with the standard ATF Form 4473 which is completed at the time a retail firearm is actually transferred to the buyer and the information in the form is used to provide ATF (by way of the FBI national crime information system) the necessary information to facilitate a criminal background check. This form captures the make, model, serial number and caliber of the weapon(s) purchased and is combined with the buyers full legal name, a complete physical description (eye and hair color, height and weight) physical street addresses, Social Security number, birthplace/birth date, drivers license number, issue and expiration dates, etc.). The paper form kept by the store may contain any other personal information the dealer adds such as a photo copy of your driver's license or military ID, your phone number, email address or other information.

There are two other forms which the average buyer is probably not aware of as they are not used during the buyers actual transaction. The first one is ATF Form 3310.4—Report of Multiple Sale or Other Disposition of Pistols and Revolvers. Any retail customer who purchases more than one hand gun in a consecutive five day period from the same dealer must be reported by the dealer to the ATF within 24 hours. Notification may be by facsimile or mail (but the mailed form must have a same day postmark). This form also contains the same personal information on the buyer which is taken from the Form 4473 and again includes the serial numbered weapons data, including make, model and caliber(s) involved in the sale. Most well-informed thugs simply buy weapons from multiple locations to avoid this reporting. The data then is largely kept on law-abiding citizens who are not making straw purchases but are merely exercising their constitutionally recognized rights.*

Also of particular note is ATF Form 3312.1—the National Tracing Center Trace Request Form. These are initiated internally by investigators who are seeking to connect a serial number of a firearm to an American buyer. Once initiated investigators use the eTrace system to first determine where the weapon originated (i.e. country of origin and the manufacturer or importer). At this point, unless the weapon(s) have been previously identified in other crimes or have been entered into the Suspect Gun Database as a result of Operation Fast and Furious or Operation Castaway, the ATF Tracing Center would normally have to contact the manufacturer or the importer for identifying information regarding specifically where those weapons were next shipped in the process of placing their firearms inventory into the market place. Manufacturers and importers are not legally allowed to transfer weapons directly to individuals or even to their own employees; they may only transfer weapons to federally licensed firearms dealers (known by the acronym FFL) or other licensed manufactures, exporters or importers.

---

* Indeed, the form and the data on law abiding citizens is of little value to law enforcement; congressional politicians originally enacted the paper trail for re-election purposes so they could say "...I fought the good fight to keep our neighborhoods safe."

Note: unless the weapon(s) were specifically confiscated from an FFL dealer who originally received or stole the weapon from the OEM manufacturer or importer, the government investigator does not have the individual retail transaction information nor the buyer's name. Neither do they have the date the weapon was sold in a retail situation. Only the retailer would have this information in a stored Form 4473 or in the ATF's warehouse of 4473 forms taken from out of business dealers.

By law, software programs like eTrace and the Suspect Gun Database are not allowed to proactively contain the names of US citizens who originally and legally purchased firearms. Information on individual citizens by federal law should be kept in a separate location; access to that information using a common computer program to view combined firearms data and private citizen's possession information would be an illegal firearms registry—and we all know the ATF never does anything illegal.

Even if the government has a separate software program containing private information on US citizens extracted from their many forms of source information, one has to wonder; does the possession and access to both eTrace software and any other private citizen program information accessed through a suite of digital portal programs within the same government agency on the same computer by any one person in the government not also constitute defacto firearms registration? Are we supposed to believe that electronic labels separated on a computer screen by less than an inch effectively compartmentalize the good from the bad and the seriously butt-ugly gun registry? The ATF has been collecting this combination of paper and electronic trails on both types of information for many years beginning with the National Firearms Act of 1934 and dramatically expanded under Title I of the 1968 Gun Control Act.* The very possession of decades of

---

* **National Firearms Act** ("**NFA**"), enacted on June 26, 1934, currently codified as amended as 26 U.S.C. ch. 53, is an Act of Congress that imposes a registration and tax on the manufacture and transfer of controlled firearms and destructive devices. The NFA is also referred to as Title II of the Federal firearms laws. The Gun Control Act of 1968 is Title I.

firearms transaction forms which contain massive amounts of privacy information on American citizens comprises a defacto paper database of information that amounts to a gun registry.

You can imagine with the access to data provided by the eTrace program and other computerized data, the two rifles found at the crime scene of Terry's murder were quickly back-tracked to a specific Arizona firearms dealer and inevitably, with the assistance of the FFL dealer, the specific sales transaction information that identified the gunrunner who purchased the weapons and the exact date they were purchased.[*]

To date, the ATF authored eTrace software allows access by approximately 30 foreign countries and nearly 3000 foreign (and often corrupt) law enforcement agencies with access to the name, make, model and serial number of every weapon purchased by law-abiding citizens, businesses, trusts, LLC's and corporations in the US since 1968 (and in the case of Title II weapons associated with the National Firearms Act, records which date to 1934). Intended to be the digital flagship of criminal Mexican cartel data-mining,[†] this program and the related suite of digital programs is potentially the greatest threat to privacy in America. The good news is, if you can believe the DOJ, it hasn't worked so well.

> *"...ATF's expansion of its automated system (eTrace) to trace guns seized in Mexico has yielded very limited information of intelligence value...Mexican law enforcement officials view gun tracing as merely a tool that ATF uses to further its own investigations."*

DOJ REPORT, Nov. 2010, Pg vi

You can read that *"...further its own political agenda"*. In 2009 the Obama administration began using the ATF, the Attorney General's

---

[*] **Two AK-47s Used to Murder Mexican Lawyer Were 'Fast and Furious' Guns From U.S.,** by William La Jeunesse, Published June 17, 2011 by FoxNews.com. Published June 17, 2011; last accessed at:
http://www.foxnews.com/politics/2011/06/17/two-ak47s-used-to-murder-mexican-lawyer-were-fast-and-furious-guns-sources-say/ June 22, 2011
[†] **"According to ATF's June 2007 Gunrunner strategy,** *tracing guns seized in Mexico is the "cornerstone" of Project Gunrunner."* DOJ/OIG Report Nov. 2010, Pg vi.

office and the Department of Homeland Security and even the President himself to peddle this new strategy in Mexico. Initially using the Bilateral Arms Trafficking Conference held in Mexico during the spring of 2009 as the media event for the public launch, the announcement stated enormous amounts of American taxpayer dollars would start flowing into Mexico.

> *"ATF is in the process of developing a Spanish version of E-trace that it will make available to the GOM (Government of Mexico) in December 2009. The Spanish version of E-trace will remain a request system that follows the same methodology as E-trace. However, programmers have expanded the list of input fields to seven, in large measure to satisfy the GOM's desire to collect and track more data."* [Complete text at Endnote[8]]

American Embassy Cable, 09MEXICO1048*

At this point I do not know what the additional fielded information was intended to do, but clearly the Government of Mexico thought it was important and fully intended to use when it became available. I also do not know the specific ATF source where the additional data was being retrieved, although no new firearms reporting forms were initiated during this period so it is likely the data already existed in either eTrace, the Suspect Gun Database or an ATF unknown source (legal or not). The eTrace program in my opinion—even in its original form—was a borderline illegal registration mechanism; adding anything to firearms data regarding buyer information would only serve to further blur that line.

To the ire of firearms owners in the US, the ATF has repeatedly thumbed its nose at federally mandated laws against firearms registration which most law-abiding American gun owners and

---

* **American Embassy Cable, 09MEXICO1048**: From an unclassified document originating from the American Embassy in Mexico; Reported in: *Bajo la mesa, Washington culpa a México del tráfico de armas,* and accessed at http://wikileaks.jornada.com.mx/notas/bajo-la-mesa-washigton-culpa-a-mexico-del-trafico-de-armas. English translation accessed on June 28, 2011 at: http://wikileaks.org/cable/2009/04/09MEXICO1048.html

firearms activists rightly see as constitutionally onerous. One example is the mandated length of time ATF is allowed to keep personal information on American citizens after a retail gun shop has requested clearance for a gun sale; originally the restriction was for a matter of days and then the record was mandated by law to be destroyed. ATF has publically stated that they can and will keep that information for dramatically longer periods. This is one example of the arrogance of officials in DOJ and ATF. Are activists and citizens alike appropriately worried that the mythical *Iron River of Guns* based on Holder's DOJ propaganda was intended from the beginning to leverage new gun control legislation? Or are we all just too jaded and paranoid from repeated government scandals to trust the government is doing all this for our benefit?

> *"eTrace has always looked perilously close to an illegal function, with massive government and LEO support, but only to keep us safe. Last I heard, 75 million out-of-business records languished in government warehouses (must have grown since then a decade ago or more), with desperate desire to simply digitize them all (for safety, security, space-saving, federal jobs program while you're at it), but the law prevented them from doing so. No way to verify if it has been done or not, and little confidence in a "no" answer".*

Alan Korwin
GunLaws.com*

To make eTrace and other information regarding ongoing investigations more accessible, Immigrations and Customs Enforcement (ICE) also ponied up a digital magnifying glass, similarly implemented in a Spanish language version at US taxpayer expense. A virtual information exchange system, this software portal is called *Armas Cruzadas*.

> *"Separately, ICE provided to the GOM an information sharing portal, in Spanish, called Armas Cruzadas. This portal facilitates easy access to information on arms trafficking, investigations, and seizures. Armas Cruzadas,*

---

* **Alan Korwin**, American firearms activist and author (Gun Laws of America by Bloomfield Press), personal communication, July 2011.

however, is not a U.S. weapons database that lends itself to tracing confiscated weapons. The intent of Armas Cruzadas is to create a virtual information exchange tool between the U.S. and Mexico."

American Embassy Cable
09MEXICO1048 *

What worries firearms activists is what exactly is being exchanged in terms of citizen privacy? While eTrace itself may originally have only contained data regarding the path of a firearm from manufacturer to distributor to retail sale outlet; investigative data when added into new identifying fields could easily compromise the integrity of American privacy.

I located another cable marked "CONFIDENTIAL" and sent to the US Secretary of State which tends to support the frightening conclusion that ATF is providing foreign countries with data on American citizens through Armas Cruzadas. As noted earlier, part of the software revision was to include new data fields specifically requested by Mexico.

The cable reads (in part)...

*"The February 27 visit by John Walters (ONDCP) helped initiate coordination with the newly installed Calderon Administration. In separate meetings with Attorney General Medina Mora and Public Security Secretary Garcia Luna, Director Walters emphasized the importance of information sharing for interdiction and for attacking drug trafficking organizations...Medina acknowledged the importance of serial number tracing, but requested a level of information sharing that would provide Mexican access to information about **purchasers** [ed. Note: emphasis added] of military-style munitions and pro-actively put them in a position to arrest and prosecute."* [Complete text at Endnote 9]

American Embassy Cable
07MEXICO1854*

---

* Ibid, American Embassy Cable, 09MEXICO1048

To me the key word in that last sentence is *purchasers*. Why would Medina Mora even be asking for information on American citizens who bought firearms if the ATF did not have this information to provide them in the first place? There is no mention in the cable of John Walters responding to the request that the US can't provide that information because 1) they don't have it or, 2) because it is illegal for them to have it. When I approached National Rifle Association attorneys with this information, they suggested it was merely to help Mexican officials more easily identify American straw buyers traveling in Mexico. While this may be the case, it remains a difficult proposition that privacy information on American citizens appears to now be available to foreign operatives.

It is one thing if ATF keeps "clean" records of serial numbers in a database for investigative purposes, it is an entirely different thing if they are now populating eTrace with information on firearms ownership (based on purchases) by American citizens and then making that information available to foreign governments who have repeatedly demonstrated not only widespread corruption but possible collusion with Middle Eastern terrorists who have a violent agenda to destroy the United States. The names, addresses and types of firearms owned by US citizens is what they call valuable intelligence in the underworld of terrorism.

The day Brian Terry was shot, ATF agents in Arizona accessed their local eTrace software connection and input the serial numbers of the weapons recovered at the scene. The software did exactly what it was designed to do and immediately told ATF personnel where and when the firearms had been manufactured, who distributed the firearm and with the aid of the Suspect Gun Database exactly what retail federal firearms dealer had made the over the counter sale. In this case, the data identified a criminal, but the vast majority of information held by ATF are the records of private citizens who are not criminals.

---

* **American Embassy Cable, 07MEXICO1854**, marked "Confidential" and sent to the Secretary of State, Washington DC March 13, 2007, accessed at: http://www.wikileaks.ch/cable/2007/04/07MEXICO1854.html

We don't know what other data eTrace provided, but ATF would normally contact the retail business first, and it would be the business who dutifully dug through their records and provided Avila's full name and address (and any other information on weapons he had purchased that day, not just the two AK47 rifles), his driver's license number, where he was born, his Social Security number, his height, weight, color of eyes and hair.

ATF may also have requested, using the Trace Request Form, any information regarding any other weapons Avila had purchased from that store at any point in their license history. They can request the same information about you.

Although it would not be required, the gun shop—f it had copied Avila's driver's license—may have chosen to FAX his photo and the other information to the ATF. But ATF really didn't need that since Avila had been under surveillance for over a year. ATF had lots of pictures of Avila, some of which may have even been streamed real-time into ATF Director Ken Melson's office in Washington D.C.

Whatever photograph they decided to use was quickly distributed throughout the state. Local law enforcement agents were mobilized and they located and arrested Avila in Phoenix the same day. The U.S. Attorney's Office in Arizona later indicted him on three counts of straw purchasing firearms, but it would be a day late and a dollar short for Terry's family.

Interestingly, these three indictments did not stem from the weapons purchased on January 16, 2010 which eventually ended up at the Terry crime scene in Peck Canyon just below Hell's Gate. Instead, Avila was indicted for rifles he bought *six months later* and which turned up at another crime scene entirely.

On May 6, 2011, DOJ also unsealed an indictment of Manuel Osorio-Arellanes for the murder of Brian Terry. Osorio-Arellanes had been wounded at the scene and was unable to flee; as it turns out, he was an expert at fleeing.

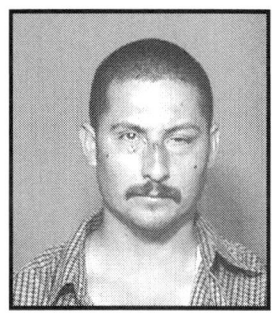

Osorio-Arellanes is an illegal Mexican thug that has been deported at least once before. Arellanes' criminal past includes domestic violence, drug and alcohol abuse, including violence against police according to arrest records in Maricopa County. With virtually no redeeming human qualities Osorio-Arellanes on the night he was involved in the murder of Brian Terry, was moon-lighting his criminal experience. Osorio-Arellanes later admitted carrying a rifle, according to an FBI search warrant, but claimed he did not fire when he realized the men they'd encountered were Border Patrol agents. I'm sure you can believe him.

Figure 11: Manuel Osorio-Arellanes.

All through this debauchery ATF and other political operatives from the White House have continued to foist the myth on the American public that this kind of thing is the fault of criminal activity by US gun dealers who do this as a lucrative adventure.

> "Assault weapons, as we now know here in Mexico, are helping to fuel extraordinary violence."

President Barack Hussein Obama

Secretary of State Hillary Clinton, on a visit to Mexico, boldly stated that America's inability to prevent weapons being smuggled across the border was causing the deaths of Mexican police officers, soldiers and civilians;* you would have thought that should have stuck in her "vast right wing conspiracy" throat but it did not. In fact, as it has been shown in this research, it was the US Government who was pushing firearms into Mexico and using the

---

* **Hillary Clinton: U.S. Fueling Mexican Drug Wars,** published March 26, 2009; (CBS/AP) "U.S. Secretary of State Hillary Rodham Clinton said Wednesday that America's "insatiable" demand for illegal drugs and its inability to stop weapons from being smuggled into Mexico are fueling an alarming spike in violence along the U.S.-Mexican border." Accessed June 23, 2011 at:
http://www.cbsnews.com/stories/2009/03/25/politics/main4891839.shtml

eTrace system (which used the Operation Fast and Furious firearms to artificially inflate arms trafficking numbers) to bolster a political agenda.

The other scary part was they were also pushing computerized information into the hands of foreign nationals; information that likely compromises the privacy of American citizens and that privacy appears to be compromised in other ways.

I was personally an arms dealer during this period and only on a few occasions did questionable people appear to attempt the purchase of firearms (admittedly I am fortunate to live in a small town that has predominantly good citizens; regrettably our proximity to Mexico is changing that). However, in 2009 a customer appeared at our sales counter casually asking what it would cost to purchase ten AK47 rifles. Without giving away our surprise at what was to us an obviously unusual request, we engaged the customer about the sale and told the individual we did not have that kind of inventory but would check to see if it was available.

When he left, I tasked my employee to contact ATF and he alerted agents in Phoenix to the situation.

> *"The Agent I spoke with was very helpful and said it sounded like I did a good job of qualifying the purchase, and stated that the purchase was lawful..."*

As part of the public expenditures related to Project Gunrunner, the ATF had provided FFL dealers with online training and glossy counter brochures which profiled potential straw sales; this sale fit the profile for several reasons, large quantity of semi-automatic firearms, cash buyer, not quibbling on price. It turns out that like a lot of Arizona gun dealers who were similarly approached during Operation Fast and Furious, when alerted ATF apparently in every case said,

> *"...go ahead, sell the guns. No problem."*
>
> **ATF Name withheld**

In our case, the buyer was re-contacted to confirm his interest in the sale and we subsequently initiated the order for the firearms;

when the customer returned to pick them up he provided us with the required Arizona driver's license for residency (and interestingly showed us an active duty US Marine Corps ID). He filled out the standard ATF Form 4473, we contacted the FBI NICS operation for a routine firearms background check which they quickly cleared.

Note that by law, since the background check cleared, all personal information taken by the FBI regarding this individual should have been destroyed within the next few hours. As you will see, this was not the case.

Although we were unaware of Operation Fast and Furious at the time and did not have information regarding any of its far-reaching implications, we met that evening and discussed the business rules associated with this sale. Both the employees and I were in agreement that no matter how the ATF felt about this and regardless that the FBI had cleared the buyer on a background check, we decided this was not the kind of business in which we wanted to participate; other firearms dealers similarly made this decision. It was a fortuitous decision, as we were subsequently approached by buyers described in the ATF profile who did not have good credentials, were clearly speaking broken English, wanted to buy a lot of guns with cash and had an appearance that could literally raise the hair implants on Vice-President Joe Biden's head.

Almost two years later in July of 2011, the ATF Tracing Center contacted me requesting a trace on one of the weapons in this sale made in 2009. Uncharacteristically, ATF offered up the actual date of the retail transaction in my store; information they could not have legally possessed. Based on previous trace requests, ATF would normally not have that information; the trace request is used to obtain that information, not to confirm it.

When it turned out a rifle in this 2009 sale was being traced I wasn't very surprised; I was angry but not really surprised. Was I scammed by an ATF operative posing as a Marine with fake ID, was the ATF doing surveillance on that buyer, or was it completely unrelated to Operation Fast and Furious? Unlike Brian Terry's family, I'll probably never know.

What I do know is that even if that customer was a straw buyer for the cartel, the only way ATF could have had the date of sale information in my store was if the FBI (who actually does the background check) illegally transferred that information to ATF when by law they should have destroyed it long ago. An illegal firearms registry is the only answer.

While some will say "...*hey, thank goodness they are keeping that information otherwise criminals would be getting away with murder*..."   The self-obvious response is that ATF is also getting away with murder.

At what point do we as Americans begin to blindly accept the inevitable consequences of rogue government? At what point do we lose our integrity as American citizens and become the tax slave chattel of power-hungry despots whose hope for change becomes a edict of power we can ill afford to abide?

Latin American Arms

*"After decades of uncontrolled proliferation, **at least 45 million to 80 million small arms and light weapons**— that is, weapons operated by an individual or small group, including handguns, assault rifles, grenades, grenade launchers, and even man portable surface to air missiles— **are circulating throughout the region**...* [ed. Note: emphasis added]

Center for Defense Information[*]

The reality is straw buyers for the cartels may be purchasing firearms in the US, but they don't actually need American gun stores to obtain those firearms. In many cases, the weapons used by the cartels are simply not for sale at Super Walmart.

In fact, the drug lords don't have to go to America in order to buy illegal arms; they stay right in Mexico and buy all the arms they want. Central and South America in general and Mexico in particular is awash in opportunities to purchase illegally trafficked firearms. To start with, there are already literally *tens of millions of weapons* available for sales that were dumped into the area during the Cold War by the US Government and the Soviet Union. This idea stands in stark contrast to the propaganda proposed by ATF who suggests straw buyers are supplying the cartels with profit centers based on US sales.

"You're going to spend $8,000 [in the US] *and sell them for $20,000 or $25,000 down in Mexico..."*

ATF agent [†]

Supposedly, these statements and others like it were based on hard evidence of ATF investigations using eTrace and other computer

---

[*] **The Small Arms Trade in Latin America**, Rachel Stohl and Doug Tuttle, accessed July 2, 2011 at: http://www.cdi.org/pdfs/Small_Arms_Latin_America.pdf
[†] **CBS News** accessed at: http://www.cbsnews.com/8301-503543_162-4893905-503543.html

71

software to uncover American complicity in Mexican drug-related violence. At best, it was preposterous propaganda. Indeed, this political agitprop fails the test of logic for several critically important reasons and is in fact insulting to anyone who honestly runs the numbers and looks at the results.

Any investment like the one described above that turns an $8000 firearms purchase into $25,000 is leveraging a three to one uptick in profit. This is a popular ratio with ATF and is used in their online straw buyer video training* describing the same ratio in illegal US street sales. But consider that the used average condition semi-automatic AK47 sells at any gun store or flea market in Arizona for about $500. Using the same 3:1 ratio, the implication is a straw buyer can quickly turn that investment into $1500 by reselling it to the drug cartel in Mexico. Ok, that's not particularly difficult math, let's see if it actually holds up.

Here is a real example of how this drivel turns into popular conventional wisdom and urban folklore. Time.com, ever the journalistic lapdog for every elected socialist program in America, actually reported in 2009 that a Mexican thug had purchased a .50 caliber rifle (Time.com enhanced the description by calling it a "killing machine") supposedly from an Arizona retailer for $21,000.† Three to one investment margins indicated by ATF would suggest this entrepreneur could resell the weapon in Mexico for about $60,000.

Hey, Time.com and ATF said so, it must be true!

In fact, it sounds like pretty good money, particularly for the gun store (how many $21,000 deals did you do on any one day last week?). But, much as I hate to introduce facts into the media's fantasy football game, let's take a closer look.

First of all, nobody pays $21,000 for a .50 caliber rifle in the US. They are expensive, but *NOT* that expensive. New retail pricing for

---

* http://www.atf.gov/training/firearms/ffl-educational-seminars/
† **Time.com** Aug. 10, 2009, last accessed on June 23, 2011 at:
http://www.time.com/time/world/article/0,8599,1915327,00.html

a top of the line weapon of this type from Barrett Arms is about $9000.*

How is it we are supposed to believe the drug cartels are able to maintain an incredibly successful $250 billion dollar international money laundering operation, supported by an even larger illegal drug and human trafficking industry and are able to get Wachovia (a Wells Fargo) Bank to participate in laundering cash amounting to nearly one-third of Mexico's entire Gross Domestic Product (GDP)†, all the while pitted against the efforts of several really smart well-armed governments but somehow the ATF wants us to believe they can't figure out how to pay retail for an over the counter firearm?

The reality of the arms trade is that the type of weapons preferred by the drug cartels (see the Appendix) cost very little in third world countries as compared with the US arms market; in any case some of these weapons are not available to US buyers at all. This is largely because third world countries are run by dictators who have no interest in the business of profit, unlike American capitalists who have to pay the bills from the profit. While run of the mill semi-automatic AK47 rifles sell for about $500 here, their fully-automatic machine gun counterpart in an American gun shop carries the hefty tag of $15,000 and only for those willing to wait the three to six months necessary to complete the ATF background check.

Here's the newsflash—the same fully-automatic Communist-made (Combloc) AK47 machine gun sells for a mere $100 in the Middle East and for cash either you or a Jihadi can sleep with it tonight.‡ Supply and demand works even in the Middle East and Mexico; when a market is flooded prices go down. Secretary General of the United Nations Kofi A. Annan once suggested an AK47 in Africa could be purchased for the cost of a chicken; I'm guessing that would be one expensive chicken, even in the context of President

---

* **Barret Arms Pricing**, Rev 2, 2011, http://www.barrett.net/pdfs/Price-List.pdf
† http://www.guardian.co.uk/world/2011/apr/03/us-bank-mexico-drug-gangs
‡ **STRAFOR Global Security and Intelligence Report**, *Mexico*, by Scott Stewart and Fred Burton, copyright July 9, 2009

Obama's bailout expenditures, but the point is taken regarding the relative cost black market arms.

But, forget the whole machine gun thing for a moment; given that you are any average consumer buying a product of almost any description and your choice is $100 bucks with immediate delivery—or $15,000, a government background check and six months delayed delivery *for EXACTLY the same thing*—which deal are you likely to choose? How stupid do they think we are?

Note that a lot of the news video I saw reporting the American retail gun connection to Mexican drug cartels last year featured the repeated sound of fully-automatic machine guns. A weapon like the M-60 machine gun recovered in a cartel raid near Falcon Lake in 2011 costs nearly $250,000 in the US (and you get the ATF's special six month waiting period). Using ATF's 3:1 ratio that one weapon would have cost the cartel three-quarters of a million dollars. In contrast, that same weapon might only be a few thousand bucks on the Beirut black market.

Hold up your hands, how many people think you get to successfully run a multi-billion dollar international operation, reporting your expenditures to the most violent criminals on earth and you become successful through excessively stupid spending? The loathsome lunatic in the White House might think that works with our tax money in a cross-eyed dream for redistribution of wealth, but it is unclear this is a model the cartels have adopted.

Let me ask you this, did you ever try to BUY a machine gun over the counter in a gun store? How many have you even seen for sale? In fact, American machine guns are rarer than abstinence in Barney Frank's bedroom, having been heavily controlled since passage of the National Firearms Act in 1936 (thank you FDR). ALL sales of newly manufactured machine guns to private citizens have been outlawed since May 1986 (thank you Ronald Reagan).

Machine guns are real hard to get even if the weapon is a used legally registered pre-'86 machine gun and you are a wealthy, honest, law-abiding American citizen living in a relatively free state with a lot of personal squeaky clean documentation on a hygienically clear criminal record and uninhibited by the type of draconian laws imposed in New Jersey, California and other socialist utopias. I am telling you this from experience; I had a federally issued Class III firearms license to sell machine guns and I made my living at this for a number of years—I do know what I'm talking about.

The inflated price here as compared to the Middle East is caused by this same government controlled coercion called the National Firearms Act administration (NFA) which currently maintains the only (arguably) legal firearms registration in America accompanied by a 'special' personal background check which takes anywhere from three to six months in order to complete before the now thoroughly vetted buyer can get his paws on the purchase. You have got to ask yourself why an honest, wealthy (and probably very busy) pillar of the community would risk everything they have worked for in order to engage in tawdry little illegal gun sales with Mexico?

To be fair, there were weapons illegally moving across the border in Arizona. It is obvious some of these small arms transactions went to the cartels but others were more likely going to individual Mexican citizens—victims trying to protect themselves and their families from the escalating violence initiated between competing drug cartels in an equipment race fueled and supplied by radical Islamic Jihadists and the ATF.

But, just to put a fine point on this, the ATF gunrunner numbers just don't make any rational sense.

Many hand gun and long gun sales are routinely based on a certain amount of paranoia associated with the Obama/Holder record of gun control. During the fall of 2008 when Obama was originally elected, prospective American gun owners who had reviewed Senator Obama's abysmal (and thankfully short) Chicago record on gun control became convinced new Draconian gun control legislation was just around the corner.

In fact, after Obama was elected in November 2008, the entire gun industry sold out of semi-automatic rifles and the ammunition in a matter of weeks; manufacturers were backordered by millions of units and gun shows were selling them at prices that would make even Donald Trump blush. In fact, at the time even old military poorly maintained bolt-action rifles from World War I completely sold out along with even slower inventory that no one in their right mind would use as a defensive weapon. Obama at the time was heralded with tongue in cheek as the "Firearms Salesman of the Year".* (See, Figure 12).

Other dealers obviously took ATF at their word and sold bulk orders of ten and twenty rifles to people who should not have had them. Note that ATF knew these people were serious trouble, should not have possession of the weapons and yet, they let them walk out the door of gun shops anyway. Reports suggest some ATF managers were absolutely giddy about being able to find the guns in Mexico.

To their credit, a lot of ATF agents in Phoenix complained internally to management who promptly and arrogantly ignored the judgment of their own agents.

Firearms Salesman of the Year

Figure 12: President Barack Hussein Obama whose election facilitated the sale of every military style semi-automatic rifle in American gun shops.

Still, ten units at a crack or twenty—while this is good profit in any business except gum balls, it is still not enough guns to correlate to the arming of large Mexican drug cartels in any real way.

---

* http://www.foxnews.com/politics/2009/01/16/obama-driving-surge-gun-sales-firearms

Consider that there are about 6000 federally licensed firearm dealers in Arizona and the greater southwest. The Washington times puts the probable number of drug cartel operatives at over 100,000 thugs for just the Sinaloa and Los Zetas cartels alone; populations for all Mexican cartels and their American gang outlets puts them at a force of almost one-quarter of a million criminals. Most criminals carry at least two guns as well as other weapons into a fight, and they own other firearms as backups. Assuming a conservative estimate of three firearms per thug, you are talking about three-quarters of a million firearms, probably more. The Mexican government as we indicated earlier is sitting on a warehouse of confiscated firearms that was estimated to be one-third of a million weapons in 2008 and this doesn't include the number of weapons corrupt officials in the Mexican government resold to the cartels. That totals nearly one-million criminal firearms afloat in Mexico or in government warehouses at any one time.

Now I know Hillary Clinton's assessment that all firearm owners are the purveyors of evil is wildly popular at Washington beltway cocktail parties, but for argument sake, let's assume that not every one of the 6000 dealers in the southwest is corrupt. In fact, I know from experience that to get a federal firearms license, you have to go through a lot of paperwork, an extensive FBI background check and an up-close personal interview with the ATF who comes to your shop and looks over you and your life with a microscope.

That's not to say the retail firearms business is free of corruption, what business is? It is just that considering it is one of the most regulated businesses in America, corruption at the retail level is probably pretty limited—let's say less than ten percent (or about sixty dealers in the entire southwest *MAY* be actively selling to Mexican straw purchasers). ATF's record of retail dealer prosecutions suggests it is far less than that, but for argument's sake, let's go with ten percent (sixty corrupt dealers).

Now do the math.

Even if you believe American firearms dealers supplied only ten percent of the cartels one million weapons, 100,000 weapons going through sixty dealers would be over 1600 illegal firearms transfers per dealer. Hey, you know somebody might notice a truck that big backing up to the local gun shop.

Since you can only get about four firearms on an ATF firearms transfer form, you'd have to say that is a lot of paperwork to keep clean in front of near-sighted ATF inspectors. ATF inspectors, who—particularly since 9-11—routinely inspect the firearms disposition books at each and every gun shop in the southwest, and they might have queried that many transfers of military weapons with some amount of vigor. Hey...I'm just guessing here...professional investigators are actually paid to notice these things.

Even if a dealer is doing all this illegally under the table, at $500 a pop for a semi-automatic AK47, that's more than a half-million dollars in hot cash they would also have to adeptly hide from those pesky IRS inspectors. That is a lot of cash even for a Democrat like William J. "Cold Cash" Jefferson (D-La.) who modeled cash stashing in his home freezer.*

American firearms dealers did NOT arm the Mexican drug cartels because it couldn't have happened this way. You and I have been lied to for political gain, admittedly not for the first nor the last time. Obama, Holder, Napolitano, Clinton and the whole cadre of idiots running the mainstream media think we are too stupid to figure this all out. I don't personally like their assessment of the American people.

So, get this: between 2005 and 2009, a total of $41 billion worth of U.S. defense arms were legally exported under the auspices of the US State Department and the Pentagon via the Foreign Military Sales (FMS) program and a total of nearly $60 billion via the Direct Commercial Sales (DCS) program according to a recent U.S. Government Accountability Office (GAO) report.†

---

* **William J. Jefferson (D-La)**, gained national attention after federal agents found $90,000 in his freezer. He was convicted in Aug. 2009 of 11 of 16 criminal counts including bribery, racketeering, money laundering and wire fraud.
† **GAO report**: http://www.gao.gov/new.items/d10952.pdf

The bulk of recent US arms exports went to multiple foreign countries, but Mexico acquired some $204 million in military arms shipments approved for export in fiscal year 2008 alone according to the GAO. Consider the following report from the Center for Defense Information in Washington DC:

> "Small arms flooded Latin America during the Cold War, most significantly during the Central American civil wars of the 1980s. Although diverse motivations, channels, and suppliers have had a hand in their proliferation, the Cold War and its legacies bear most of the responsibility. Both the United States and the Soviet Union supplied their Latin American allies with mass quantities of weapons through proxy arms dealers. The Soviets and their Warsaw Pact allies sent weapons to Cuba, which then passed them to the Sandinistas in Nicaragua.
>
> "In response, the United States often provided its Central American allies, like the counterrevolutionary Nicaraguan Contras, with Soviet weaponry, most notably the AK-47, in order to maintain official "deniability" of its involvement in the conflicts. **The U.S. military allegedly maintained warehouses of Soviet-bloc weapons that were distributed throughout the region.** [ed. Note: emphasis added and Soviet-bloc weapons are AK47's and SKS models] The United States also used third countries, including Israel, to supply the Contras. In El Salvador, the Farabundo Martí National Liberation Front received AK-47s from the Honduran military, which had raided the CIA's Nicaraguan supplies. Caches of Cold War–origin weapons are still being found in Latin America...
>
> "According to data provided by the Norwegian Initiative on Small Arms Transfers, **in 2005 Latin America legally imported at least $175 million worth of small arms and light weapons, as well as ammunition and spare parts.** [ed. Note: emphasis added] The United States was the main supplier to the region, exporting almost $50 million worth of these weapons. Other major suppliers to Latin America that

year included Belgium, the Czech Republic, Germany, Israel, Italy, Russia, South Africa, and Spain. The same 2005 data reveals that the vast majority of the $29 million worth of U.S. small arms flowing to South America went to Colombia. Mexico imported $10 million worth of small arms, almost as much as all the small arms that Central America and the Caribbean imported combined."

This 2008 report referenced here pretty much puts the pin in the party pig. Between the US, the former Soviet Union and Hezbollah terrorists trafficking every imaginable weapon into Mexico, Central and South America, it is difficult to believe the cartels are seriously interested in buying overpriced American rifles from a few low level border thugs; not that they wouldn't do it but it seems like a stretch (you'd have to be on drugs or something).

Many of the M16 machine guns captured or left behind in our hasty retreat from Viet Nam similarly ended up in El Salvador years later.

"The American military had left them in Asia, where they had been collected...and shipped back across the sea ...M16s had been provided to the Salvadoran government as part of the American foreign military sales program and had leaked from government possession to the insurgency. In sum, the United States had armed its foes, indirectly but surely."

C.J. Chivers*

Weapons "leak" into insurgencies from all corners of the world; Africa, Asia, Central and South America and the ubiquitous Middle East. This is fundamentally why there were never any high profile drug cartel "kingpin" arrests directly associated with Operation Fast and Furious (I'm sure that some of those same 'kingpins' were on the payroll of DEA and the FBI had nothing to do with that). Most of the time these kingpins were too busy negotiating orders for millions of automatic weapons, ammunition, grenades, portable surface to air missiles and rocket launchers—things that just aren't available in your average home town "Mom and Pop" gun shop.

---

* **The Gun,** C.J. Chivers, Simon and Schuster, Copyright 2010, pg. 363

But they do continue to be available and from *"...all the usual suspects"* which now include the United States as well as rogue nations and disintegrating nations in rebellion. Particularly in the cases of rebellion automatic weapons are shipped legally, lost in the heat of battle or left behind, captured and resold time and time again. AK47 weapons originally manufactured in Russia which turn up at crime scenes used by the Mexican drug cartels often bear manufacturing date stamps from the 1950's.

The principal force-multiplier for Osama Bin Laden when he was fighting with the Afghani Mujahideen in their successful attempt to oust the Russians from their homeland was a real river of iron that moved AK47s and other military arms in such enormous quantities they were measured in tons of weight rather than numbers of arms. In 1983 Karachi insurgents backed by the US received 10,000 tons of arms in one year; an amount increased by 1987 to shipments totaling 65,000 tons of military grade weapons annually.*

During the Albanian conflict in 1997, citizens ran roughshod across a terrain of failed government that had promised a rational transformation of Communist inspired coercion to a market economy; like a lot of plans laid by socialist lap-dog state planners, it went south on them. Riots broke out and the Albanian Combloc factory locally producing AK47s was ransacked for its inventory. After the blood bath, government officials conservatively estimated that the arms loss was on the order of 700,000 weapons and probably 1.5 billion rounds of ammunition, although their estimates were considered low.† Some of the materiel was returned, most of it went into the black market, which of course precipitated the Albanian government to negotiate a new arms deal for "defensive purposes."

The US, since the Islamic terrorist attack in 2001, has become one of the largest known purchasers of AK47s in the world,

---

* **Ibid**, The Gun, pg. 362
† **Turning the Page: Small Arms and Light Weapons in Albania**, Center for Peace and Disarmament Education/Saferworld, December 2005, pg. 6

"...which it has handed out by the tens of thousands in Afghanistan and Iraq."*

Among those documents released through WikiLeaks was a provocative cable communication marked "Secret"; the cable was sent by the American Embassy in Monterey Mex. and directed to the Secretary of State, FBI and the Department of Justice dated 3 March 2009. In the cable, authored by Bruce Williamson, Principal Officer at the American Embassy at that time, diplomatic officers attempted to respond to the discovery and origin of various US-made grenades and other explosive devices recovered at the site of several terrorist attacks in Mexico. Something neither your neighbor nor your local Wal-Mart gun counter is likely to have for sale.

The weapons identified in the cable included an M26A2 fragmentation grenade, 21 other grenades, twenty-five 40mm explosive projectiles, a U.S. M203 40mm grenade launcher, M-67 fragmentation grenades and three South Korean K75 and K400 fragmentation grenades. The cable read in part,

> *"The lot numbers of some of the grenades recovered, including the grenade used in the attack on Televisa†, indicate that previously ordnance with these same lot numbers may have been sold by the US to the El Salvadoran military in the early 1990s via the Foreign Military Sales program. Local Mexican law enforcement has recovered a Grenade spoon and pull ring from an exploded hand grenade used in a January 6, 2009 attack on Televisa Monterrey, a Monterrey television station. Based upon ATF examination, it appears that the grenade used in the attack on the Consulate has the same lot number, and is of similar design and style, as the three of the grenades found at the narco-warehouse in Guadalupe. On January 7, 2009, the Mexican*

---

* **Ibid**, The Gun, pg. 411
† **Televisa**: Mexican multimedia conglomerate, the largest mass media company in Latin America and in the Spanish-speaking world. It is a major international entertainment business, with much of its programming airing in the United States on Univision, with which it has an exclusive contract.

Army recovered 14 M-67 fragmentation grenades and 1 K400 fragmentation grenade in Durango City, Durango. Finally and perhaps most disturbing, on January 31, 2009 three men tossed a K-75 grenade into a night club near Pharr, Texas..." [Complete text in Endnote[10]]

Bruce Williamson[*]

With the Cold War days over; most people would assume the US and former Soviet Union would have long ago completed the gunrunning associated with that period; unfortunately this is a very dangerous assumption. Hillary's US State Department in FY2010 (the most recent data available) was still authorizing large scale foreign weapons sales into many places in Central and South America as well as weapons sales directly to the Government of Mexico.

> *"Last year, the U.S. State Department's Direct Commercial Sales Program doled-out some $416.5million worth of weapons and equipment to the Mexican military. U.S. taxpayers have stumped up more than a billion dollars to fund the so-called Merida Initiative, providing equipment and training to Mexico's security agencies."*

Robert Farago and Ralph Dixon[†]

Mexico has one of the most corrupt military and police networks in the world, which isn't really saying much in Chicago, but they are in fact at least a shared source of their own problem. One of the drug cartel enforcement units (Los Zetas) is comprised entirely of ex-Mexican military that deserted and took their weapons with them.

Calderón and other Mexican officials have been repeatedly accused of having ties to the Sinaloa Cartel whose blood enemy includes Los

---

[*] **Bruce Williamson**, Principal Officer at the American Embassy in Monterey, Mex. Cable accessed on July 5, 2011 at:
http://www.wikileaks.ch/cable/2009/03/09MONTERREY100.html
[†] The Truth About Guns, http://thetruthaboutguns.com/2011/08/robert-farago-and-ralph-dixon/atf-death-watch-53-the-truth-about-operation-fast-and-furious/ 8/10/2011

Zetas; that rivalry—and the Mexican federal corruption—has a long history.

In fact, fore-shadowing the military enforcement background of the Zetas, the "original" illegal Mexican drug organization created in the 1980's was the Guadalajara crime syndicate led by Miguel Ángel Félix Gallardo.* Gallardo was himself a trained law enforcement officer who at one time was the bodyguard for the governor of Sinaloa and knew first-hand the ins and outs of illegal trafficking. Using this knowledge he began to smuggle local Mexican-sourced marijuana to aging hippies and other criminal gang organizations inside the US—eventually becoming the first major connection for the Columbian cocaine trade. He later became the principal Mexican trafficker for the *Medellin* cartel, which was run by the infamous and brutal Pablo Escobar.† Eventually Gallardo would become the "Godfather" of Mexican drug cartels.‡

Documentation suggests both Gallardo and his Mexican Columbian-based trafficking success was at least partially due to what the CIA calls an "asset". Assets are essentially operatives willing to take US taxpayer money (under the table) in trade for information or

---

* **Miguel Ángel Félix Gallardo** (born January 8, 1946) is a convicted Mexican drug lord known as "*El Padrino*" (*"The Godfather"*) who in the 1980s formed the Guadalajara Cartel and became the first drug czar in Mexico to control all illegal drug traffic in Mexico and the corridors along the Mexico-U.S.A. border.

† **Pablo Emilio Escobar Gaviria** (December 1, 1949 – December 2, 1993) was a Colombian drug lord. Often referred to as the "World's Greatest Outlaw", he was the most elusive cocaine trafficker ever to have lived. He is regarded as the richest and most successful criminal in world history. Some other sources state that he was the second richest criminal ever, after Amado Carrillo Fuentes. In 1989, *Forbes* magazine declared Escobar as the seventh richest man in the world, with an estimated personal fortune of $25 billion (USD). He attempted to enter Colombian politics, even offering to pay off the nation's $10 billion national debt.

‡ **"The Godfather"** convened the nation's top drug narco-traffickers at a house in Acapulco where he designated the *plazas* or territories. The Tijuana route would go to the Arellano Felix brothers. The Ciudad Juárez route would go to the Carrillo Fuentes family. Miguel Caro Quintero would run the Sonora corridor. The control of the Matamoros, Tamaulipas corridor - then becoming the Gulf Cartel- would be left undisturbed to Juan García Abrego. Meanwhile, Joaquín Guzmán Loera and Ismael Zambada García would take over Pacific coast operations, becoming the Sinaloa Cartel.

willing to help action certain events deemed "necessary" by the CIA.

In the case of the Gallardo syndicate (which eventually morphed into the Sinaloa Cartel) the paid asset was Miguel Nassar Haro.[*] As head of the Government of Mexico's intelligence agency (called the *Dirección Federal de Seguridad* or DFS[†]) Haro was uniquely able to offer Gallardo government protection. The DFS organization itself was considered from inception to be a CIA invention and many officials, Haro among them, were assets trading cash for favors. The CIA's closest government allies were for years in the DFS and who blatantly handed out DFS badges and credentials to top-level Mexican drug-traffickers; badges of authority that have been labeled by DEA agents a virtual "license to traffic" In Mexico.

> "...the DFS was in part a CIA creation; and the CIA presence in the DFS became so dominant that some of its intelligence, according to the famous Mexican journalist Manuel Buend'ia,[‡] was seen only by American eyes."

Peter Dale Scott[§]

Most of this dirty criminal history between the CIA and the Mexican drug cartels is unknown to the average American as it doesn't make the six o'clock news in any real way. However, Gallardo's criminal syndicate operating as the principal drug trafficker in the CIA's infamous Contra scandal involving Manuel Noriega is considerably closer to home. Noriega was repeatedly shielded by the CIA against DEA investigations.[**] This unholy arrangement of US Government protection for Mexican thugs was widespread at the time.

---

[*] **Cocaine Politics** by Peter Dale Scott and Jonathan Marshall, (Berkeley and Los Angeles: University of California Press, 1991)

[†] **Dirección Federal de Seguridad,** (Directorate of Federal Security) or DFS; Created in 1947 it was merged into the *Centro de Investigación y Seguridad Nacional* (CISEN) in 1985.

[‡] **Manuel Buend'ia**, *La CIA en Mexico* (Mexico City: Oceano Magazine, 1983).

[§] **Washington and the Politics of Drugs** by UK journalist Peter Dale Scott, appearing in Variant Volume 2, issue No. 11 (summer 2000) and accessed at: http://www.variant.org.uk/pdfs/issue11/Variant11.pdf

[**] **Ibid**, Cocaine Politics, Scott and Marshall

In 1981 William Kennedy was appointed U.S. Attorney in San Diego. Preparing to bring charges against a large scale car thief ring which was moving autos into Mexico, Kennedy was about to file a warrant for the arrest of none other than Miguel Nassar Haro, the CIA's favorite stoolie in the Mexican DFS.* Washington held up the indictment for months after which Kennedy was unceremoniously fired. It is clear the CIA will go to leviathan depths to wash their laundry.

One ex-CIA agent† suggests the reason cartels are even remotely interested in small purchases of weapons by straw buyers in the US is that Los Zetas has organized a *coup d'état* scheduled to depose Philipé Calderón and potentially overthrow the entire Mexican state in 2012. Their goal—a seat at the founders feast— is to achieve the legitimized political status in Mexico that Pablo Escobar failed to establish in Columbia. It is supposedly this "finding" that authorized the CIA to use ATF resources to funnel guns to the competing Sinaloa cartel.

Stockpiling any and every weapon cartels can lay their hands on in order to facilitate a *coup d'état* would explain what would normally be a disinterested approach to small arms purchases. They appear to be organizing this partially under the nose of the DEA and especially the ATF who is clearly too busy harassing small US gun stores.

> *"(MEXICO CITY) - Los Zetas use the Alliance Airport in Ft. Worth, Texas -the same airport where the DEA's Air Operations Center is located—to fly weapons to Columbus, NM., El Paso, and Laredo, TX. to be later smuggled into Mexico. CIA analysts say the weapons, which are purchased*

---

* **Doing His Job Too Well,** Time Magazine, Monday, Apr. 12, 1982 accessed at: http://www.time.com/time/magazine/article/0,9171,922837,00.html

† **Salem News:** Former DEA and CIA Operatives: Los Zetas May Attempt to Overthrow Mexican Government in 2012 (Using U.S. Government Weapons), Carmen Álvarez, Translated by Mario Andrade, DeadlineLive.info, July 2011. Robert Plumlee, a former CIA pilot and Phil Jordan, a former CIA operative and DEA director, claim Los Zetas have stockpiled thousands of weapons to disrupt and influence Mexico's national elections in 2012., accessed at: http://www.salem-news.com/articles/july202011/los-zetas-ca.php

from the U.S. Government according to captured Zeta leader Jesus Enrique Rejon Aguilar, aka. El Mamito, are being stockpiled throughout Mexico for a potential upcoming overthrow of the Mexican government in 2012...The report is corroborated with an interview with Phil Jordan, former director of the DEA in El Paso, who stated that the stockpiles, which include anti-aircraft missiles, are transported from a Dallas-Fort Worth Airport. The consultant added that the criminals set up (phony) companies to buy weapons directly through a State Department program."

Carmen Álvarez*

The shipments of firearms and ammunition are enormous and the amount of money is huge (detailed at Endnote[11]). Total authorizations by the State Department in FY2009 were over $35 billion and increased substantially during 2010. Authorized sales into the South American radical tri-border Islamic hotbed of arms and drug trafficking in FY2010 resulted in $6,416,445 in sales of arms and technology deliverables to Argentina, $1,825,134 to Paraguay and a whopping $37,134,259[†] to Brazil whose population from Middle Eastern Lebanese descent alone is estimated to be ten million.[‡]

A similar situation had occurred in 2008 when US military ordnance was recovered in both Mexico and Columbia and was traced to US Government sales to the government of Honduras who frankly had a harder time explaining this than Lucille Ball trying to tell Ricky how the toaster caught fire. Problematically this situation was further complicated by our Mike Vanderboegh's reporting that ATF agents in Tampa Florida were also trafficking arms into Honduras as part of a copy-cat program called Operation Castaway and run under the leadership of a former Phoenix ATF official.

---

[*] **Ibid**, Salem News
[†] **FY2010 Weapons sales** from US Department of State accessed at: http://www.pmddtc.state.gov/reports/documents/rpt655_FY10.pdf
[‡] **Brazilian Lebanese population**, accessed at:
http://en.wikipedia.org/wiki/Lebanese_Brazilian

*"On July 9, 2008, the Defense Intelligence Agency (DIA) published a report entitled "Honduras: Military Weapons Fuel Black Arms Market". According to the DIA report, three light anti-tank weapons (LAWs) were recovered in Mexico City in January 2008..Six more LAWs were recovered...in March 2008. Factory markings analysis of lot and serial numbers...indicates that these LAWs were part of a shipment of fifty sent to the Honduran 2nd Infantry Battalion's TESON training element. **The LAWs were originally transferred to Honduras in 1992 as part of a U.S. Foreign Military Sales program.**"* [ed. Note: emphasis added]

Rice*

Analysis in Columbia by the Antiterrorist Analysis Inter-institutional Group (GIAT) documented a turn of terrorist weapons that occurred during the peace process being brokered between November 2004 and April 2006. Paramilitary organizations and militias turned approximately 9,521 rifles and 195 machine guns. The data revealed a virtual smorgasbord of international weapons manufacturers involved in arming the Columbian lords.

All were illicit weapons clandestinely introduced into the violent conflict by the ever familiar arms traffickers from Honduras, Nicaragua and El Salvador—not US gun shops. There aren't enough guns or gun shops in the southwestern US to support the lucrative high volume gunrunning schemes that are fueling the cartel violence and rogue governments all over the world have filled this vacuum.

"Of these, 1,877 were made in the United States and brought into Colombia by trafficking rings. Most of the rifles were made in the former Soviet Union (3,547), Bulgaria (2,333), North Korea (1,764), and Poland (47). The machine guns were made in Romania (75), Russia (60), Germany (37), Colombia (20), and Venezuela (3). The majority of the

---

* **LAW Ordinance**: Cable originated from the US Department of State, 2 October 2008 and accessed at:
http://www.wikileaks.ch/cable/2008/10/08STATE105491.html

weapons originated from Nicaragua, El Salvador, and Honduras, acquired legally during Central America's internal conflicts in the 1980s and later were sent illegally to Colombia via air and sea."

Wood[*]

There is no way of calling these weapons back. While it would seem prudent to combat terror at its source and that combat inevitably is going to require time, technology, money and weapons, none the less the continued injection of weapons into countries with corrupt governments and known sponsors of terror is going to eventually result in throwing high-octane gasoline on the problem and then lighting the proverbial covert match.

Note that there are very few Central American countries with large numbers of illegals moving across the US border that do not have access to eTrace. (i.e. Guatemala, El Salvador and Honduras all have huge numbers of illegal crossings through Mexico).

Figure 13: Tri-Border region of South America

The tri-border area of Paraguay, Brazil, and Argentina has become a particularly lucrative cross-border smuggling region. Smuggled goods in this area, including weapons and narcotics, are valued between $2 billion and $3 billion annually. **Hezbollah runs much of the area's smuggling activities, using profits to support activities in the western hemisphere and the Middle East** [ed. Note: emphasis added]"

Center for Defense Information[*]

[*] **Columbian** smorgasbord of weapons from Central America: http://www.wikileaks.ch/cable/2006/06/06BOGOTA5526.html

It would be a simple matter for corrupt officials in Mexico to provide Islamic terrorists in South America with forged passports and other documents; they are already supplying cartels with forged certificates to purchase weapons directly from the US State Department. Their access to e-Trace documentation regarding the location of firearms owners in the US would be valuable data for Islamic radicals who covet in the US the same Zeta-style takeover planned for Mexico. Elections are frequently the tipping point for violence in both Islamic and socialist agendas; the occurrence of major US and Mexican elections in 2012 may spell double trouble.

Hezbollah as indicated in the Center for Defense Information report cited earlier is not the last terrorist standing in this international nightmare, but they are the biggest. And this is the real story; not only of gun trafficking, human bondage and drug cartels in Mexico, but of how Islamic terrorists colluding with cartels provide both of them with new markets for illicit drug sales, money laundering opportunities and the prospect for political power. In return Middle Eastern terrorists are able to move large amounts of cash out of American mosques and Muslim centers. The cash, the drugs and the guns are moving in both directions on the border and it's the cash that's leaving the US that is funding terrorism.

> *"You tell me what you know, and I'll confirm. I'll keep you in the right direction if I can, but that's all. Just... follow the money..."*
>
> **Deep Throat**

It travels through the Tohono O'odham Nation and other well-known crossings along the Arizona/Mexican border, back along the arms trafficking routes in the Tri-Border region of South American and into the Jihadist hands of Middle Eastern terrorists. The drug cartels are also doing this for the Islamic terrorists in return for large quantities of Combloc weapons which move from Iran and Syria, again into South America's tri-border region and up into Mexico.

---

* **Ibid,** The Small Arms Trade in Latin America

The most active point of exchange is this tri-border area where Brazil, Argentina and Paraguay borders intersect in South America. It is this little known enclave of Islamic communities where most of the drugs from the Middle East, the arms trafficking for the cartels and a lot of hard cash trade hands faster than Eric Holder can dodge interviews with congress.

The Islamic Disconnect

"What will remain of your Lebanon after a century? Tell me!
Except bragging, lying and stupidity? Do you expect the ages
to keep in its memory the traces of deceit and cheating and
hypocrisy? Do you think the atmosphere will preserve in its
pockets the shadows of death and the stench of graves?"

Khalil Gibran, c. 1920[*]

The terrain of terrorism in the Middle East is at once enormous and unfamiliar to American audiences. In particular, terrorist groups in and around Beirut, Lebanon are now viewed as principal actors in the Islamic world of international arms trafficking, political intrigue, and violent mysticism. However, another even more insidious organization called the Muslim Brotherhood which provides radical spiritual direction to all Islamic Jihad groups; both are examined here.

Since the 9-11-2001 attack, the terrorist groups we routinely hear about are Islamic Sunni radicals in *al-Qaida* and the misogynistic Afghani *Taliban*. Unfortunately, it is extremely difficult for the average American citizen to keep up with the alphabet soup of media-hyped terrorist organizations that are daily planning violent mayhem for both our troops overseas and Americans here at home. Palestinian Islamic Jihad (PIJ), Palestinian Liberation Organization (PLO), Abu Nidal Organization (ANO), Islamic Movement of Uzbekistan (IMU), al-Qaida in the Arabian Peninsula (AQAP), al-Qaida in Iraq (AQI)—formally Tanzim Qa'idat al-Jihad fi Bilad al-Rafidayn (QJBR), and who could forget the Kongra-Gel (a.k.a. the KGK, formerly PKK, formally the KADEK, etc., etc...)—and there are the terrorist front organizations actually operating inside the US including the Council for American Islamic Relations (CAIR), Holy

---

[*] **Khalil Gibran** (b. January 6, 1883 – d. April 10, 1931); Lebanese American artist, poet, and writer born in the town of Bsharri in modern-day Lebanon. He is chiefly known in the English speaking world for his 1923 book *The Prophet*; Gibran is the third most widely read author in history behind Shakespeare and Lao-Tzu.

Land Foundation (HLF), Benevolence International Foundation (BIF), Global Relief Foundation (GRF), Kind Hearts and the North American Islamic Trust (NAIT), all of whom are numbered among a very much longer list[12] of terror organizations that completely defy initials.

Importantly, all of the radical Islamic terror groups are tied together by a mystical allegiance of violence, corruption and misogynistic human bondage called Shariah Law which is based on the so-called Holy Islamic Qur'an.

> "...prepare for Jihad and be the lovers of death. Life itself shall come searching after you."

Hasan al-Banna*
Founder of the Muslim Brotherhood

Contrary to the propaganda that has been shoved down our throats by a complicit media, socialist blogs, politicians soft on terrorism and their fawning popular and academic constituencies, Shariah Law is not a work of faith, nor is it a rational implementation of jurisprudence—it is an agenda for implementing a mystical form of world-wide totalitarianism and uses the guise of religion to hide behind the US Constitution and in particular the First Amendment freedoms of speech and religion.

> "...The only way you can stop us is by giving up your democracy. If you give up democracy and Freedom of Speech, and start to stop us and ban us the way you started to do, that is the way you can stop us. But that means we succeed. We say to the people: 'You see? Democracy is Hypocrisy'."

And this tidbit which pretty much says it all...

> "...We will use your democracy to destroy your democracy."

Sheikh Omar Bakri Mohammed†

---

* **Hasan al-Banna** Founder, Muslim Brotherhood [c. 1928]
† **Bakri** interview, Cybercast News Service, 2000

If you have ever read any of the classic works of Marxist/Leninist Socialism, or the writing of Woodrow Wilson, the Sheikh's comment on democracy sounds eerily familiar to these misguided political hacks who have led vulnerable Americans down the primrose path of political totalitarianism for over 100 years.

> *"[Capitalists]...will work on the preparation of their own suicide..."*

Vladimir Ilyich Ulyanov Lenin

> *"For it is very clear, that in fundamental theory socialism and democracy are almost if not quite one and the same. They both rest at bottom upon the absolute right of the community to determine its own destiny and that of its members.*
>
> *Men as communities are supreme over men as individuals...Democracy is bound by no principle of its own nature to say itself nay as to the exercise of any power...*
>
> *The difference between democracy and socialism is not an essential difference, but only a practical difference—is a difference of organization and policy, not a difference of primary motive."*

Woodrow Wilson*

The same can be said of Shariah Law which is in reality a brutal enforcement mechanism animated by fanatical terrorist organizations intent on destroying not only the US and the freedoms recognized in our Constitution but similar aspirations for freedom anywhere they find them. This mystical form of terrorism—like Socialism—effectively eliminates the American way of life, freedom of religion and any chance for individual liberty, achievement and human dignity anywhere in the world. This is the 'minimal' difference in policy and organization between

---

* Socialism and Democracy, Woodrow Wilson, 1887, accessed at:
http://teachingamericanhistory.org/library/index.asp?document=2208

Shariah and Socialism unidentified by Woodrow Wilson's psychotic vision of democracy and collectivist destiny.

While the OIC will continue to advocate for the Muslim happy-face, at the spiritual forefront of this world syndicate of violence is another umbrella group called the Muslim Brotherhood (a.k.a. *Ikhwan*). The Ikhwan movement was first organized in 1928 after the collapse of the Ottoman Empire by *Hasan al-Banna*—the original psychotic-Islamic version of Dr. Demento. It was al-Banna who created a rigidly conservative and highly secretive Egyptian-based organization dedicated to resurrecting a new Muslim empire (caliphate). According to al-Banna,

> *"...It is the nature of Islam to dominate, not to be dominated, to impose its law on all nations and to extend its power to the entire planet."*

Hasan al-Banna*

Hasan al-Banna was born out of the radical Muslim desire to counter the ideology of modernization, the Brotherhood's platform included a strict interpretation of the Qur'an; one that demeaned the status of women in society, exalted a glorification of suicidal violence and formed the basis for what has come to be known as Shariah Law. Along with al-Banna, the grand Mufti of Jerusalem *Haj-al Amin Al-Husseini* was also an enormously influential Muslim leader of the time. Together, the two created a powerful and popular Islamist organization by pandering to fundamentalist Islamic principals which largely blamed the world's problems on Infidels in general and the Jewish people in particular.

Figure 14: Hasan al-Banna, founder of the Muslim Brotherhood.

---

* **The Broken Crescent**, Hoveryda Fereydoun, Praegar Publishers, 2002

Al-Banna also gave the group the catchy club motto it still uses today:

> *"Allah is our purpose, the Prophet our leader, the Qur'an our constitution, jihad our way and dying for God our supreme objective."*

Hasan al-Banna*

This has been widely adopted by many terrorist organizations as the principal mantra of violence; a chant of terror heard from the Middle East to New England. While under surveillance as a possible terrorist, *Ismail Salim Elbarasse* was arrested on August 20, 2004, in Maryland, suspiciously taking pictures of important structural elements of the Chesapeake Bay Bridge. Subsequent search of Elbarasse's home revealed the archives of the Muslim Brotherhood in North America. Among these documents was the "Explanatory Memorandum" (completely detailed in Endnote[13])—the Muslim Brotherhood's plan for the overthrow of the United States. In addition to the plan, the document confirmed...

> *"...the myriad Muslim American groups in the United States...nearly all of them are controlled by the Muslim Brotherhood and therefore as Shariah dictates, are hostile to this country, its constitution and freedoms..."*

Center for Security Policy†

Former National Security Council Counter-Terrorism Adviser Richard Clarke testified before congress on the ideological connection between various terrorist groups:

> *"...the common link here is the extremist Muslim Brotherhood—all of these organizations are descendents of the membership and ideology of the Muslim Brothers."*

Richard Clark*

---

* **Muslim Brotherhood website**, accessed at:
http://www.ummah.org.uk/ikhwan/index.html
† **Center for Security Policy:** Shariah—The Threat to America
http://www.centerforsecuritypolicy.org/

The 9/11 Commission Report explores the Ikhwan's violent influence on terrorist Osama bin Laden as well as the "Blind" Sheik Omar Abdel Rahman—the man responsible for the 1993 attack on the World Trade Center. An important aspect of the Muslim Brotherhood ideology is the sanctioning of violent Jihad like the famous fatwa issued by Sheikh Yousef al-Qaradhawi making it a religious obligation of Muslims to abduct and kill U.S. citizens.[†][‡]

The Ikhwan opposes the secular tendencies of Islamic nations (e.g. Egypt) and wants to leverage a return to what they believe are the original precepts of the Qur'an, and the rejection of virtually all Western influences—particularly individual freedom and private property ownership. Their operational plan is called "Civilization Jihad" and it is very, very violent.

> *"The general strategic goal of the Group in America which was approved by the Shura Council and the Organizational Conference for the year is "Enablement of Islam in North America, meaning: establishing an effective and a stable Islamic Movement led by the Muslim Brotherhood which adopts Muslims' causes domestically and globally, and which works to expand the observant Muslim base, aims at unifying and directing Muslims' efforts, presents Islam as a civilization alternative, and supports the global Islamic State wherever it is.*

> *"In order for Islam and its Movement to become "a part of the homeland" in which it lives, "stable" in its land, "rooted" in the spirits and minds of its people, "enabled" in the live [sic] of its society and has firmly-established "organizations" on which the Islamic structure is built and with which the testimony of civilization is achieved, the Movement must*

---

[*] **Testimony** of Richard Clarke before the Senate Committee on Banking, Housing, and Urban Affairs, (Oct. 22, 2003).
[†] **The Rise of Nuclear Iran**: How Tehran Defies the West, Dore Gold 2009; Regnery Publishing, ISBN 1596985712.
[‡] **Jihad Against Non-Muslims Is Obligatory,** Report 2877 extracted from The Muslim Brotherhood website on The Jihad and Terrorism Threat Monitor at MEMRI, http://www.memrijttm.org/content/en/report.htm?report=2877

plan and struggle to obtain "the keys" and the tools of this process in carry [sic] out this grand mission as a "Civilization Jihadist" responsibility which lies on the shoulders of Muslims and – on top of them – the Muslim Brotherhood in this country...The process of settlement is a "Civilization-Jihadist Process" with all the word means. The Ikhwan must understand that their work in America is a kind of grand Jihad in eliminating and destroying the Western civilization from within and "sabotaging" its miserable house by their hands... and Allah's religion is made victorious over all other religions."

Muslim Brotherhood*

One of the most amazing things to me has been the incessant drivel from the Obama White House denial-factory and from other players complicit in a charade that pre-supposes radical Muslims will suddenly soften and join hands with Christians and members of all faiths to sing choruses of Cum-by-ya, if we would just sit down and talk things out, importantly to Obama, without any pre-conditions. Unfortunately, the terrorist organizations and their state sponsors just don't know the tune.

" ... We don't make a distinction between civilians and non-civilians, innocents and non-innocents; only between Muslims and unbelievers...and the life of an unbeliever has no value, it has no sanctity."

Sheikh Omar Bakri Mohammed

For those unfamiliar with radical Islamic code-speak, the term *'unbelievers'* (in any Islamic context) translates into what may be the more familiar term *Infidel.* The literal Arabic translation is *Kafir,* a pejorative term referring to one who covers up the truth (specifically in this case, the truth of Mohammed and the Qur'an). All Islamic-extremists (as well as Bill Maher and a few other hacks

---

* **Explanatory Memorandum on the General Strategic Goal for the Brotherhood in North America**, accessed at:
http://www.investigativeproject.org/document/id/20

at the *New York Times*) use the term to insult Christians, Native Americans, Hebrews and other non-Muslims.

Similar to Marxist socialist revolution, Islamic extremism has its own three distinct stages in re-establishing the Islamic caliphate; these are:

> *Dawa*— missionary work, persuading individuals to agree with the basic tenets and principals of Islam. Often accomplished through Imam Indoctrination at local mosques, community centers or *madrasah* schools, it is also facilitated in public school policy, prisons and jails.

> *Hejira*—spreading the faith through large-scale emigration and then birthing massive numbers of new-born 'believers' (better known in our Arizona illegal alien Campesina communities as Anchor Babies).

> *Jihad*—Without any qualifiers the term is generally understood to refer to a holy war on behalf of Islam. A person engaged in jihad is called a *mujahid*, the plural is *mujahideen*. The best-known pre-9-11 mujahideen were the various loosely-aligned Afghan opposition groups led by Osama bin Laden (among others) who initially fought against the incumbent pro-Soviet Afghan government and the Soviet Union during the 1970s, largely supported by covert US aid during the Jimmy Carter, Ronald Reagan and George H.W. Bush administration. Their principal advocate in Congress at that time was Charlie Wilson (D-TX).

Contrary to what the news media would have us believe, when an Islamic-terrorist decides he is going to go visit Mohammad and take the lives of innocent Americans with him, that individual act of terrorism is merely an agenda item on the "to-do" list for Socialism in establishing the next Islamic world caliphate. It is on a list with many other items including a philosophical takeover of the public schools, a material redistribution of wealth from those who have earned it to those who have not, inevitable economic collapse and the ultimate bondage of Christian, Buddhist, Pueblo and Jewish *Infidels*.

This is the Muslim Brotherhood's approach to the takeover of the United States; other radical Jihadi terrorists have similar intentions. Hezbollah is the best example.

Lebanon holds some of the first local evidence of stone-craft by Lower Palaeolithic humans in the Middle East and appears to date back perhaps 2.5 million years. The country contains primordial ruins that date to at least 5000 BC. Its ancient villages* originally comprised of fishing communities on the Mediterranean, both pre-historic and historic evidence suggest conflict is deeply rooted in a very troubled and complex record of religious fanaticism.

Beirut, the capital of Lebanon and its largest city has seen the shadow of many rulers, most of them brutal empires; among them were Egyptian, Persian, Assyrian, Hellenistic, Roman, and beginning with the violent hegemony of Mohammad in 635 AD— Islam became a major long-term player. With few exceptions, Muslim leaders of the Ottoman Empire wielding the iron boot of Islamic Shariah Law controlled the area for over 1200 years until 1923 when the last caliphate collapsed.

The Ottoman Empire was in principle tolerant towards Christians and Jews; however this tolerance, in accord with the Muslim *dhimmi* †system has always been subject to a special Muslim tax called the *Jizya*. Christians and Jews were not considered equals to Muslims, an institutionalized form of discrimination based on Islamic Shariah Law which has continued unabated to this day.

For instance, as part of dhimmitude, legal complaints against Muslims by Christians and Jews were inadmissible in Islamic courts of law. They were forbidden to carry weapons or ride horses and their houses could not be elevated above the preferred homes of Muslims. After more than 1000 years of religious repression by Islam, it is unlikely dhimmitude will disappear from Muslim jurisprudence. The radical and mystically regressive Ayatollah Khomeini, who overthrew the secular Shah of Iran in 1979, led a

---

* The 7000 year old Lebanese city of Byblos is considered to be one of the oldest continuously inhabited cities in the world.

† **Dhimmi**; the word means "one whose responsibility has been taken."

reactionary revolution that was partially based on the advocacy of dhimmitude slavery and its Jizya revenue stream.*

Early in World War I, France and Great Britain who had predetermined their military success in the Middle East, concluded a secret 1916 pact called the Sykes-Picot agreement. It negated promises made to Arabs by T. E. Lawrence (a.k.a. "Lawrence of Arabia")† for a national independent Arab homeland located in the area of modern Lebanon and Syria, in exchange for their siding with British forces against the Ottoman Empire.

Figure 15: Prince Faisal (center front) at Versailles during the Paris Peace Conference of 1919. T.E. Lawrence is behind Faisal, second from the right.

The agreement's terms ceded political control of the area to France and Great Britain and were later affirmed officially by the Council of the League of Nations in 1922.

---

* *On Islamic Government* by Ayatollah Khomeini indicates unequivocally that non-Muslims should be required to pay the poll tax, in return for which they would profit from the protection and services of the state; they would, however, be excluded from all participation in the political process
† **Lt. Colonel Thomas Edward Lawrence** (b.~16 August 1888–d. 19 May 1935), known professionally as T. E. Lawrence, was a British Army officer renowned especially for his liaison role during the Arab Revolt against Ottoman Turkish rule of 1916–18.

Great Britain's Arab Foreign Office had originally embraced the notion that internal tribal insurgence within the Ottoman Empire would absorb enormous resources that could not be fielded against the British army. With the help of Lawrence and heavily supplied by the British, local partisan tribes—led by Lawrence's co-conspirator Prince Faisal bin Hussein* (Figure 15) and based on promises of future Arab independence—sided with the British army and organized the Arab revolt against the Ottoman Empire, all of which eventually facilitated the end of the caliphate albeit at enormous cost of life to the Arab tribal forces. Although Faisal was a descendant of the Islamic prophet Muhammad and received considerable criticism for partnering with Christian infidels, pan-Arab nationalism coupled with Lawrence's notions of independence, not religion, were Faisal's main motivations.

Lawrence's self-drafted map of an independent Middle East had been presented to both Britain's War Cabinet and to Arab leaders throughout the Lebanese-Syrian deserts. The map was designed with the intention to marginalize the post-war role of France in the region by limiting direct French colonial control over the Lebanon area in particular. It included a separate state for the Armenians, a separate state of Palestine and grouped the people of present-day Syria, Jordan and parts of Saudi Arabia into yet another state based on tribal patterns and commercial trade routes.

The secret Sykes-Picot agreement, publically exposed in November 1917 by the Russian Bolsheviks (who had actually acquiesced to the clandestine agreement in hopes of obtaining Ottoman lands for themselves) is seen by many as a turning point in Western/Arab relations. The betrayal was deep and continues to reverberate in modern terrorist motivations.

The perfidy and treachery of the British government in cahoots with France and Russia would transform Islamic motivations in the

---

* **Faisal bin Hussein bin Ali al-Hashemi**, (b. 20 May 1885–d. September 8, 1933) was for a short time King of the Arab Kingdom of Syria in 1920 and was King of Iraq from August 1921 to 1933. He was a member of the Hashemite dynasty, a descendant of the family of Muhammad.

Middle East from Arab independence into what has become a world-wide threat doctrine of terrorism leveled not only at Great Britain, but indeed the entire diaspora of western civilization. Even more than a decade after the September 11 terrorist attack on the US, it is a threat the US does not wholly comprehend.

> *"Mr. Chairman, the plain fact of the matter is that we have institutionally failed to meet our duty to become well-informed on the Threat Doctrine of our enemy. And without a clear understanding of the Enemy Threat Doctrine, victory is likely impossible. The reasons for our paucity in this area are many but they stem from two serious and connected obstacles. The first is a misguided belief that the religious character of the enemy's ideology should not be discussed, and that we need not address it, but should instead use the phrase "Violent Extremism" to describe our foe and thus avoid any unnecessary unpleasantness. The second is that even if we could demonstrate clear-headedness on the issue and recognize the religious ideology of al Qaeda and its associate movements for what it is: a form of hybrid totalitarianism, we still drastically lack the institutional ability to analyze and comprehend the worldview of the enemy and therefore its strategic mindset and ultimate objectives."*

Dr. Sebastian Gorka[*]

Hezbollah, a Shi'ite[14] terrorist organization bankrolled by Iran, has a racehorse lineage of violence. Formed in early 1980's as a result of the Israeli war with Lebanon, their violent leaders were inspired by radical revolutionary cleric Ayatollah Khomeini.[†] The Ayatollah was deeply involved with the *Fedayeen* Islam, a network of *holy killers* engaged in repeated attempts at political assassinations. In

---

[*] **THE EVOLUTION OF THE TERRORIST THREAT,** Prepared Testimony for House Armed Services Committee, Subcommittee on Emerging Threats and Capabilities by Dr. Sebastian L. v. Gorka, June 22, 2011.
[†] **Grand Ayatollah Sayyed Ayatollah As-Sayyid Ruhollah Mostafavi Musavi Khomeini** (b. 24 September 1902–d. 3 June 1989) Iranian Imam, religious fanatic, politician and leader of the 1979 Iranian Revolution which saw the overthrow of the Shah of Iran. He is considered a "champion of Islamic revival" by Shi'a scholars.

1944 Khomeini published: *Kashf al-Asrar* ("the Revealing of Secrets"), which served as an irrational intellectual guide for the terror tactics adopted by Hezbollah.[*]

> *"...Every part of the body of a non-Muslim individual is impure, even the hair on his hand and his body hair, his nails, and all the secretions of his body.*
>
> *Islam makes it incumbent on all adult males, provided they are not disabled and incapacitated, to prepare themselves for the conquest of countries so that the writ of Islam is obeyed in every country in the world. But those who study Islamic Holy War will understand why Islam wants to conquer the whole world...*
>
> *Those who know nothing of Islam pretend that Islam counsels against war. They are witless. There are hundreds of other Quranic verses and a hadith urging Muslims to value war and to fight. Does all that mean that Islam is a religion that prevents men from waging war? I spit upon those foolish souls who make such a claim.*
>
> *Whatever good there is exists thanks to the sword and in the shadow of the sword! People cannot be made obedient except with the sword! The sword is the key to Paradise, which can be opened only for Holy Warriors!"*

Ayatollah Khomeini
***Kashf al-Asrar* ("the Revealing of Secrets")**

It was in the tone of this violent liturgy Hezbollah militia forces were originally trained and organized by the Iranian Revolutionary Guard. Hezbollah is reputed to have been among the first Islamic resistance groups to use tactical suicide bombing, assassination, and kidnapping foreign soldiers in the Middle East to leverage a radical mystical agenda. The political side of the organization

---

[*] **International Terrorism: An Introduction to Concepts and Actors:** by Donna M. Schlagheck (1988); Lexington Books. pg. 58, ISBN 0669154547.

maintains strong support among Lebanon's Shi'a population*, and is able to mobilize demonstrations of hundreds of thousands on a moment's notice utilizing their vast telecommunications network which includes a satellite television station and associated website called *al-Manar* (The Beacon of Light).† Originally launched in 1991, *al-Manar* was designated as a "Specially Designated Global Terrorist entity," and banned by the Bush administration in December 2004.

A national unity government was formed in Lebanon in June 2008, giving Hezbollah and its radical opposition defacto veto power through dictatorial control of eleven of the thirty cabinet seats. While eleven out of thirty seats does not sound like clout, the balance is not necessarily in disagreement when it comes to the destruction of Israel and the United States. In August, only a few months after the election, Lebanon's new Cabinet *unanimously* approved a draft policy statement which secures Hezbollah's existence as an armed organization and guarantees its right to:

"...liberate or recover occupied lands."
Lebanese Government Policy, 2008

This is not an insignificant phrase to be ignored as part of a larger and significantly boring policy statement; Shariah Law, based on what Muslim's call the Holy Islamic Qur'an, dictates that *anywhere* an Islamic mosque or community center has been built is—by Islamic law—Islamic land, regardless of whether that land is in Lebanon, Israel, New York's ground zero or Tucson, Arizona. It is important to understand, many radical terrorists already consider parts of America—not just like Islam—they actually consider these places part of Islam.

---

* **Shi'a population in Lebanon** is estimated to be about 40%, outnumbering both Sunni and Christian communities.

† **Al-Manar:** registered as *Lebanese Media Group Company* and broadcasting from Beirut, Lebanon, the self-proclaimed "Station of the Resistance" (*qanat al-muqawama*) is an integral component of the psychological warfare they leverage against the state of Israel, and an important part of Hezbollah's agenda to spread its propaganda to the rest of the pan-Arab world.

With an annual budget estimated at over $100 million dollars, Hezbollah is truly a model for terrorism everywhere. Since at least 2009 (when it was first reported by ABC News and the Washington Times[*]) Hezbollah terrorists have been sharing Mexican Drug Cartel land routes to move people, weapons, drugs and other contraband across the US border and using the profits to finance terror operations in the Middle East.

> "Hezbollah is using the same southern narcotics routes that Mexican drug kingpins do to smuggle drugs and people into the United States, reaping money to finance its operations and threatening U.S. national security, current and former U.S. law enforcement, defense and counterterrorism...The Iran-backed Lebanese group has long been involved in narcotics and human trafficking in South America's tri-border region of Paraguay, Argentina and Brazil. Increasingly, however, it is relying on Mexican narcotics syndicates that control access to transit routes into the U.S. Hezbollah relies on "the same criminal weapons smugglers, document traffickers and transportation experts as the drug cartels..."

Washington Times, 2009

Both Mexican narco-terrorists and Hezbollah have illicit materials to trade and, neither shares even a passing interest in the sovereignty of the United States.

Hezbollah has a wide variety of illegal Middle Eastern drugs not produced in Mexico (i.e. high grade Afghan hashish, opium and Asian heroin), access to European drug markets for Mexican marijuana and they have inexpensive Combloc weapons (e.g. AK47's, ammunition and other weapons) which they are trafficking through the tri-border region of Brazil, Paraguay and Argentina. With this operation Hezbollah terrorists are able to routinely re-supply the cartels with the necessary drugs, cash and firepower to

---

[*] Hezbollah Using Mexican Drug Routes, Washington Times March 2009, http://www.washingtontimes.com/news/2009/mar/27/hezbollah-uses-mexican-drug-routes-into-us

animate their illicit activities while Hezbollah obtains a base for radical recruiting for Jihad, money laundering and large scale arms trafficking.

The Drug Cartels also provide Hezbollah with land access to US markets, street gang drug distribution, American-based Islamic terror cells and importantly a return path for cash extracted from the mandatory mystical tax on Islamic Americans donating Zakat* to Mosques, Islamic-based community centers and 501c3 Islamic "charities" which can be directed back into the Middle East to finance terror.† Both organizations are able to broker additional arms deals in Central and South America for military grade machine guns, ammunition, grenades and grenade launchers, anti-tank weapons, sniper rifles and rockets.

Two other actors besides Lebanon participate in this trifecta of terror and bear some additional examination; Syria and Iran. Considered part of antediluvian Mesopotamia, these two sponsors of terror play an integral role in the arms trafficking that connects the fertile crescent of the Middle East and Central and South America to Mexico and the United States.

Syria, like many Islamic nations experiences constant religious tension within its borders between Shia and Sunni[15] extremists; both embrace agendas of terror inside and outside of Syria. Sunni Islam is often referred to as the orthodox version of the religion and comprises the largest single religious following in Islam; three-quarters of the Syrian population are Sunni. Syria has been under "Emergency Law" since 1962, effectively suspending what little constitutional protections were afforded citizens, and its system of government, based on Shariah Law, is considered non-democratic.

Even older than Lebanon, Syrian archaeological artifacts demonstrate a center of Neolithic culture dating back 10,000 years

---

* **Zakat**: Mandatory cash donations made by all Muslims. Islam earmarks large amounts of Zakat for terrorist activities.
† **Hezbollah-Cartel Partnership**: Source, Michael Braun Retired assistant administrator and chief of operations U.S. Drug Enforcement Administration (DEA) .http://www.washingtontimes.com/news/2009/mar/27/hezbollah-uses-mexican-drug-routes-into-us/

to a time when agriculture and cattle breeding appeared for the first time in the world. After the death of Mohammad, Syria was conquered by the Rashidun army and became an integral part of the Islamic empire. In the mid-7th century, the Umayyad dynasty, then rulers of the Muslim empire placed their Islamic capital in the ancient city of Damascus setting the stage for centuries of conflict. Modern tribulations relating to Syrian arms trafficking through Lebanon began in the 1970's.

The Constitution of Syria was adopted 13 March 1971. In the most contradictory definitions possible between secular government and mystical radicalism, it defines Syria as a socialist state with Islam recognized as the majority religion.

In early 1976, the Lebanese civil war which gave rise to Hezbollah was going poorly for the Lebanese government; with the approval of the Arab league Syria sent 40,000 troops into Lebanon beginning a 30 year Syrian military presence. Many crimes in Lebanon, including the high profile assassination of *Rafik Hariri,** were attributed to the Syrian forces and intelligence services. Over the following 15 years of civil war, Syria fought for and gained much control over Lebanon, and attempted to undermine Israeli influences in southern Lebanon, through extensive use of proxy militias; a model similarly adopted by Hezbollah operatives of Iran.

From 1976 until its suppression in 1982, the radical Muslim Brotherhood led an armed insurgency against the government. In response to an attempted uprising by the brotherhood in February 1982, the government crushed the fundamentalist opposition centered in the city of Hama, leveling parts of the city with artillery fire and leaving between 10,000 and 25,000 people either dead or wounded, mostly civilians. The Syrian government's actions at Hama have been described as the single deadliest act by any Arab

---

* **Rafic Baha El Deen Al-Hariri** (b. November 1, 1944–d. February 14, 2005): business tycoon and the Prime Minister of Lebanon from 1992 to 1998 and again from 2000 until his resignation in 2004. Hariri was assassinated on 14 February 2005 when explosives equivalent to around 1000 kilos of explosives were detonated as his motorcade drove through Beirut. Syrian operatives have been blamed for the assassination.

government against its own people in the modern Middle East.* It also graphically demonstrates the value of life in Syria. Syria's human rights situation is among the worst in the world, according to human rights organizations such as Human Rights Watch.† The authorities routinely arrest democracy and human rights activists, censor websites, detain bloggers, and impose travel bans. Arbitrary detention, torture, and disappearances are widespread.‡

Syria remained a political and military power in Lebanon until 2005, exerting a jack-booted hegemony over Lebanese politics that has contributed heavily to political unrest. In 2005 the bulk of the Syrian forces withdrew from Lebanon but some of its intelligence operatives remained, drawing further international rebuke. Although dissent has been limited, Syrian activists did participate in the so-called Arab Spring uprisings occurring across the Middle East in 2011 and demanding an end to the coercive 1962 Emergency Law, political reform and importantly reinstatement of civil rights.

Syria is a strategic player in the arms trafficking land routes used between Lebanon and Iran; it is as well a frightening harbinger of the Islamic marriage of terror between Shia and Sunni extremists. While the two Islamic sects have been beating in each other's head for over 1000 years, they have jointly embraced a combined goal which views the destruction of western civilization as more important than individual disagreements over religious doctrinal narrative.

The public face of this new form of trans-national Islamic terror is called the Organization of the Islamic Conference (OIC) and purports to represent Muslims worldwide; its membership includes 56 Islamic states (57 if you count Palestine). As a sort of more violent mystical version of the United Nations, the OIC is the

---

* **Dreams and Shadows**: the Future of the Middle East, by Robin Wright, Penguin Press, 2008, p.243-4
† **Syria among worst for rights abuses**: Reuters, 2011-01-24, accessed at:
http://www.reuters.com/article/2011/01/24/us-syria-rights-idUSTRE70N5S620110124.
‡ **Human Rights Watch Annual Report** accessed at:
http://www.hrw.org/en/node/79303

second largest supra-national organization in the world. Publications of OIC include the sort of intellectual terrorism that actually exempts Islamic Jihad from the definition of terrorism.* This is the same model of terrorism-denial used by Janet Napolitano ("man-caused disasters") and the US Dept. of Defense analysis of the Islamic terror attack at Ft. Hood, Texas by Army Maj. Nidal Hasan, a self-professed soldier of Allah. The terrorists have issue of denial when it comes to murdering Americans or Nidal's purpose in the US Army.

> *"...the only way a Muslim could Islamically justify serving as a soldier in the U.S. army is if his intention is to follow the footsteps of men like Nidal..."*

Anwar al-Awlaki†

Encouraged by the success of OIC, Iran's President Mahmoud Ahmadinejad has called for a further strengthening of bilateral ties with Syria, saying the two countries already enjoy close brotherly and sustainable relations. Speaking at a meeting with the visiting Syria's Prime Minister Muhammed Naji Otri in the capital Tehran on Thursday, Ahmadinejad stated that Iran and Syria have wide-ranging plans for boosting the level of bilateral economic and political cooperation

> *"Iran's President Mahmoud Ahmadinejad has called for a further strengthening of bilateral ties with Syria, saying the two countries already enjoy close brotherly and sustainable relations. Speaking at a meeting with the visiting Syria's Prime Minister Muhammed Naji Otri in the capital Tehran on Thursday, Ahmadinejad stated that Iran and Syria have wide-ranging plans for boosting the level of bilateral*

---

* **Terrorism: Factors and Countermeasures**, Journal Islam Today, by Mohammed Ali Al Taskhiri, Copyright 2010, accessed at:
http://www.isesco.org.ma/english/publications/Islamtoday/26/P2.php
† **Anwar al-Awlaki** (b. April 22, 1971) al-Qaeda terrorist and dual citizen of the U.S. and Yemen, originally of Yemeni descent born in New Mexico. He is a radical Islamic lecturer, mystical leader, and former imam. According to U.S. officials, he is a senior talent recruiter and motivator, who has become "operational" as a planner and trainer for al-Qaeda and all of its terror franchises. Maj. Hasan attended his lectures.

economic and political cooperation...Iran and Syria, which share a common position on many regional and international issues, have enjoyed a boost in strategic political, economic and cultural ties in recent years. Bilateral trade volumes between the two countries is currently valued at $3 billion and is expected to hit $5 billion in the near future."

Press TV, an Iranian News Service[*]

Although public alliances between national sponsors of terror may be news to the world, covert alliances have been long-standing particularly in arms trafficking. Syria is virtually a member of the Soviet bloc who provides a variety of financial and military assistance to Syrian-backed terrorism. This includes Combloc weapons, explosives and training. The materiel Syria does not receive from Communist sources are fulfilled by Iran.

"Within the Middle East, Damascus affiliates primarily with the Iranian and Libyan governments. The Iranian connection has particular importance in Lebanon. Boeing 747s belonging to the Iranian Air Force fly to Damascus carrying manpower, arms, and funds for Iran's operations in Lebanon. These are then taken by convoys of trucks, using military roads to avoid custom checks and border searches, to the Beka'a Valley in Lebanon. Radical fundamentalist Muslim groups such as Islamic Jihad, Islamic Amal, and Hezbollah depend on this arrangement for nearly all their supplies."

Daniel Pipes[†]

Although Daniel Pipe's description of arms trafficking dates to 1989, it continues to this day in exactly the same fashion.

"Syria plays a key role in Iranian efforts to supply arms to Hezbollah. Typically, shipments of such arms arrive at

---

[*] **Iran calls for boosting ties with Syria,** Iranian News Service: Thu Mar 10, 2011
http://www.presstv.ir/detail/169262.html
[†] **National Interest,** Terrorism: The Syrian Connection by Daniel Pipes, Spring 1989

Damascus airport and are then trucked to the Beka'a valley and other Hezbollah strongholds. The importance of this overland route is evident in the successful interception by Israel or the United States of ships carrying arms from Iran on new fewer than six different occasions between 2001 and 2010."

Center for Security Policy[*]

According to the Center for Security Policy report, Beka'a valley is also the home for both Lebanese poppy-producing heroin and an enormous counterfeiting operation known to have produced prolific numbers of US $100 bills. Both operations are used to further fund terrorism. However, drugs and counterfeiting are not the only criminal industries actively pursued by these terrorist organizations and their sponsor states. Illegal endeavors include connections to US cigarette smuggling, extortion, fraud, diamond smuggling and human trafficking; all of which contributes to financing Islamic Jihad.

Their international transportation routes begin with the Islamic diaspora throughout western Africa. Hezbollah's criminal outreach in Africa is supported by both Syria and Iran and principally leverages Lebanese Shia business populations throughout the continent and their family and business relationships in South America, particularly the Tri-Border Region of Brazil, Paraguay and Argentina. Warnings of this connection have been frequently raised at the highest levels of US government but almost wholly ignored by the US media.

In 2007, the Bush Administration's chairman of the Joint Chiefs of Staff, Marine General Peter Pace, warned members of the Senate Armed Services Committee that elements of radical Islamic groups were active in South America recruiting and training terrorists. In July 2011, the Committee on Homeland Security's Subcommittee on Counterterrorism and Intelligence held a hearing entitled "Hezbollah in Latin America –Implications for U.S. Homeland

---

[*] **Shariah, The Threat to America**, An Exercise in Competitive Analysis, Copyright 2010 by the Center for Security Policy. Shariahhthethreat.com

Security." Hezbollah, the Muslim Brotherhood's Explanatory Memorandum on Civilization Jihad and the al-Qaida declaration of war and Military Manual for American Muslims (used as training materials for Mexican Drug Cartels) as well as other terrorist groups and radical documents have repeatedly been mentioned in both the US Congress and the conservative press, duly noted and largely ignored by the Democrats and the liberal mainstream media. This is the kind of abject denial that has brought together the criminal elements of illegal drugs, arms trafficking and Islamic terrorism to the borders of Arizona and other southwestern states.

The Ikhwan doctrinal approach to trans-national mysticism, coupled with al-Qaida, Hamas and the Iranian-backed syndicate of thugs called Hezbollah are all dangerously operating out of the Tri-Border Region (TBR) of South America and using this area as a staging area for radical recruitment to Jihad, money laundering and arms trafficking.

> *"Ahmed Muhammed Dhakane...admitted to running a smuggling ring from Brazil to transport Al-Shabaab Somali terrorists into the United States to wage jihad. As Poole and others have pointed out, this is just the latest revelation about the extent to which terrorist operatives have entered the United States -- including several who have crossed the southwest border acting on behalf of groups such as Al Shabaab, Hezbollah, and Hamas."*

American Spectator[*]

The US government has known about terrorist-based violence, arms and drug trafficking in South America's Tri-Border Region for a very long time; some federal investigations of arms trafficking go back to the 1970's. It is not surprising—given the enormous number of arms authorized by the US government for sale to corrupt foreign regimes—that US officials would be in denial regarding complicity in fueling the violence in Mexico.

---

[*] **American Spectator**, Walking Too Softly by Ben Lerner on 5-5, 2011, accessed at: http://spectator.org/archives/2011/05/05/walking-too-softly#

The Tri-Border Region (TBR) in South America is one of the last lawless frontiers on the planet. Although there is evidence that Hamas has also been active in this region as well as Central America and Mexico, it is Hezbollah* that has largely cultivated and actively inspired the violent aspirations of Muslim communities in the TBR. Paraguay became so rogue that Bill Clinton took time out from his sexual predations to suspend US arms sales as illicit trafficking increased through the Paraguayan corridor.

> "...[During] *the mid-1990s the United States applied its export control laws to suspend arms sales to Paraguay because of their likely diversion to Brazil. Brazilian police regularly seized U.S. guns from crime scenes, guns that had not been legally supplied to Brazil. The U.S. Bureau for Alcohol, Tobacco, Firearms, and Explosives (BATF), with the assistance of the State Department and the then Office of Defense Trade Controls, worked with the Brazilian police to trace the weapons' origins. They discovered that the seized weapons had been legally transferred from the United States to Paraguay, but illegally diverted to Brazil. The United States requested that Paraguay enact tighter controls over its weapons imports, but Paraguay neglected to do so. In 1996, after several warnings, the United States suspended small-arms exports to Paraguay..."*

Center for Defense Information†

Those communities in the TBR comprise in excess of about 25,000 predominantly Middle Eastern-born residents and their descendants many of whom originally immigrated from Lebanon in two waves, the first occurred just after the 1948 Arab-Israeli war and the second was activated as a result of the Lebanese civil war which began in 1982 and served as the crucible for Hezbollah hegemony in Lebanon and beyond.

---

* **Hezbollah:** literally "Party of God," is a Shi'a Muslim radical militant terrorist group and a political party based in Lebanon.
† http://www.cdi.org/pdfs/Small_Arms_Latin_America.pdf

Since at least the 1970's, the US Drug Enforcement Administration (DEA) has been aware of significant arms trafficking originating with Middle East terrorist organizations and occurring in this remote area of South America, an Islamic hotbed at the tripartite intersection where Brazil, Argentina and Paraguay merge.

Now, public documents from the National Drug Intelligence Center (NDIC) confirm these investigations which at the time were reviewed and analyzed by the NDIC Document Exploitation program (Doc Ex) as early as 2007.

> *"NDIC's Doc Ex Branch supported DEA's Special Operations Division by analyzing information on* **a high-level drug trafficker, money launderer, arms dealer, and terrorist who is documented in 74 DEA investigations*** *dating* **back to the 1970's** [ed. Note: emphasis added] *Historical evidence indicated that this individual and his associates have trafficked multi-ton quantities of hashish and heroin and laundered tens of millions of dollars in drug proceeds. In addition, this individual had also brokered international multimillion dollar arms deals for Yemen, Kuwait, Syria, Argentina, Brazil, Bulgaria, and Colombia and has supported several Middle Eastern terrorist groups including the Palestine Liberation Front, the Palestine Liberation Organization, and the Popular Front for the Liberation of Palestine."* [Full text is at Endnote[16]]

NDIC, 2007†

NDIC's Doc Ex Branch contributed to drug-terror investigations aimed at disrupting and dismantling at least five Arab TBR drug trafficking organizations (DTOs) that operate in Argentina, Brazil, and Paraguay as well as in surrounding areas and in Europe and the Middle East. All five DTO's have since been linked to Islamic Radical Groups.

---

* **Mexican Drug Cartels & Islamic Radicals Working Together**, by J. Jesús Esquivel, Copyright, Proceso, July 16, 2008.
† **NDIC Accomplishments FY2007,** published by the Department of Justice, accessed at: http://www.justice.gov/ndic/accomp/06-07/acomp07.htm

The enormous selection of drug cartel weapons are not coming from US gun shops as the Obama/Holder administration had repeatedly suggested and as has been refuted here; military grade weapons are getting into Mexican drug cartel operations largely through a lucrative connection with Islamic terrorists and rogue governments.

As a direct result of this international weapons trafficking, drug related violence and money laundering is particularly egregious along the borders of the US directly south of California Arizona, New Mexico, and Texas.

In 2008 *Salim Boughader Mucharrafille* was sentenced to 60 years in prison by Mexican authorities on charges of organized crime and immigrant smuggling. Mucharrafille, a Mexican of Lebanese descent owned a cafe in the city of Tijuana, across the border from San Diego. He was arrested in 2002 for smuggling 200 people, including Hezbollah supporters, into the U.S.

In 2001, *Mahmoud Youssef Kourani* crossed the border from Mexico in a car and traveled to Dearborn, Mich. Kourani was later charged with and convicted of providing "material support and resources ... to Hezbollah," according to a 2003 indictment. These crossings were systemic of 38 other documented illegal crossings by Lebanese immigrants in FY2007, FY2008 and FY2009, although we do not by any means catch them all, not even most of them. The Ikhwan, Hezbollah, Hamas, al-Qaida and all the other mystically-based terrorist groups are operating with the same play book; its called the Holy Qur'an and forms the basis for several levels of Shariah Law used to justify a wide range of illegal activity in the US, all of which are a clear and present danger to the US Constitution. You won't see this in the news, but you can see this threat for yourself in these references:

- **Qur'an***
- **Sunna ahadith: Bukari** [†]

---

* **Qur'an]** accessed at: http://quod.lib.umich.edu/k/koran/browse.html
[†] **Sunna ahadith** at http://www.searchtruth.com/

- **Reliance of the Traveler**[*]
- **Milestones by Sayyaid Qutb**[†]
- **Explanatory Memorandum**[‡]
- **Principals of Islamic Jurisprudence** [§]

The following statement from the Council on American Islamic Relations proposes the Qur'an should be the law of the land in America, a clear problem of constitutional law and a threat to our sovereignty.

> *"The Quran should be the highest authority in America, and Islam the only accepted religion on earth."*

CAIR, 1998

The text of Islamic Jurisprudence also suggests issues not only with international sovereignty but with freedom of religion in the Establishment Clause of the first amendment:[**]

> *"Sovereignty...is the prerogative of Almighty Allah alone."*

Principals of Islamic Jurisprudence [1:8]

---

[*] **Reliance of the Traveler accessed at:**
http://canaryinthecoalmine.typepad.com/Shariah
[†] **Milestones by Sayyaid Qutb accessed at:**
http://majalla.org/books/2005/qutb-nilestone.pdf
[‡] **Explanatory Memorandum accessed at:**
http://www.investigativeproject.org/document/id/20
[§] **Principals of Islamic Jurisprudence accessed at:**
http://www.islamicperspective.net/Pictures/Book%20File/b7s2s5.pdf

[**] **First Amendment**: Two clauses in the First Amendment guarantee freedom of religion. The establishment clause prohibits the government from passing legislation to establish an official religion or preferring one religion over another. It enforces the "separation of church and state." Some governmental activity related to religion has been declared constitutional by the Supreme Court. For example, providing bus transportation for parochial school students and the enforcement of "blue laws" is not prohibited. The free exercise clause prohibits the government, in most instances, from interfering with a person's practice of their religion.

"Fight...(anyone who holds secular law superior to Allah) until there is no persecution and the religion is Allah's entirely."

Qur'an, 8:39

The Qur'an in particular has profound disagreements with liberty, particularly with discrimination as concerns the 14th amendment, Federal hate laws, civil rights and equal protection under the constitution.

"[Non-Muslims are]...the most vile of created beings."

Qur'an, 98:6

"Be merciful to one another but <u>ruthless to the infidels</u>."

Qur'an, 48:29

"Allah thus directs you as regards your children's inheritance: to the male, a portion equal to that of two females."

Qur'an, 4:11

The Qur'an is often advocated as a book of peace. However, violence is an ever present theme in Islamic law with hate targeted on anyone who is not Muslim (a.k.a. an infidel) the apostasy of anyone who rejects Islam. Islamic law recognizes no authority except that which comes from Allah (Islam is not just a religion but a complete way of life governed by Shariah law that comes from Allah who alone is sovereign in Islamic jurisprudence).

"Fight and kill the infidels wherever you find them, and seize them, beleaguer them and lie in wait for them in every stratagem of war."

Qur'an, 9:5

"When a person who has reached puberty and is sane voluntarily apostatizes from Islam, he deserves to be killed...There is no indemnity for killing an apostate."

Reliance of the Traveler, o8.0—8.4

"Honor Killing]...is *not subject to retaliation...a father or mother (or their fathers or mothers) for killing their offspring, or their offspring's offspring.*"

Reliance of the Traveler, o1.0—1.2

Casey Anthony had better hope her parents don't find Islam in the near future. Domestic abuse is another very difficult subject for Islam as they endorse its use as a marital tool for domestic negotiation.

"*As to those women on whose part ye fear disloyalty and ill conduct, admonish them first, next refuse to share their beds, and last...beat them.*"

Qur'an, 4:34

Treason in U.S. Code Title 18, Section 2385 is another one of those pesky issues for radical Imams who are trying to recruit new Jihadi terrorists in local American mosques:

"*Against them* [the infidels] *make ready your strength to the utmost of your power, including steeds of war, to strike terror into the hearts of the enemies of Allah, your enemies, and others besides...*"*

Qur'an, 8:60

Women are unusually singled out in Shariah not only for misogyny and condoned child abuse but brutal gender-based violence such as female genital mutilation, forced sterilization and endorsed polygamy. In the writings of the Sunna hadith, Islamic scholars documented;

"*...the Prophet...consummated his marriage when she was nine years old.*"

Bukari: Vol.7

---

* **Enemies**: This is the creed displayed on the Muslim Brotherhood coat of arms.

"Circumcision is obligatory ...for both men and women."
Reliance of the Traveler, e4.3

"Marry women of your choice, two , or three, or four...or a captive that your right hands possess."

Crossing other lines of legality include: taxation/money-laundering and federal racketeering statutes supported by passages in Reliance of the Traveler h8.7—h8.17 and the Qur'an, 9:29, tax evasion indentified in Qur'an text 9:60, illegal immigration, drug/weapons trafficking, fraud [credit, mail, bank, wire, mortgage], cigarette smuggling,* internet/retail sales of counterfeit/pirated designer products,† and illegal Fund Raising.‡

Because Zakat (re: Qur'an 9:60) is one of the five pillars of Islam, American Muslims are required to donate to charity; HLF, Al Aqsa Education Fund, UASR, CAIR, Islamic Association for Palestine, WISE and other 501c3 'charitable' Islamic organizations fill the middle-man void between this forced taxation of American Muslims and the need for terrorist financing. It is Zakat that crosses each year through the Tohono O'odham lands, travels across Mexico into the Tri-Border Region of South America and finally to the Middle East where it is used to kill American soldiers.

Much of this effort is sanctioned by Shariah Law and is supported by threats to the US Constitution and the rule of law. Specifically

---

* **Smuggling**: Mohamad Hammoud funneled millions of dollars to Hezbollah in addition to domestic smuggling of night vision equipment, GPS devices, stun guns, nitrogen cutters, laser range finders, compasses and blasting equipment—all destined for the Middle East. One truck load of smuggled cigarettes can yield up to $2 million profit for terrorists.

† **Fake goods** range from counterfeit power tools to designer clothing, pharmaceutical products such as Viagra, Prozac, and Xenical, Gucci handbag knockoffs, Prada shoes, T-shirts, DVD's, digital game software, etc. The FBI estimates counterfeiting costs US businesses $200-250 BILLION/yr.

‡ **Illegal Fund Raising**: The Holy Land Foundation: largest terrorist trial in history. Working under non-profit, tax-exempt status as a charitable organization, HLF funneled millions of dollars from 1987 until 2006 to Hamas, one of the most virulent terrorist organizations in the Middle East.

this research suggests Shariah's assault on America includes attacks on:

Article VI, Sovereignty

Emancipation Proclamation

Amend:1, Establishment Clause, Freedom of Religion

Amend:1, Freedom of Speech

Amend:14, Equal Protection (Sex/Race)

Model Penal Code § 230.1: Polygamy (nationwide)

US Constitutional Treason & Sedition Laws

U.S. Code Title 18, Section 2383-85

Radical Islam and Shariah continue to embrace an ideology that routinely breaks federal Hate and Civil Rights Laws, Domestic Abuse Laws, Taxation/Money laundering, Tax evasion, Illegal immigration, Drug/Weapons trafficking , Fraud [credit, mail, bank, wire, mortgage, smuggling, counterfeit/pirated products and Illegal Fund Raising not to mention common sense and decency.

Regrettably this is the political position on social justice and sovereignty taken up by the Obama administration; their consistent response (when they are not too busy looking the other way) is to either remain outwardly soft on terrorism or blame rank and file Americans for the problem. It is the blame-game Obama and Holder have chosen to use as the principal leveraging arm to cover up Operation Fast and Furious.

Project Cover-up

"I know nothing! NOTHING..."
Sgt. Schultz*

Brian Terry's BORTAC team, following well-practiced law enforcement procedure, announced themselves as Border Patrol agents and ordered the suspects to lay down their weapons. An intense fire-fight erupted during which Terry was mortally wounded in the lower pelvis. As his life ebbed away that night, he was unaware that ATF agents had been personally responsible for placing the AK47 rifle that killed him into the hands of the cartel bandit who pulled the trigger.

Even though it has only recently come into public view as a result of the death of Agent Terry, the tragic activities surrounding the arms trafficking known as Operation Fast and Furious (under the auspices of Project Gun Runner) actually began in Laredo TX as a Department of Justice program in 2005 under the George W. Bush administration; it was one element in a larger program called the Southwest Border Initiative.

The "blue-sky" strategy of the program as a whole was to identify, prosecute and end illegal weapons trafficking. Overall, from a public relations aspect, the larger problem was very few prosecutions actually resulted from a program that routinely allowed gun traffickers to "walk" firearms across the border. After four years, millions of taxpayer dollars† and a lot of wasted time

---

* **Sgt. Schultz** played by actor John Banner (28 January 1910 – 28 January 1973), born Johann Banner, was an American film and television actor. He is best known for his role as the World War II German Master Sergeant Hans Georg Schultz in the situation comedy *Hogan's Heroes* (1965–1971).

† **FY2006 and FY2007**, ATFE had dedicated approximately 100 special agents and 25 industry operations investigators to the Southwest Border Initiative. During FY2008, ATF deployed 146 special agents and 68 industry operations investigators to the program to bolster that initiative at a conservatively estimated cost of $32.2 million.

and energy, the program was essentially deemed a failure in early 2009 by newly confirmed Attorney General Eric Holder* a critical player of the incoming Obama administration of spare change.

Throughout their career, ATF agents are thoroughly cross-trained in both US manufactured weapons systems as well as many foreign firearms designs including the AK47 and are entirely aware of its reputation, reliability and lethality. To their credit, when the message was passed down to agents in Arizona that ATF management wanted them to let these weapons cross the border into cartel hands, they immediately balked. Ironically, more than one agent heatedly voiced his disbelief and asked superiors if they were prepared to attend the funeral and face the family of an American who is killed by one of these weapons?

> *"When I made complaints against the ATF, they were completely ignored and whitewashed and they left the same people in place to operate Project Gunrunner."*

> **ATF Tucson Agent Jay Dobyns**

The complaints went without note or action by management except to threaten agents with career limiting retaliation for not "...*being on the team.*"

> *"We have learned that ATF field agents strongly objected to the program, but that their opposition was dismissed."*

> **Rep. Darrell Issa†**

Worse than being ignored, some agents feared the inevitable downside of whistle-blowing; career retribution from an irrational management team can have a certain finality to it. ATF historically has a rather short conversation that goes something like,

---

* **Eric Himpton Holder, Jr.** (b. January 21, 1951) On December 1, 2008, President-elect Barack Hussein Obama announced Holder would be his nominee for Attorney General. Holder was formally nominated on January 20, 2009 and approved by the Senate Judiciary Committee on January 28. Following his confirmation by the full Senate on February 2, 2009, he became the 82nd Attorney General of the United States.

† **Congressional Oversight Hearings** 6-15-11 "Operation Fast and Furious: Reckless Decisions, Tragic Outcomes."

"...turn in your badge and your gun, turn over your briefcase and don't slam your ass in the door on the way out."

With the ATF it can get a lot uglier than just forced career changes. After two grueling years undercover with the Hell's Angels, Agent Jay Dobyns management leveraged the danger of gang retaliation in an attempt to put a lid on Dobyns' complaints about the agency.

"You are gonna spend the rest of your life running from the Hells Angels. We know who you are, we know where you live."

The ATF office in Phoenix, specifically Agent-in-Charge Bill Newell and his deputy, Assistant Special Agent George Gillette, had both promised to protect Dobyns, but Dobyns says they didn't. He says the Hells Angels threatened to rape his wife and behead his children. Weeks later, Dobyns says the gang, who could not otherwise have known where he lived, burned down his house with his family inside. Miraculously, they escaped.

"They (ATF) abandoned us, they ignored us". *

In December 2010 an ATF agent named Vince Cefalu began contacting FoxNews and going public with the scandal of lost guns in Project Gunrunner. Since then, other ATF agents have stepped up to the plate and corroborated Cefalu's allegations. But in June 2011 Cefalu, a 24 year veteran of ATF operations, was given his walking papers.

US Representative Darrell Issa who, along with Senator Grassley have been putting a magnifying glass on ATF since the story broke in early 2011.† They jointly wrote a letter to ATF's Deputy Director William J. Hoover urging his cooperation in not retaliating against

---

* FoxNews: accessed on June 28, 2011 at:
http://www.foxnews.com/politics/2011/05/04/friction-grows-lawmakers-doj-project-gunrunner-probe
† This scandal only came to the attention of the mainstream media through the efforts of two citizen journalists, David Codrea at Examiner.com and Mike Vanderboegh of the Sipsey Street Irregulars. Their original stories can be read at: http://www.examiner.com/gun-rights-in-national/a-journalist-s-guide-to-project-gunwalker

ATF employees who provide testimony to the Committee on Oversight and Government Reform.

> *"I write to request your assurance that the Bureau of Alcohol, Tobacco, Firearms, and Explosives (ATF) will not retaliate against witnesses who have provided information to this Committee. I make this request in light of the fact that on June 15, 2011, in a hearing before the Committee entitled "Operation Fast and Furious: Reckless Decisions, Tragic Outcomes," three veteran ATF special agents gave testimony highly critical of the ATF. They should not face reprisals of any kind for their testimony. No other ATF employees who cooperate with Congress should face retaliation either. The Committee relies on whistleblowers to conduct unvarnished and thorough oversight. Witnesses who choose to cooperate with the Committee must be confident that they can provide information without fear of punishment."*

> **Rep. Darrell Issa**

Apparently Issa's letter and Cefalu's new employment opportunity letter must have crossed in the congressional mailroom.

As a direct result of Eric Holder clamming up and stonewalling initial inquiries by Issa, Grassley and others, the Committee on Oversight and Government Reform began proceedings to bring out the "unvarnished" truth. The DOJ's actions in preventing witnesses from testifying and withholding documents in official congressional investigations are themselves a federal crime.*

The committee's concern, almost from the beginning was that ATF acting director Ken Melson was set to be the fall-guy in the cover-up; indeed this was reported by the media. Although this turned out not to be the case, the committee on July 5, 2011 began to warn Holder that using Melson to cover up DOJ involvement would be a serious overstepping of his authority.

> *"Technically, Mr. Melson no longer enjoys the due process protections afforded to career officials. Given his testimony,*

---

* **Obstructing or impeding a Congressional inquiry** is a criminal violation under 18 U.S.C. § 1505.

unless a permanent director is confirmed, it would be inappropriate for the Justice Department to take action against him that could have the effect of intimidating others who might want to provide additional information to the Committees...Knowing what we know so far, we believe it would be inappropriate to make Mr. Melson the fall guy in an attempt to prevent further congressional oversight."

Joint letter by Grassley and Issa to Eric Holder*

The warning came about in a letter written after a secret meeting with Grassley and Issa on July 4, 2011. With only his personal lawyer present, Melson finally began to open the kimono on the involvement in the cover-up by ATF management at DOJ as well as the inter-agency collusion in Operation Fast and Furious by paid informants of the DEA and FBI.

"ATF leadership appears to have been effectively muzzled while the DOJ sent over false denials and buried its head in the sand. That approach distorted the truth and obstructed our investigation. The Department's inability or unwillingness to be more forthcoming served to conceal critical information that we are now learning about the involvement of other agencies, including the DEA and the FBI....The Acting Director said that ATF was kept in the dark about certain activities of other agencies, including DEA and FBI. Mr. Melson said that he learned from ATF agents in the field that information obtained by these agencies could have had a material impact on the Fast and Furious Government investigation as far back as late 2009 or early 2010. After learning about the possible role of DEA and FBI, he [Melson] testified that he reported this information in April 2011 to the Acting Inspector General and directly to then-Acting Deputy Attorney General James Cole on June 16, 2011.

Joint letter by Grassley and Issa to Eric Holder†

---

* **Congressional Letter** from Senator Charles Grassley and Rep. Darrell Issa to Attorney General Eric Holder: July 5, 2011 Committee on Oversight and Government Reform (the complete letter is reprinted as part of the Endnotes).
† **Ibid**, Congressional Letter, July 5, 2011

And Melson did not arrive at the meeting empty handed. The committee had repeatedly subpoenaed ATF and DOJ documents throughout the first half of their investigation in 2011; what they got from Holder were either outright refusals or heavily redacted documents that were of little use. Melson handed them an eye-opener regarding documents he submitted to the official in the Office of the Deputy Attorney General (ODAG) who was specifically put in charge of the DOJ effort in providing subpoenaed documents to Grassley and Issa's committee.

> *"Mr. Melson provided documents months ago supporting his concerns to the official in the ODAG responsible for document production to the Committees, but those documents have not been provided to us."*

Joint letter by Grassley and Issa to Eric Holder*

And this was neither the most shocking nor the most damning testimony given by Melson. As Brian Terry lay bleeding from a fatal gunshot wound near Hell's Gate, I am sure he was equally unaware the illegally trafficked rifles used at the crime scene had been purchased using taxpayer funds. Further, that not only were federal indictments for the supposed 'kingpins' sought in Operation Fast and Furious delayed by DOJ, but those individuals were on the payroll of the FBI and DEA.

> *"The evidence we have gathered raises the disturbing possibility that the Justice Department not only allowed criminals to smuggle weapons but that taxpayer dollars from other agencies may have financed those engaging in such activities.*
>
> *"...Mr. Melson's responses tended to corroborate what others had said. Specifically, we have very real indications from several sources that some of the gun trafficking "higher-ups" that the ATF sought to identify were already known to other agencies and may even have been paid as informants.*

---

* **Ibid**, Congressional Letter, July 5, 2011

"...According to Acting Director Melson, he became aware of this startling possibility only after the murder of Border Patrol Agent Brian Terry and the indictments of the straw purchasers, which we now know were substantially delayed by the U.S. Attorney's Office and Main Justice.

"...It is one thing to argue that the ends justify the means in an attempt to defend a policy that puts building a big case ahead of stopping known criminals from getting guns. Yet it is a much more serious matter to conceal from Congress the possible involvement of other agencies in identifying and maybe even working with the same criminals that Operation Fast and Furious was trying to identify.

"...If agencies within the same Department, co-located at the same facilities, had simply communicated with one another, then ATF might have known that gun trafficking "higher-ups" had been already identified. This raises new and serious questions about the role of DEA, FBI, the United States Attorney's Office in Arizona, and Main Justice in coordinating this effort."

Letter* from Grassley and Issa to Eric Holder[17]

In fact, Agent Newell testified to Issa's committee on July 27, 2011 that ATF never had any plans to extradite drug kingpins from Mexico. A shocked committee sat stunned at the testimony which on one hand suggested ATF's plan was to put drug kingpins into jail, (i.e. "disrupt, dismantle, destroy") but on the other hand had absolutely no extradition strategy to do so. Newell's only response to further inquiry of how exactly ATF was going to jail anybody In Mexico without extradition proceedings was,

"...one of the things we wanted to do...as soon as we had solid information on who the drug kingpin in Mexico was...was to share that information with the Government of Mexico."

---

* Complete text of this letter appears in the Endnotes beginning on Page 134.

On the surface, this appears to be an eminently reasoned argument with both planning and expected results. The problem is that after spending years of "investigative" resources, millions of taxpayer dollars ATF never once got around to telling the Government of Mexico anything. Newell seems to have great intentions after indictments are flying all over the place; where were the intentions before people started dying for this program?

Newell apparently did tell a government national security advisor, but it was not a security advisor in Mexico; it was Kevin O'Reilly, the National Security Advisor to the President, an advisor whose office is in the White House. O'Reilly's position is not insignificant, nor is his feigned ignorance of the subject any more palatable than Holder's or Melson's incessant denials in blocking the investigation.

> *"O'Reilly was national security director for North America tasked with monitoring the activities of Mexican drug cartels. We are asked to believe he inquired about a program that was providing the cartels with guns but kept what he found out to himself."*

> **Investors.com**[*]

The email correspondence sent two attachments to O'Reilly, apparently in response to a request for information NSA could use to brief White House officials regarding Project Gunrunner in preparation for a pending trip to Mexico. The NSA holds weekly meetings in the White House situation room and may include not only the Secretary of State, the Vice-President and Security Council members but may include the President as well. It was this startling revelation between ATF and the NSA that has put President Obama and perhaps others back onto the roadmap of scandal.

---

[*] **ATF: The White House Knew** Posted 07/28/2011 07:02 PM ET, accessed on July 29, 2011 at:
http://www.investors.com/NewsAndAnalysis/Article/579822/201107281902/AT F-The-White-House-Knew.htm

Figure 16: Email from ATF Agent William Newell to White House National Security Advisor Kevin O'Reilly.

When this interchange occurred between Issa's committee and Newell, they were asking if he had shared information on the illegal Operation Fast and Furious investigation with anyone in the White House. The first sentence in the email which contained the subject line "GRIT" (Gun Runner Interdiction Team) and was sent to O'Reilly states,

> "...You didn't get these from me."

Somehow that opening comment just doesn't ring like a lucid bell of legality, ethics or integrity.

The truth behind the cover-up and the bullet that killed Agent Brian Terry is a remarkably poignant tragedy that is forever linked in the infamy of failed ideology. The dark alley of arms trafficking, narco-terrorism and deceit that resulted in so many killings and the subsequent cover-up was initiated to foster a failed political ideology, an uncaring ideology focused on an irrational totalitarian program that is willing to trade the lives of Americans, our precious individual freedom, personal wealth and our guns for an uncaring secular privileged class in Washington and a mystical elite in Beirut and Tehran.

That ideology now and always has included the political use of gun control as an effective agent of both change and power; a subject to which we will now turn.

Getting Gun Control Under Control

"I just want you to know that we are working on it. We have to go through a few processes, but...under the radar."

**President Barack Hussein Obama
to Sarah Brady, Spring 2011***

Historically gun control is an insidious methodology that Adolph Hitler used in part of the plan to exterminate the Jewish communities in Germany during WWII; Hitler's NAZI† atrocities were inspired by the coercive and racist government programs first instituted in the US by Democrat Woodrow Wilson prior to and during WWI. With Hitler doing the heavy lifting in Europe for Fascism, his gun control ideals were adopted during the 1930's by Franklin Roosevelt's principal cheerleader for federal control of firearms—Attorney General Homer Cummings.

It was Cummings inherent fear of handguns coupled with Roosevelt's juice for social justice that first sent the proposal for a national firearms registration to the US Congress in 1934. The House of Representatives, already wary of a progressive populist movement in Roosevelt's fawning media and trumpeted by the White House itself to both condemn and glorify the dreaded machine gun in gangster hands, so found reason to delete the

---

* **March 30, 2011** Meeting with Jim and Sarah Brady, White House press secretary Jay Carney and the President as reported in the Washington Post. During the meeting the President himself brought up the issue of gun control according to Sarah Brady, "*...to fill us in that it was very much on his agenda.*" The meeting was precipitated by the shooting of Arizona Rep. Gabrielle Giffords and occasioned by the anniversary of the attempted assassination of President Reagan during which Jim Brady was seriously wounded.
http://www.washingtonpost.com/lifestyle/style/over-a-barrel-meet-white-house-gun-policy-adviser-steve-croley/2011/04/04/AFt9EKND_story_2.html
† **NAZI** is an acronym for National Socialist Workers Party.

handgun registration from the original bill. The registration of machine guns and other 'destructive devices' did pass both the US House and the Senate and was eventually signed into the history of Roosevelt's New Deal accomplishments as the National Firearms Act of 1934 (commonly referred to as the NFA).

Modeled on the Harrison Narcotics Act, the NFA based regulatory powers on a tax imposed on trafficking in the weapons within and across state lines, thus generating federal jurisdiction for intrastate as well as interstate transactions. Cummings, undaunted, continued to author handgun control legislation long after Roosevelt and the public had dismissed it as unimportant. Still, Cummings had accomplished the first broad implementation of federal firearms authority through restrictions initiated by the office of the US Attorney General, a model for generations to come.

Parts of the NFA were eventually overturned by the Supreme Court in 1968, ironically the same year Thomas J. Dodd's (D-CT)* famous 1968 Gun Control Act was put in place. Further coercive actions were increased in sweeping measures by the Clinton administration's semi-automatic firearms ban in 1994. Their principal mechanism then as now is the well-worn path of socialist elites everywhere—that of legislated gun control.

During the meeting from which we draw the quotation at the beginning of this chapter, President Obama also volunteered information regarding how firearms records get into the government's system and what can be done about it relative to firearms retailers; the first concerns eTrace which we discuss elsewhere in this research; the second is all about gun control. The Sarah Brady and her lobbying efforts over the years have focused on one myopic issue to the complete exclusion of all others; disarming the American public through accelerated institutionalization of national gun control legislation.

Obama as well as Eric Holder has a long and ugly record impinging on the rights of law-abiding citizens to own firearms. On the

---

* **Thomas Joseph Dodd** (May 15, 1907 – May 24, 1971) United States Senator and Representative from Connecticut.

campaign trail in 2008, candidate Obama spoke openly of his support for reinstituting the 1994 Clinton gun control legislation (which was originally authored by Holder) and his support for a total ban on the manufacture, sale and possession of all handguns and the registration of long gun owners.[*] The long gun registration issue is one that would repeat itself time and again.

Candidate Obama also stated he would close the infamous gun-show loophole and importantly overturn the Federal law requiring ATF to destroy privacy records of law abiding citizens who pass routine background checks in the purchase of firearms.[†]

In point of fact, ATF has been thumbing their nose at the records destruction requirement for some time, illegally maintaining an enormous warehouse of information on firearms possessed by Americans. That law specifically states:

> *"...the [background check] system shall -(A) assign a unique identification number to the transfer; (B) provide the licensee with the number; and (C)* ***destroy all records of the system with respect to the call (other than the identifying number and the date the number was assigned) and all records of the system relating to the person or the transfer.*** *"* [ed. Note: emphasis added]

18 U.S.C. § 922: US Code - Section 922: Unlawful acts

The multiple firearm reporting requirements are an integral part of every retail firearms transfer and routinely occur after the FBI background check has cleared the individual for possession of the weapon(s). The wording of the law clearly states *"destroy all records of the system"*, there is no exception (beyond retaining the ID number of the transaction and the date it occurred). It does not say within thirty days, or twenty-four hours, or even five minutes; it says destroy them, period.

---

[*] **Townhall.com**: accessed at
http://townhall.com/tipsheet/chrisfield/2011/06/01/misfire_obamas_scandalous_secret_gun_control_agenda
[†] **Ibid,** Washington Post

Another leading advocate in eliminating the ATF records restriction has been Socialist sock-puppet Sen. Frank Lautenberg (D-NJ) who in 2009 introduced legislation not only to completely scuttle the requirement but to actually mandate ATF to maintain the records on legal transfers to law-abiding citizens for up to six months.* He was joined in this legislative fiat against American liberties of privacy by all the usual suspects in the cabal of rabid anti-rights, anti-gun co-conspirators; among them Sen. Charles Schumer (D-NY) and Sen. Diane Feinstein (D-CA).

Much of this liberal empowerment mechanism for rogue gun control began in the middle part of the last century with an unlikely war hero who had a penchant for loose women and fast boats.

In 1958 a youthful US Senator and naval war hero named John F. Kennedy† (D-MA)—at the time representing the lucrative firearms-manufacturing state of Massachusetts—proposed a bill to prohibit "*the importation of firearms originally manufactured for military purposes.*" This blatantly protectionist bill did not pass into law, but the Congress did subsequently prohibit the re-importation of weapons that the United States had sent abroad under its foreign-assistance act and the WWII lend-lease program.‡

Ironically, after enormous efforts on the part of New Deal socialists to outlaw and register machine guns, Kennedy, who later became the 35th President of the United States, was assassinated in 1963 by

---

* **S. 2820,** 111TH Congress, 1ST Session The legislation exercised the usual fear-mongering umbrella of terrorism has the excuse for implementation; the records were to be retained for up to 10 years for individuals who received firearms and appeared on various terrorist lists maintained by the government "...*all records generated in the course of the check of the national criminal back ground check system, including the ATF Form 4473, that are obtained by Federal and State officials shall be retained for a minimum of 10 years.*" In fact, any records involved in any criminal investigation may already be maintained by law enforcement and did not need this legislation to do so.

† **John Fitzgerald "Jack" Kennedy** (May 29, 1917 – November 22, 1963), often referred to by his initials JFK, was the 35th President of the United States, serving from 1961 until his assassination in 1963.

‡ England, who had been caught unprepared for World War II had directly benefited from Americans who had sent firearms out of their personal gun collections to assist in the defense of old Britannia.

an unregulated and fairly uncomplicated imported military bolt action rifle purchased and delivered through the US Postal Service mail. Kennedy's assassination would become an icon for gun control legislation led by yet another liberal from New England.

Thomas J. Dodd had become chairman of the Senate Subcommittee on juvenile Delinquency in 1961. By the time of the first Kennedy assassination, Dodd had already "...*directed the staff of the Subcommittee to initiate a full-scale inquiry into the interstate mail order gun problem.*" Staff studies of mail order guns sold to residents of the District of Columbia supported Dodd's conviction that,

> "...*criminals, immature juveniles, and other irresponsible persons were using the relative secrecy of the mail order-common carrier method of obtaining firearms, because they could not purchase guns under the laws in their own jurisdictions.*"

Congressional Report*

Dodd held hearings in 1963 largely using the data he had accumulated through his staff reports and subsequently drafted a bill restricting mail-order sales of handguns. Within days of the John Kennedy assassination, Dodd had redrafted the bill to include rifles and shotguns. The legislation languished in committee and was finally scuttled in 1964, but Dodd—like many socialists—was undeterred by temporary setbacks.

Beginning in 1965 Dodd would get a series of indelible crises which would serve to put his draconian legislation over the top. Among them were the Watts Riots in Los Angeles in 1965, Bloody Sunday in Selma,[18] the march at Marquette Park in Chicago,[19] twenty thousand anti-war demonstrators marched in New York in March 1966, 10,000 picketed the White House in May 1966. On April 15, 1967, 400,000 people marched from Central Park to the UN building in New York City to protest the war while 100,000 marched in San Francisco on the same day and on April 17, 1968

---

* Thomas Dodd report prepared for the Subcommittee. to Investigate Juvenile Delinquency of the S. Comm. on the Judiciary, 90th Cong., 2d Sess., 1968.

national media broadcast the anti-war riot that erupted in Berkeley, California; the over-reaction by the police in Berkeley was shown in both Berlin and Paris, sparking street reactions in those cities.

As a consequence of wide-spread racial fear fueled by a cadre of media who lives for violence and an appetite for civil disobedience by liberal anti-war apologists and activists of the period, a much more prophylactic version of the bill finally became *Title IV of the Omnibus Crime Control Act of 1968*. It was passed by the Senate in May 1968 and by the House on June 6, the day after the shooting of Attorney General Robert F. Kennedy.*

Strangely—although one of Dodd's original hot buttons and further leveraged by the assassination of John Kennedy was the use of the Post Office in delivering weapons to individual buyers—incredibly the bill did not restrict interstate mail-order of rifles. However, in the aftermath of Attorney General Robert Kennedy's death in June 1968 and coupled with the various permutations of urban riots and political demonstrations, a number of revisions were proposed to the original Omnibus bill. In the fall of 1968 an amended bill which did restrict interstate sale of long guns through the mail was signed into law by President Lyndon B. Johnson.

The Gun Control Act signed by President Johnson on October 22, 1968, was another omnibus measure; included in the Act were amendments to the National Firearms Act of 1934, extending its coverage to newly defined "destructive devices" (now including bombs, hand grenades, land mines, and similar mechanisms most of which are now in the hands of Mexican drug cartels).

The major objectives of the legislation were:

---

* **Robert Francis "Bobby" Kennedy** (November 20, 1925 – June 6, 1968), also referred to by his initials RFK, was an American politician, a Democratic senator from New York, and a noted civil rights activist. An icon of modern American liberalism, he was a younger brother of President John F. Kennedy and acted as one of his advisors during his presidency. From 1961 to 1964, he was the U.S. Attorney General.

(1) Eliminating the interstate traffic in firearms and ammunition that had previously frustrated state and local efforts to license, register, or restrict ownership of guns.

(2) Denying access to firearms to certain congressionally defined groups, including minors, convicted felons, and persons who had been adjudicated as mental defectives or committed to mental institutions.

(3) Ending the importation of all surplus military firearms and all other guns unless certified by the Secretary of the Treasury as "particularly suitable for...sporting purposes."

The first goal was a clear federalization of local law enforcement efforts; although the Federal government has rarely demonstrated any ability to deal with local law enforcement (note: Washington D.C.—with both local and Federal laws outlawing any possession of any type of firearm—has the most egregious record of firearms homicide in the US). It also served notice those firearms laws were newly subject to interstate transportation regulation and enforcement.

The second goal was based on the German model of identifying, isolating and regulating specific constituencies in a larger agenda to affect overall gun control in the more general population (a.k.a. "divide and conquer"). Adolph Hitler's NAZI political party first isolated through propaganda and later disarmed the Jewish communities prior to launching the holocaust; the US Democrat's socialistic political party (with a little bit of help from liberal GOP Republicans) have to date similarly disarmed segmented American populations of teachers, hospital workers, most civilian government employees and anyone working a voting booth (unless of course you are a Black Panther attempting to influence the outcome of an Obama election*, in which case you receive a "get out of jail free card" courtesy of Eric Holder and the DOJ). Tragically, they have also disarmed soldiers on US military bases, the result of which were the deaths at Fort Hood, TX instigated by Islamic

* **2008 voter-intimidation case against New Black Panthers riles the right**
By *Krissah Thompson* Washington Post Staff Writer Thursday, July 15, 2010

terrorist Capt. Hassan Nidal; a crime like so many which is perpetrated against the coercively regulated and unarmed populace.

The third item was a purely new model for anti-rights propaganda. By planting the idea in the public mind that certain types of weapons *ONLY* become politically acceptable if used by hunters exercising good sportsmanship; this becomes an agile leap of agitprop to condemn and outlaw any weapon that does not meet the purely arbitrary "sporting" criterion of an appointed government official.

Comparison to the old 'German' model of gun control is not lightly offered. Thomas Dodd, the principal author of the 1968 legislation, used Hitler's 1938 German gun control law as the boilerplate to compose new American restrictions; line by line comparisons of matching language have been done. Dodd had extensive background in and about Germany as he was a principal in the famous Nuremburg Trials of NAZI war criminals*. It has been shown† he was not only in possession of a translation of the German gun control law but the translation was done for him by the US Library of Congress.[20] Hitler's pogrom against the Jewish people and Dodd's 1968 legislation both used the "sporting purpose" criteria. It is a methodology that Obama and Holder continue to advocate in their anti-rights agenda for America.

By identifying "acceptable" weapons and the definition and criteria of their use, "unacceptable" weapons becomes a defacto category and their owners the unrelenting target of totalitarian government intervention. As it is an effective, arbitrary and politically motivated effort designed to fail, increasing calls for new and ever more restrictive regulation is inevitable. It is a short step from there to complete registration and finally—confiscation.

A disarmed populace is a controlled populace.

---

* **Dodd** served as a senior member of the team of U.S. prosecutors at the Nuremberg trials of Nazi war criminals in 1945-46.
† **Jews for the Preservation of Firearms Ownership**: GCA '68: What Your Politician Never Told You, http://jpfo.org/common-sense/cs34.htm

Although a similar Canadian gun registration law was sold to taxpayers using a highly emotional and media-visible support mechanism, results in Canada have been anything but stellar in this recent warning from a journalist there:

> *"...it is hard to say just how effective it has been in preventing long-gun deaths. Kimveer Gill's gun was registered under the much more restrictive handgun category, yet it didn't stop his deadly rampage at Dawson College five years ago. Nor did the long gun registry stop James Roszko from killing four Mounties the year before. And had the registry been in force in 1989, it's hard to see how it would have kept a rifle out of Marc Lepine's hands."*

The Montreal Gazette*

Although most American readers are unfamiliar with the specific news stories cited in the Montreal Gazette's story, I think you get the point; firearm registration is both an expensive as well as a failed approach to crime. It does offer a very nice revenue stream for politicians as it costs a great deal of money to manufacture programs intended to get politicians re-elected and the community disarmed, all in one fell bill.

The Canadian law was originally expected to cost about $2 million. Recent revelations in the Canadian press suggest the registry has actually cost our northern friends in excess of $1 billion in only the last few years and is predicted to expense an eye-popping $80 million in FY2011alone. Politics can easily shortchange you, and as with high school employees running the cash register you have to be careful what you pay for and be sure to count your change.

In the end President Obama did get what he paid for—all the Democratic Party socialists merrily dancing around his myopic May pole chanting *"...gun control...gun control."* Never mind they are dancing on the blood of Brian Terry.

---

* **Montreal Gazette Editorial**: Consider the gun-registry decision carefully, July 15, 2011, accessed at:
http://www.montrealgazette.com/opinion/editorials/Consider+registry+decision+carefully/5105822/story.html

Here is a sampling of the headlines from just one day in June 2011:

ATF Mexico debacle triggers new gun control debate
Houston Chronicle June 30, 2011 Byline: Dan Freedman[*]

Democrats to Take Aim at Gun Laws Amid ATF Probe
The Wall Street Journal June 30, 2011 Byline: Evan Perez[†]

Weak laws cited in gun-trafficking fight
The Washington Post June 30, 2011, Byline: Sari Horwitz[‡]

Dems Call for More Gun Control in Light of Operation Fast and Furious

Town Hall June 30, 2011 Byline: Katie Pavlich[§]

ATF's 'Fast and Furious' gun-tracking program prompts gun laws debate
The Hill June 30, 2011 Byline: Jordy Yager[**]

In many ways it strains the imagination that Holder, a career gun control wonk, did not foresee the opportunity inherent in this debacle. His good old boy partner in crime from Chicago (no, not Obama, I'm talking about President Obama's favorite hit man— Rahm Emanuel) had a favorite strategy Holder has maximized,

"Never let a serious crisis go to waste. What I mean by that is it's an opportunity to do things you couldn't do before."

Rahm "Dead Fish" Emanuel[††]

---

[*] **Houston Chronicle**
http://www.chron.com/disp/story.mpl/chronicle/7633343.html
[†] **Wall Street Journal**
http://online.wsj.com/article/SB10001424052702304450604576416630876667142.html
[‡] **Washington Post**
 http://www.washingtonpost.com/investigations/democrat-weak-us-laws-hurt-gun-trafficking-fight-in-mexico/2011/06/29/AG7TxbrH_story.html
[§] **Town Hall**
http://townhall.com/columnists/katiepavlich/2011/06/30/dems_call_for_more_gun_control_in_light_of_operation_fast_and_furious
[**] **The Hill** accessed at:
http://thehill.com/homenews/house/169145-fast-and-furious-program-prompts-gun-laws-debate
[††] **Wall Street Journal**: accessed at
http://online.wsj.com/article/SB123310466514522309.html

It's become a mantra in government these days and there is no shortage of dupes willing to chant that party line. You rarely run across a quiet unassuming politician that is part of the Democratic Party machine; Elijah Cummings is a good example. After Rep. Darrell Issa began to hold the first official hearings on Project Gunrunner in June 2011, Cummings—who does not have the ranking party authority to hold hearings—called what he referred to as a "summit" on the problem. At issue was the party invitations; the only people he invited were gun-control lapdogs and anti-rights advocates who proceeded to put on their own little serendipitous dog and pony show for the media blitzkrieg before issuing a report.* Incredibly, the report makes no mention of Brian Terry's death or that of Agent Jamie Zapata or even the hundreds of Mexican police officers or innocent Mexican citizens that died as a result of Project Gunrunner.

So what did the report talk about?

> "...the substantial body count that resulted from this operation is something that Democratic Rep. Elijah Cummings and his colleagues avoid mentioning. The report simply does not include the two American federal law enforcement officers killed in ambushes with Gunwalker firearms, and does not mention the Mexican casualties of this Obama administration-created fiasco. Instead, the minority report minimizes the magnitude of the crimes perpetrated under the guise of law enforcement, while building the case for gun control—an interesting development, as gun control may have been the ulterior motive for Gunwalker all along."

Bob Owens, Pajama Media†

---

* **OUTGUNNED** Law Enforcement Agents Warn Congress They Lack Adequate Tools to Counter Illegal Firearms Trafficking http://media.washingtonpost.com/wp-srv/investigative/documents/firearms_report_063011.pdf

† **Rep. Cummings' Gunwalker Report Neglects To Mention ... Gunwalker**, by Bob Owens, Pajama Media, accessed June 30, 2011 at:
http://pajamasmedia.com/blog/rep-cummings-gunrunner-report-neglects-to-mention-gunrunner

Without too much surprise Cummings report also dutifully cites the now bogus and hysterical 90% gun trace number. You know how you can tell a fool...but you just can't tell him much?

Cummings as the principal player in this charade is acting as a cheerleader for new ATF regulations that he proposes in his summit paper; most of it is old hat, but the proposal to implement a database of multiple long gun sales to American citizens (this would be data not currently obtained by ATF often due to permits for discrete carry of defensive weapons). This is not Cummings own idea; and it is similarly not new to the gun control debate. This incarnation of the regulation was put online at the ATF website as an Emergency Demand Letter[21] the same month Brian Terry was murdered. Emergency demands by the government always carry special exemptions.

ATF had in fact been intending on implementing this long gun reporting demand on privacy for some time—unfortunately unaware Operation Fast and Furious was going to hit the airwaves—they had been slapping themselves on the back for doing very well blaming gun shops with the whole 90% trace thing.

Two ATF emails revealed the long term plan for gun control and the tactical elements officials were manipulating in order to achieve that end. Katie Pavlich at Townhall.com broke the story on the existence of the emails between ATF officials Mark R Chait (assistant director for field operations with ATF) and deputy assistant director for field operations William Newell.

Mentioned earlier, Agent Newell was the special agent in charge (SAC) of the Phoenix Field Division and ultimately held local Arizona responsibility for Operation Fast and Furious. As you recall, Newell was the one who notified the White House via email about Project Gunrunner. This email is dated six months prior to Brian Terry's murder.

From:	Chait, Mark R.
Sent:	Wednesday, July 14, 2010 10:25 AM
To:	Newell, William D.
Cc:	McMahon, William G.
Subject:	Re: SIR

Bill - can you see if these guns were all purchased from same FFL and at one time. We are looking at anecdotal cases to support a demand letter on long gun multiple sales. Thanks Mark R. Chait Assistant Director Field Operations

Figure 17: The smoking gun email from Chait to Newell

After the initial freak-out at ATF due to whistle-blowers exposing the illegal gun trafficking operation in January 2011, Newell was involved in the early effort to put a lid on the media frenzy. Once again Chait emails Newell with a shout out for a job well done and another request for anecdotal evidence to support the agenda for multiple long gun reporting. Obviously, both the agenda for gun control and the demand letter were clearly in process by July 2010.

From: Chait, Mark R.
To: Newell, William D.
Cc: McMahon, William G.
Sent: Wed Jan 26 09:30:54 2011
Subject: F & F
Bill – well done yesterday on the F & F takedown and press conference...in light of our request for Demand letter 3, this case could be a strong supporting factor if we can determine how many multiple sales of long guns occurred during the course of this case. Could you have this information pulled for us to see if this may provide concrete info of a recent case. Thanks again..

Mark R. Chait
Assistant Director
Field Operations

Figure 18: Jan. 26, 2011, a second email from Chait referring to the Demand Letter and the need for a cause and affect case for multiple long gun sales.

The new regulation referred to in the demand letter was intended as a paper burden on dealers and not individual citizens (in fact, only on dealers in four states); their sense was that almost any new gun control that was not congressionally approved could fly "under the radar" as a new ATF regulation; and it might have worked except for a dirt-bag named Osorio-Arellanes and the other rip-crew thugs at Hell's Gate that brought those two pesky AK47's back across the border.

But even before the death of Agent Terry, the wheels were starting to come off the wonk's gun control wagon. The overseeing agency for the ATF is Holder's Department of Justice; the Office of Inspector General's (OIG) review of ATF and provided to DOJ in November 2010 did not have a happy face on it. Although the OIG was not aware of illegal aspects of Operation Fast and Furious, the review specifically indicated that ATF's legal umbrella—Project Gunrunner—was just not effectively targeting the kind of complex firearms trafficking for which the money had been ear-marked in the first place as part of the public strategy.

> *"...we found that 68 percent of Project Gunrunner cases are single-defendant cases, and some ATF managers discourage field personnel from conducting the types of complex conspiracy investigations that target higher-level members of trafficking rings...directing the efforts of Project Gunrunner toward building larger, multi-defendant conspiracy cases would better disrupt trafficking organizations...Although ATF has had a long-stated intent to make fuller use of the resources of the Department's Organized Crime Drug Enforcement Task Force Program to conduct more complex conspiracy investigations, **it has not done so** [ed. Note: emphasis added]."*

OIG Report, Nov. 2010, Pg v

To assess the impact of Project Gunrunner, DOJ's Office of Inspector General (OIG) examined data on ATF's actual performance in tracing guns, conducting criminal investigations, conducting compliance inspections of gun dealers in the region, and referring leads to ATF's criminal enforcement personnel for prosecution. Data in these areas was reviewed from fiscal year (FY) 2004 through FY 2006 (three years prior to ATF's implementation of Project Gunrunner), with data from FY 2007 through FY 2009 (the initial three full years of Project Gunrunner). Results of the review were more mind-numbing than a YouTube video of Charlie Sheen's hangover and not nearly as entertaining.

> *"...we found weaknesses in how ATF implemented Project Gunrunner as a multi-agency effort. Although, as noted...ATF has increased some program activities during Project Gunrunner, **ATF's focus remains largely on inspections of gun dealers and investigations of straw purchasers**, [ed. Note: emphasis added] rather than on higher-level traffickers, smugglers, and the ultimate recipients of the trafficked guns."*
>
> ### OIG Report, Nov. 2010, Pg v

The number of actual convicted felons who served jail time was not particularly dramatic; from 2006 to 2009 on average only about 150 people went to jail for firearms trafficking;* not unsurprisingly none of them were considered drug cartel kingpins. Nor did the efforts lead to recovery of large numbers of firearms in either the US or Mexico. ATF data indicated only 195 firearms were recovered in Mexico as a result of Project Gunrunner and only 372 in the US. Not really what you would call a big haul, but it was a good deal for the Mexican drug cartels considering ATF illicitly put over 1000 weapons into their bloody hands. And, with methodic timing, President Obama personally endorsed the new ATF long gun reporting regulation in June 2011 with a beautiful hand-signed Executive Order.

> *"The Justice Department on Monday ordered that all gun dealers in California, Arizona, New Mexico and Texas be required to notify the federal government about frequent buyers of high-powered rifles, saying that violence along the Southwest border has expanded to a point that it poses a 'significant threat' to the United States...the timing of the new mandate seems a little too convenient; as it's not yet clear how much of this supposed gunrunning "problem" originates in Washington."*
>
> ### The Washington Times†

---

* **OIG Source**: AFTE response to OIG Report, Nov. 2010 Pg. 117
† **Justice Department orders more reports on border arms sales**, by Jerry Seper, The Washington Times, July 11, 2011

So...ATF has just figured out that violence is a threat on the border; well you knew they had to catch up to reality at some point. I wonder if this means we'll get a nice shiny new sign on the south side of Phoenix warning tourists about the newly designated 'significant threat'? I wonder what the schedule is for signage in Kansas City?

Although it might not seem immediately relevant considering the otherwise weighty context of pervasive gun control, but the fact that President Obama facilitated this through Executive Order is not insignificant. The other multiple weapon purchase reporting requirement on hand guns was enacted by congressional fiat some years ago; even at that time congressional authorship of the law was questioned as unconstitutional. Although much has been made of the language of the constitution, the words of the second amendment are not really that hard to absorb,

> *"A well regulated militia being necessary to the security of a free State, the right of the People to keep and bear arms shall not be infringed."*

US Bill of Rights

The Second Amendment*

It is not like that sentence is constructed with esoteric formulas for the theory of nuclear physics; it says you and I have the right—not only to possess firearms—but we have the right to wear them around town. Importantly, it says those rights shall not be compromised. This is of course incredibly interesting considering

---

* **Second Amendment (Amendment II)** to the United States Constitution is the part of the United States Bill of Rights that recognizes the right of the people to keep and bear arms. It was adopted on December 15, 1791, along with nine other elements in the Bill of Rights. There are several versions of the text of the Second Amendment, each with slight capitalization and punctuation differences, found in the official documents surrounding the adoption of the Bill of Rights. One version was passed by the Congress, while another (shown in the text above) is found in the copies distributed to the several states and then ratified by them.   Accessed at: http://en.wikipedia.org/wiki/Second_Amendment_to_the_United_States_Constitutio n - cite_note-6

the state of affairs we are in today with relatively large, coercively unarmed populations in the US.

I remember being interviewed once by a young reporter who was anxious to do a story on the gun rights recognized in the second amendment. We met for lunch in a restaurant and after the usual exchanges the reporter acknowledged—even though he did not normally involve himself with constitutional politics—that as a teenager he had done a lot of hunting with his father and therefore he was a supporter of the second amendment. Then in a more official tone signaling the beginning of the interview, he asked me,

> "For the record, what is the purpose of the second amendment?"

I watched as he wrote his own question down on a notepad, wrote my name and then looked up at me. My response was short.

> "The second amendment is about shooting corrupt politicians."

I thought his eyebrows were going to push his ball cap off the top of his head.

This is a fine point that I believe a lot of good Americans who are not gun owners (and some Democrats who do own guns) miss when they see well-educated and normally glib political idiots like John Kerry trying to win the "gun vote" on the campaign trail by mimicking gun owners with broken English like we are all a bunch of ignorant Elmer Fudds in a Saturday matinee Looney Tune.

> "Ah wanna buy me a huntin' license..."
>
> **Sen. John Kerry**
> **Candidate for the White House**

Although there is an important element in the history of personal liberty that includes a long tradition of hunting that goes back to the rights of Englishmen to hunt on royal lands, the second amendment in revolutionary context was never about quail or deer. The US Bill of Rights has always been the recognition of a free people's right to defend themselves from corrupt politicians and other loathsome criminals who use government coercion and despotism to enact an anti-rights agenda for the American people.

Nowhere, in the US Constitution, nor in the Bill of Rights does it make ANY exception for the US Congress (or the ATF, DOJ or the President) to enact sweeping rules regarding the specificity of either hand guns or long guns or any other kind of gun; those are the tools of freedom relative to the right of self-defense and the preservation of our republic.

Another pervasive adage in firearms activism:

"What part of '...shall not be infringed' don't you get?"

But, even if we disregard those enabling constitutional restrictions on what government can do to us, and further putting aside both history and reality, the US Congress has already claimed authority over weapons reporting in this turf battle between political thugs. It was congress that debated and then voted on the previous multiple hand guns reporting scheme. At least in congress there are often public hearings, public debate, some degree of oversight and the scrutiny of the people via the media (however flawed and miniscule that process might seem). Indeed, 'equal protection under the law'* would preclude elements in Obama's Executive Order from passing muster in congress. You just can't pass congressional law against minority populations—segregating firearms dealers in only four states to the exclusion of all others. That used to be called discrimination, now it's called social engineering.

It is, however, another example of a classic and well-worn 'divide and conquer' strategy. Because it affects very few businesses (all of whom have already been vilified by the cheerleading press corps),

---

* **Equal Protection Clause**, part of the Fourteenth Amendment to the United States Constitution, provides that *"no state shall ... deny to any person within its jurisdiction the equal protection of the laws"*. The Equal Protection Clause is seen as an attempt to secure the promise of the United States' professed commitment to the proposition that "all men are created equal" and empowers the judiciary to enforce that principle against the states. As originally written it applied only to state governments, but it has since been interpreted to apply to the Federal Government of the United States as well. Yeah, equal, I get it.

very few people really look at the impact. The incessant argument from the socialist side of the congressional aisle is this:

> *"...why would honest citizens object to law enforcement knowing they were purchasing multiple firearms?"*

Of course, it was never about honest citizens supporting the efforts of a law-abiding law enforcement community. This political feign has always been about using an illogical and significantly flawed redirection of the anti-rights gun control argument—from an agenda of socialist control—to guilt-tripping honest people into assembling their own gallows (as Comrade Lenin so aptly put it).

The argument can and should be turned around,

> *"...why would honest politicians object to law-abiding citizens buying a thousand guns?"*

A thousand firearms in the hands of each and every honest, law-abiding, patriotic American can be described—not only as a good start to more secure American neighborhoods—but also as a high return investment in a war of coercion, prosecuted against honest citizens and illegally waged by corrupt governments and their anti-rights lackeys.

But even more importantly, the *legal precedent* of enacting anti-rights regulations through discriminatory gun control—not only contrary to the constitution, the rule of law and completely without congressional oversight, but—enacted purely at the fiat discretion of Executive Order by the President has now been established.

Increasingly, every time Obama wins with a new plank of Socialism, liberty loses.

This was not the first anti-rights firearms related gun control put in place by the Obama administration. Again, done largely under the radar and implemented against only a small segment of the shooting community, early in the Obama administration, once-fired military brass ammunition casings—traditionally offered for sale to shooters on limited or fixed retirement income and who reload their own ammunition economically to save money—the military casings (originally purchased at taxpayer expense) were suddenly removed from public sale in order to be preferentially destroyed by the government. This was really a minor inconvenience for a very few shooters, but it was a toe in the water for larger strategies to use regulations rather than congressional legislation to implement gun control agenda items as part of a larger anti-rights agenda.

Although they eventually relinquished their intent to destroy the brass casings, they were not forced to do so by any legal or congressional direction, and in any event had proven their point— Holder and the ATF had learned regulations could clearly be imposed to enact gun control that need not pass muster in congressional review.

The new ATF multiple long gun reporting rule requires firearms dealers to notify ATF of multiple sales to the same person if any of those sales included semiautomatic rifles—using ammunition of .22 caliber or larger and contained in removable magazines—if those sales occurred within five days of each other.

No self-respecting rocket scientist (or terrorist straw buyer) could fail to miss the six day loop hole in this reporting scheme.

It should not be missed that gun dealers—exercising the due diligence Americans would expect of honest businessmen—were already *voluntarily* trying to alert ATF agents on the SAME DAY to the multiple long gun sales drug cartel straw buyers were initiating under the approval of ATF—and they were flatly ignored in favor of a political agenda that put Brian Terry's blood on the hands of ATF, DOJ and the White House.

Only two days after the Chicago-trained thug in the White House ignored American rights of privacy and buttressed business discrimination with his Executive Order, US House of Representative members of the appropriations committee voted 25-16 to insert a rider into the Justice Department's appropriations spending bill, specifically prohibiting ATF from spending any taxpayer dollars implementing this egregious regulation.* Of course, we all now know ATF follows all the laws, right?

---

* Thank you Rep. Denny Rehberg (R-MT) for stepping up to the plate.

In August 2011, the National Rifle Association and the National Shooting Sports Foundation filed suit to prevent ATF from collecting data on Americans purchasing multiple long guns in the four southwestern states. The lawsuit (detailed in Endnote[22]) was co-authored by Stephen Halbrook who is one of the best second amendment lawyers in the country. Even in the short afternoon I spent with Halbrook at an Arizona shooting range I was immediately impressed not only with the depth of his legal knowledge but his commitment to preserving second amendment rights for Americans. Halbrook's many scholarly books on the subject reflect this multifaceted commitment and make him a formidable champion against the draconian boot of the ATF.

Halbrook is no stranger to Arizona nor to weighty lawsuits concerning an over-reaching federal juggernaut. As the principal attorney who ultimately overturned elements of the Clinton Assault Weapons bill in the Supreme Court based on 10th Amendment sovereignty of the states, Halbrook did so on behalf of Arizona Sheriff Richard Mack.

> *"So here's the U.S. Congress making an unconstitutional gun control law, requiring a county official to enforce it and pay for it, and then threatening to arrest him if he refuses! What a government!"*

> **Sheriff Richard Mack**
> **Graham County, AZ**

Mack was the first sheriff in the US to file suit against the Clinton administration for trying to make local law enforcement bend to an ideological agenda; he probably won't be the last. Basically, in a well-worded document by Halbrook, the NRA/NSSF lawsuit asserts the ATF lacks authority to require federally licensed dealers to submit data on multiple long arm sales.

> *"This is a bait-and-switch scheme by an administration and a bureau frantically trying to distract lawmakers and the general public from the deadly 'Fast and Furious' debacle. This is a serious problem with deadly consequences, yet the Obama administration wants you to believe it can deter $40 billion transnational criminal enterprises by imposing*

paperwork requirements on honest American firearms dealers. This scheme will unjustly burden law-abiding retailers in these four border states. It will not affect drug cartels and it won't prevent violence along our borders. It will only divert scarce law enforcement resources from legitimate criminal investigations and squander them on policing law-abiding retailers."

Chris Cox, NRA-ILA

Regrettably, socialists ideologues have long used a strategy called *'two steps forward-one step back'* based on the well-known definition of conservative politics which includes a model of non-confrontation. The model has bruises all over it from being thrashed by ten foot poles. Socialists push hard for something that is *patently* ridiculous and when the dust settles, conservatives—in order to avoid the ugliness of appearing like they have a spine—push back only a little bit and the net result is the socialists get part of what they want (a part they did not have before) and only the conservatives have given up any ground. And, like Thomas J. Dodd, they are patient; they will bide their time, waiting for the right crisis to leverage a newly worded version of increasingly onerous regulations. While their intent is not only to ignore the scandal and the conditions which precipitated it, they also believe that by foisting this regulation on the four southwestern states, it will as well begin to divide the gun community, and a divided community is a vulnerable community. Once it does go down, how long do you think it will be before the good folks in Montana get the same well-greased end of the stick? To be sure, the Mexican syndicate has absorbed many of the illicit weapons that have crossed the border, but these are tragically small tears shed in a monsoon of terror that threatens to destroy Mexico and with it any shred of credibility for the Obama administration. For President Obama and Eric Holder's Justice Department to leverage ATF resources and taxpayer dollars against federally licensed firearms dealers in a political charade which results in the death of good people like Brian Terry and Jamie Zapata—a program wholly launched in order to advance a gun control plank in a Socialist agenda for America—this is surely the shallow vendetta of irrational fools.

Going Home...

Bring your alibis
Mirrors on the ceiling, the pink champagne on ice
And she said, "We are all just prisoners here of our own device"
And in the master's chambers they gathered for the feast
They stab it with their steely knives but they just can't kill the beast
Last thing I remember I was running for the door
I had to find the passage back to the place I was before"
Relax," said the night man, "We are programmed to receive...
You can check out any time you like...but you can never leave."

The Eagles
Hotel California

ATF agents testifying in the hearings on Operation Fast and Furious, have repeatedly stated that directions from management to "stand down" and not interdict weapons known to be heading for Mexican drug trafficking organizations, was completely against not only standard law enforcement training but their ethics and intuition as dedicated professionals.

> *"...when the straw purchaser makes the purchase at the counter, you don't have to land on them right there at the counter or as soon as he walks out the door, that it is okay to allow it to happen, to allow him to go with that gun under your surveillance to the ultimate purchaser of it or whom he is delivering it to, or if he is taking it to a gang or a stash house or whomever, it is okay to allow it to happen, to go there, to be delivered.* **But you don't get to go home.** *You get the gun, is my understanding, what I have been taught..."*

ATF Special Agent John Dodson*

Col. Jeff Cooper once said, "...is gun? Is dangerous." Firearms instructors, soldiers, sporting arms enthusiasts, hunters,

---

* The Department of Justice's Operation Fast and Furious: Accounts of ATF Agents, JOINT STAFF REPORT, 112th Congress, June 14 2011

155

competitors, and law enforcement professionals nationwide know you don't fool around with firearms. Deadly weapons have the moniker of "deadly" for profound reasons. These reasons are not excused by ideology or political agendas. Once a bullet exits a rifle barrel, the person pulling the trigger is responsible for the damages caused by that act from that moment onward.

One of the great dilemmas of modern crime is not only how responsible the person is who pulls the trigger, but the culpability of the individual who put the firearm in that person's hands. There are both legal and ethical questions to be answered and arguably much depends on circumstances; negligence is high on the list of guilt and is one of the first words that comes to mind when discussing ATF responsibility in the deadly results of Operation Fast and Furious.

There is no good place on the human body for a bullet wound, but some places and bullets types are better than others. Bullets typically fired by one of the AK47 variants are referred to as full-metal jackets (FMJ)—usually gilded copper jackets surrounding a lead-based projectile—they were originally designed in the late 19th century to provide deep wounding penetration at higher velocities than lead bullets alone could provide. Although bullets are frequently sleek in appearance, often resembling miniature rocketry, once they contact almost anything at high velocity, their form and characteristics change dramatically.

Unlike military style projectiles, hunting bullets typically expose the soft lead core at the nose of bullet; this design is intended to force the projectile to "mushroom" into a larger diameter thus causing a more effective wound. Military FMJ's rely on a different ballistic theory called "tumbling". While hunting bullets are effective animal killers, military ammunition designs are traditionally more interested in wounding human adversaries than killing them. The idea is that if you wound the enemy it is likely one or two of their companions will stop fighting in order to assist the wounded soldier. In this way, by wounding one you take three out of the fight.

When a FMJ bullet tumbles without mushrooming as it traverses the human body at high velocity (the typical AK47 pushes a .312" bullet out of the gun muzzle at about 2500 foot seconds and produces about 1800 foot pounds of knock down energy), that sort of energy facilitates the type of ballistic trauma the designers intended. Catching one of these as a surface laceration (e.g. "it's only a scratch") typically causes bleeding and eventual scarring of the tissue, but excepting extraordinary circumstances the wound is easily treated with First Aid and is rarely life-threatening. However as bullets begin to more solidly contact parts of the human body the more damage is done—bones are broken, appendages lost or destroyed and lethal outcomes called terminal ballistics can result, usually from blood loss.

In particular, as bullets rip and tear unpredictably through vital organs such as the heart, lungs or central nervous system (components such as the spinal cord or brain), often do so by launching bone fragments with the bullet doing additional tissue or organ damage. While the bullet may initially cause a very small entry wound equal to the diameter of the bullet, an additional hydraulic effect of suddenly displacing both blood and tissue creates a temporary wound cavity that can be many times the size of the bullet; death under these circumstances may become an unavoidable result regardless of bullet design.

Although the bullet that hit Brian Terry was a FMJ, designed to wound rather than kill, Terry was hit in a particularly vulnerable and dangerous area in the abdominal pelvic area. Prone to bleeding, gunshot wounds to this area are extremely painful; unlike President Reagan who was unaware he had even been shot, Terry would have been immediately aware of the damage as the AK47 bullet tore through his lower body damaging a great many internal organs and rendering him almost instantly immobile. Even though he would have effectively been taken out of the running gunfight in pursuit of the Mexican rip crews, he would have been conscious for some minutes before his blood pressure dropped enough from the internal and external bleeding to induce unconsciousness. The gunfight itself, raging before him on the high desert would have exacerbated the ability of his BORTAC companions to assist him.

As Terry's life blood ebbed he would have preferred to be fighting Mexican rip crews; instead, due to blood loss he was very likely starting to fight what would turn into the long sleep. The remote location, the bullet wound itself and the ongoing gunfight all added precious time to the potentially treatable but ultimately deadly wound that would take the life of Brian Terry.

Time is one thing there is no abundance of in a gunfight.

Terry's family shared with congressional investigators the poignant personal narrative of how he was due for time-off during that particular Christmas holiday; in fact, the day he died—after that awful night bleeding on the desert floor below Hell's Gate— that next day was supposed to be his first scheduled off-duty time with his family. Terry had meticulously picked out family Christmas presents and shipped them ahead of time so they would be sure to arrive in time for the family gathering.

As the family walked through the psychological fog of an unexpected funeral that week, waiting for the casket to arrive, Terry's presents slowly began to show up; each one a caring message from the man they had loved, a loving husband and the voice of a great American they would never hear again.

In the end, Brian Terry did go home; they buried him on Christmas Eve not far from where he grew up.

==<>==

Sometimes I feel like America is living in fish bowl. We have had this wonderfully full life with clean water, ample food and relative (if dwindling) freedom within the boundaries of the fragile glass border that separates us from the rest of the world. Even the poorest of Americans experience life on a scale of affluence unparalleled in human history. But on the outside lives a world not really of our making but as different and scary as our glass bowl is familiar and secure. That world has its emaciated, corrupt, drugged and mystically motivated face pressed tightly against the glass, patiently watching us, waiting with the focus of a house-pet who knows he cannot take food off our plate while we are there—but with perseverance also knows he will eventually get some small part of it. To a man who is both intellectually and physically starved, the amount is never the issue; they only know we have more than they do.

With few exceptions, radicals in the so-called "third world" (the one third of the planet on starvation watch) have over the last few years recruited more than half the world in terms of intellectual deprivation, misguided mysticism and criminal terrorism—and most of the rest of the world population, while not starving, is not exactly eating regularly either. A century ago, the poverty of the Middle East that has repeatedly given voice to devastating and localized revolutions was rarely heard in other parts of the world; no Facebook, Twitter or other social media was in place to amplify those tragedies. Islam, for all its profound and fundamental faults, remained an isolated and stoic form of corrupt mysticism; Socialism might have suffered the same fate if it had not been taught in developing nations and given voice by the ignorance of a poorly educated journalistic cadre.

Today things are decidedly different; the internet elements of social media act as force multipliers both in terms of activists who would otherwise be denied the eyes and ears of protest; in early August 2011 the information darkness in Syria is complete as officials there throw the dead switch on both the Internet and city power systems. As well, the social media amplify our affluence and our burgeoning waistlines to an audience of emaciated radical mystics and ideological despots and other feral dogs intent on taking what we have.

To be sure, we fought for and earned everything we have, but the argument that this is "...my T-bone steak" is of little consequence to those who have been promised either secular or mystical Utopia and have been delivered only slavery in the guise of hope— brutality in the place of change they can believe in.

Someone once said that if you run for office on a platform that you are going to rob Peter in order to pay Paul, you can pretty much count on Paul's vote all day long—I'm guessing this person probably came from Chicago or the current White House, or both. This is at once the foundation of both secular and mystical collectivism; it is a formula for the destruction of the only real liberty and success the world has ever known. Right now, "important people" in the White House, the Department of Justice, Homeland Security, CIA, DEA, and the ATF are complicit in this nexus of national nincompoops.

No less guilty is the mainstream news media that is at once both ignorant and dangerous. Trumpeting parroted talking points from the White House and other federal agencies, few of them have any notion of the implications of coercive government legislation that destroys the Bill of Rights they routinely hide behind. Rarely do they have a glimmer that when our government annually ships billions of dollars of automatic weapons into third-world countries—all the while regulating and in some cases outright outlawing the same weapons possession by law-abiding American citizens—the resiliency of our republic is deeply eroded and the integrity of journalism is fundamentally dead.

> *"Brian Terry is not the last guy, okay... Let's put it out there right now. Nobody wants to talk about that. Brian Terry is not the last guy...Unfortunately, there are hundreds of Brian Terry's probably in Mexico...we ATF armed the [Sinaloa] cartel. It is disgusting."*
>
> **Carlos Canino Testimony**
> **ATF Attaché in Mexico**

Inevitably, this story as I publish it is a snapshot. My Father used to say, "...son, you don't know what you don't know." But it is clear that with more than a thousand unrecovered ATF firearms from Operation Fast and Furious and millions more high power military grade weapons on the black market in Mexico, the perceived death toll at this point is only the beginning. Continuing rumors of an accelerated arms buildup by cartels planning to overthrow the government of Mexico speaks to both the power and arrogance of drug trafficking organizations and the confidence they have in the training they received from their ongoing partnership with Islamic terrorist organizations such as Hezbollah and Hamas whose well-documented agenda for the overthrow of the US is sacrosanct.

There ought to be a better ending to all this; Brian Terry should have lived to play with his grandchildren. Our border and our children should be secure from the poison of drugs and the terror of Islamic radicalism (and our children should be taught the connections between the two). Our government should actually be the representative of a free people and the servant of a strong republic—not a coercive socialistic cabal of power-hungry fools redistributing the wealth of a victimized nation while advocating with a wink and a nod the ultimate destruction of our constitution, the republic and our individual rights.

Instead of the cultural and national achievement of rationality, productivity and pride envisioned by our ancestors as the beacon of value-added virtue in the world, our government, led by a dangerous and intellectually corrupt White House, is making decisions that are both ethically and legally beyond the pale, morally misguided and based on an historically failed ideology that contributes to this "...perfect storm of idiocy."*

The scary part is...I think the storm is only just now gathering and we're sitting here watching it through this very fragile pane of glass. Its full force has yet to be felt. When it finally arrives in the rush of irrational insanity that is inevitable with the historical breakdown of government integrity and the fracturing of the fragile illusion of "hope and change," you can only hope that you are not the only person in your neighborhood that doesn't have an AK47.

There is time to change.

Unlike President Obama and Eric Holder, I believe in American exceptionalism. I believe reasoned argument, patriotism as a purpose-driven intellectual light, the self-esteem of American citizens as well as superior firepower is far stronger than Islamic mystical terrorism or socialist strong-arming by the Democratic Party. I believe in foundations of American liberty that suggests individual freedoms and private property, flourishing under the protection of the rule of law and unhampered by coercive

---

* Carlos Canino, Acting ATF Attaché in Mexico

governments will create the innovations necessary to produce wealth, secure our children's future and eliminate human misery.

Scandal may be a hallmark of modern governance and misinformation the calling card of a failed mainstream media; but this scandal was brought to our attention by journalists outside the mainstream, journalists who care about an informed electorate, who care enough to put their own lives and reputations on the line for an America they believe is worthy. Our ancestors made the same decision to stand up to coercive and corrupt government in 1775. Neither is this the first time we have been required to stand up to Islamic terrorism. Indeed, the first time America's military defense of freedom and autonomy was put to the test, we were required to put down no less than two wars[23] with Islamic criminals during the 1801-1805 period (these were the North African Berber Muslim states known collectively as the Barbary States and included what is now known as Morocco, Algeria, Tunisia, and Libya). Islam in general and Libya in particular seems not to have gotten the memo regarding American freedoms and sovereign boundaries. But we have explained this to them before and I believe we are up to doing it again.

Our border remains problematic but the issues are not insurmountable—as long as we recognize the hard truths. We must put behind us our collective ignorance of a ventilated border that we have incorrectly perceived and fostered by a corrupt media as an issue of mere economic impact to our increasing tax burden and the threat of illegal drugs; both are virulent symptoms of a much larger disease of ideology. We must realize that if international criminal elements of radical mysticism can move thousands of terrorists across a border that our Federal government refuses to control, if narco-terrorists can forge papers allowing them to purchase whole aircraft shipments of weapons directly from our State Department and fly those weapons with impunity out of our own airports, what devices of mass destruction might these criminal partnerships also be able to fly into America? Operation Fast and Furious has finally connected all these issues of gun control, drug trafficking and Islamic terrorism for the American public in a way that will be difficult to ignore.

Clear-thinking Americans must begin to view Socialism as well as radical Islamic terrorism as a prosecutable crime and recognize those who conspire to advance it are in fact criminals to be adjudicated in courts of Federal law. We must embrace the notion our Founding Fathers defined high crimes because they are real, they are being perpetrated against America and they must be stopped. As of November 2008 we lost America to the Socialists and the Islamic radical apologists and we lost it because we were unwilling to hit below the belt when we had the chance.

Brian Terry and Jamie Zapata would tell you there is no compromise in combat and this is combat, make no mistake about it; as in the defense of our homes, our families and our lives, those who would promote quiet, passive resistance are either innocents who have never been in a real fight, are ignoring the realities of combat, or are part of the conspiracy to destroy us.

Our very existence as a free nation is under attack from outside our borders; the onslaught from within is even more scurrilous and insidious as it comes from officials in the highest levels of government—officials who have forfeited our trust and their honor in exchange for a nightmare of a socialist utopia and the enslaving fraud and sexual predation of an Islamic theocracy that has not and never will exist as long as free people are willing to stand up for liberty.

Mark Twain once said that "...twenty years from now you will be more disappointed by the things you didn't do than by the ones you did do."

This is not the time to be sitting out reality. You cannot negotiate with the unwavering intent of evil. Members of our present Federal government, unelected operatives in Czar-controlled agencies and their complicit lapdogs in the mainstream media have dropped the ball of liberty because as treasonous co-conspirators and haters of American exceptionalism they never had a right to carry it.

Our task is to pick it up and run with it. It's what Brian Terry and Jamie Zapata would have wanted us to do.

"I want whoever decided this program and knew about it to be held responsible. I want justice for my son. He served his country. He was a Marine. He was a police officer. He was a border patrol agent. My son was a true American hero..."

Josephine Terry

Appendix A: Congressional Oversight Report, June 2011

The Department of Justice's Operation Fast and Furious: Accounts of ATF Agents

JOINT STAFF REPORT Prepared for:
Rep. Darrell E. Issa, Chairman
United States House of Representatives
Committee on Oversight and Government Reform &

Senator Charles E. Grassley, Ranking Member
United States Senate
Committee on the Judiciary
112th Congress, June 14 2011

TABLE OF CONTENTS

B. Tragic, Yet Foreseeable Results

C. Catastrophe Becomes Reality

Witnessing Gunwalking: "We Did Not Stop Them."

A. Watching Guns Walk

B. Ordered to Stand Down

C. "We Were Walking Guns. It was Our Decision."

Collateral Damage: A Fast and Furious Inevitability

A. Increasing Volume Equals Increasing Success

B. "You Need to Scramble Some Eggs"

C. An Inevitable and Horrible Outcome

D. The Pucker Factor

The Tragic Death of U.S. Border Patrol Agent Brian Terry

The Beginning of DOJ's Denials: "Hell, No!"

DOJ's Continued Denials: "That is False."

A. "Of Course Not"

B. More Denials

Conclusion

==<>==

EXECUTIVE SUMMARY:

In the fall of 2009, the Department of Justice (DOJ) developed a risky new strategy to combat gun trafficking along the Southwest Border. The new strategy directed federal law enforcement to shift its focus away from seizing firearms from criminals as soon as possible—and to focus instead on identifying members of trafficking networks. The Bureau of Alcohol, Tobacco, Firearms and Explosives (ATF) implemented that strategy using a reckless investigative technique that street agents call "gunwalking." ATF's Phoenix Field Division began allowing suspects to walk away with illegally purchased guns. The purpose was to wait and watch, in the hope that law enforcement could identify other members of a trafficking network and build a large, complex conspiracy case.

This shift in strategy was known and authorized at the highest levels of the Justice Department. Through both the U.S. Attorney's Office in Arizona and "Main Justice," headquarters in Washington, D.C., the Department closely monitored and supervised the activities of the ATF. The Phoenix Field Division established a Gun Trafficking group, called Group VII, to focus on firearms trafficking. Group VII initially began using the new gunwalking tactics in one of its investigations to further the Department's strategy. The case was soon renamed "Operation Fast and Furious," and expanded dramatically. It received approval for Organized Crime Drug Enforcement Task Force (OCDETF) funding on January 26, 2010. ATF led a strike force comprised of agents from ATF, Drug Enforcement Administration (DEA), Federal Bureau of Investigation (FBI), Immigration and Customs Enforcement (ICE), and the Internal Revenue Service (IRS). The operation's goal was to establish a nexus between straw purchasers of assault-style weapons in the United States and Mexican drug-trafficking organizations (DTOs) operating on both sides of the United States-Mexico border. Straw purchasers are individuals who are legally entitled to purchase firearms for themselves, but who unlawfully purchase weapons with the intent to transfer them into the hands of DTOs or other criminals.

Operation Fast and Furious was a response to increasing violence fostered by the DTOs in Mexico and their increasing need to purchase ever-growing numbers of more powerful weapons in the U.S. An integral component of Fast and Furious was to work with gun shop merchants, or "Federal Firearms Licensees" (FFLs) to track known straw purchasers through the unique serial number of each firearm sold. ATF agents entered the serial numbers of the weapons purchased into the agency's Suspect Gun Database. These weapons bought by the straw purchasers included AK-47 variants, Barrett .50 caliber sniper rifles, .38 caliber revolvers, and the FN Five-seveN.

During Fast and Furious, ATF frequently monitored actual transactions between the FFLs and straw purchasers. After the purchases, ATF sometimes conducted surveillance of these weapons with assistance from local police departments. Such surveillance included following the vehicles of the straw purchasers. Frequently, the straw purchasers transferred the weapons they bought to stash houses. In other instances, they transferred the weapons to third parties.

The volume, frequency, and circumstances of these transactions clearly established reasonable suspicion to stop and question the buyers. Agents are trained to use such interactions to develop probable cause to arrest the suspect or otherwise interdict the weapons and deter future illegal purchases. Operation Fast and Furious sought instead to *allow* the flow of guns from straw purchasers to the third parties. Instead of trying to interdict the weapons, ATF purposely avoided contact with known straw purchasers or curtailed surveillance, allowing guns to fall into the hands of criminals and bandits on both sides of the border.

Though many line agents objected vociferously, ATF and DOJ leadership continued to prevent them from making every effort to interdict illegally purchased firearms. Instead, leadership's focus was on trying to identify additional conspirators, as directed by the Department's strategy for combating Mexican Drug Cartels. ATF and DOJ leadership were interested in seeing where these guns would ultimately end up. They hoped to establish a connection between the local straw buyers in Arizona and the Mexico-based DTOs. By entering serial numbers from suspicious transactions into the Suspect Gun Database, ATF would be quickly notified as each one was later recovered at crime scenes and traced, either in the United States or in Mexico.

The Department's leadership allowed the ATF to implement this flawed strategy, fully aware of what was taking place on the ground. The U.S. Attorney's Office for the District of Arizona encouraged and supported every single facet of Fast and Furious. Main Justice was involved in providing support and approving various aspects of the Operation, including wiretap applications that would necessarily include painstakingly detailed descriptions of what ATF knew about the straw buyers it was monitoring.

This hapless plan allowed the guns in question to disappear out of the agency's view. As a result, this chain of events inevitably placed the guns in the hands of violent criminals. ATF would only see these guns again after they turned up at a crime scene. Tragically, many of these recoveries involved loss of life. While leadership at ATF and DOJ no doubt regard these deaths as tragic, the deaths were a clearly foreseeable result of the strategy. Both line agents and gun dealers who cooperated with the ATF repeatedly expressed concerns about that risk, but ATF supervisors did not heed those warnings. Instead, they told agents to follow orders because this was sanctioned from above. They told gun dealers not to worry because they would make sure the guns didn't fall into the wrong hands.

Unfortunately, ATF never achieved the laudable goal of dismantling a drug cartel. In fact, ATF never even got close. After months and months of investigative work, Fast and Furious resulted only in indictments of 20 straw purchasers. Those indictments came only after the death of U.S. Border Patrol Agent Brian Terry. The indictments, filed January 19, 2011, focus mainly on what is known as "lying and buying." Lying and buying involves a straw purchaser falsely filling out ATF Form 4473, which is to be completed truthfully in order to legally acquire a firearm. Even worse, ATF knew most of the indicted straw purchasers to be straw purchasers *before Fast and Furious even began.*

In response to criticism, ATF and DOJ leadership denied allegations that gunwalking occurred in Fast and Furious by adopting an overly narrow definition of the term. They argue that gunwalking is limited to cases in which ATF itself supplied the guns directly. As field agents understood the term, however, gunwalking includes situations in which ATF had contemporaneous knowledge of illegal gun purchases and purposely decided not to attempt any interdiction. The agents also described situations in which ATF facilitated or approved transactions to known straw buyers. Both situations are even more disturbing in light of the ATF's certain knowledge that weapons previously purchased by the same straw buyers had been trafficked into Mexico and may have reached the DTOs. When the full parameters of this program became clear to the agents assigned to Group VII, a rift formed among Group VII's agents in Phoenix. Several agents blew the whistle on this reckless operation only to face punishment and retaliation from ATF leadership. Sadly, only the tragic murder of Border Patrol Agent Brian Terry provided the necessary impetus for DOJ and ATF leadership to finally indict the straw buyers whose regular purchases they had monitored for 14 months. Even then, it was not until after whistleblowers later reported the issue to Congress that the Justice Department finally issued a policy directive that prohibited gunwalking. This report is the first in a series regarding Operation Fast and Furious. Possible future reports and hearings will likely focus on the actions of the United States Attorney's Office for the District of Arizona, the decisions faced by gun shop owners (FFLs) as a result of ATF's actions, and the remarkably ill-fated decisions made by Justice Department officials in Washington, especially within the Criminal Division and the Office of the Deputy Attorney General. This first installment focuses on ATF's misguided approach of letting guns walk. The report describes the agents' outrage about the use of gunwalking as an investigative technique and the continued denials and stonewalling by DOJ and ATF leadership. It provides some answers as to what went wrong with Operation Fast and Furious. Further questions for key ATF and DOJ decision makers remain unanswered. For example, what leadership failures within the Department of Justice allowed this program to thrive? Who will be held accountable and when?

TABLE OF NAMES:

John Dodson

Special Agent, ATF Phoenix Field Division

Agent Dodson is the original whistleblower who exposed Operation Fast and Furious. A seven year veteran of ATF, Dodson also worked in the sheriff's offices in Loudoun County and other Virginia municipalities for 12 years. Agent Dodson was removed from Phoenix Group VII in the summer of 2010 for complaining to ATF supervisors about the dangerous tactics used in Operation Fast and Furious.

Brian Terry

U.S. Border Patrol Agent

Brian Terry was an agent with the U.S. Border Patrol's Search, Trauma, and Rescue team, known as BORSTAR. He served in the military and was a Border Patrol agent for three years. On December 14, 2010, during a routine patrol, Terry was confronted by armed bandits. He was shot once and killed. Two weapons found at the scene traced back to Operation Fast and Furious.

Jaime Avila

Straw Purchaser

Jaime Avila was the straw purchaser who bought the two AK-47 variant weapons that were found at the murder scene of Brian Terry. Avila bought the weapons on January 16, 2010. ATF, however, began conducting surveillance of Avila as early as November 25, 2009. On January 19, 2011, Avila was indicted on three counts of "lying and buying" for weapons purchased in January, April, and June 2010.

David Voth

Phoenix Group VII Supervisor

Agent Voth was the former supervisor of the Phoenix Group VII, which conducted Operation Fast and Furious. As Group VII Supervisor, Voth controlled many operational aspects of Fast and Furious. Voth is no longer in Phoenix.

Pete Forcelli

Group Supervisor, ATF Phoenix Field Division

Since 2007, Agent Forcelli has been the Group Supervisor for Phoenix Group I. Before Phoenix Group VII was formed in October 2009, Group I was the primary southwest border firearms group. Before joining ATF in 2001, Agent Forcelli worked for twelve years in the New York City Police Department as a police officer and detective.

Olindo Casa

Special Agent, ATF Phoenix Field Division

Agent Casa served in Phoenix Group VII during Operation Fast and Furious. Agent Casa is an 18-year veteran of ATF, having worked in Chicago, California, and Florida. In Chicago, Agent Casa worked on numerous firearms trafficking cases, including a joint international case. Agent Casa had never seen a gun walk until he arrived at Group VII in Phoenix and participated in Operation Fast and Furious.

William Newell

Special Agent in Charge, ATF Phoenix Field Division

Agent Newell was the former head of the ATF Phoenix Field Division during Operation Fast and Furious. Newell is no longer in Phoenix.

Emory Hurley

Assistant U.S. Attorney, District of Arizona

Emory Hurley is the lead prosecutor for Operation Fast and Furious. Hurley advised the ATF Phoenix Field Division on the Operation, including instructing agents when they were and were not able to interdict weapons.

Larry Alt

Special Agent, ATF Phoenix Field Division

Agent Alt served in Phoenix Group VII during Operation Fast and Furious. An 11-year veteran of ATF, Agent Alt worked as a police officer for five years before joining ATF. Agent Alt is also a lawyer, having served as deputy county attorney in Maricopa County, a county of nearly 4 million people that encompasses the Phoenix metro area.

FINDINGS:

- DOJ and ATF inappropriately and recklessly relied on a 20-year old ATF Order to allow guns to walk. DOJ and ATF knew from an early date that guns were being trafficked to the DTOs.

- ATF agents are trained to "follow the gun" and interdict weapons whenever possible. Operation Fast and Furious required agents to abandon this training.

- DOJ relies on a narrow, untenable definition of gunwalking to claim that guns were never walked during Operation Fast and Furious. Agents disagree with this definition, acknowledging that hundreds or possibly thousands of guns were in fact walked. DOJ's misplaced reliance on this definition does not change the fact that it knew that ATF could have interdicted thousands of guns that were being trafficked to Mexico, yet chose to do nothing.

- ATF agents complained about the strategy of allowing guns to walk in Operation Fast and Furious. Leadership ignored their concerns. Instead, supervisors told the agents to "get with the program" because senior ATF officials had sanctioned the operation.

- Agents knew that given the large numbers of weapons being trafficked to Mexico, tragic results were a near certainty.

- Agents expected to interdict weapons, yet were told to stand down and "just surveil." Agents therefore did not act. They watched straw purchasers buy hundreds of weapons illegally and transfer those weapons to unknown third parties and stash houses.

- Operation Fast and Furious contributed to the increasing violence and deaths in Mexico. This result was regarded with giddy optimism by ATF supervisors hoping that guns recovered at crime scenes in Mexico would provide the nexus to straw purchasers in Phoenix.

- Every time a law enforcement official in Arizona was assaulted or shot by a firearm, ATF agents in Group VII had great anxiety that guns used to perpetrate the crimes may trace back to Operation Fast and Furious.!

- Jaime Avila was entered as a suspect in the investigation by ATF on November 25, 2009, after purchasing weapons alongside Uriel Patino, who had been identified as a suspect in October 2009. Over the next month and a half, Avila purchased 13 more weapons, each recorded by the ATF in its database within days of the purchase. Then on January 16, 2010, Avila purchased three AK-47 style rifles, two of which ended up being found at the murder scene of U.S. Border Patrol Agent Brian Terry. The death of Border Agent Brian Terry was likely a preventable tragedy. !

- Phoenix ATF Special Agent in Charge (SAC) William Newell's statement that the indictments represent the take-down of a firearms trafficking ring from top to bottom, and his statement that ATF never allowed guns to walk are incredible, false, and a source of much frustration to the agents.

- Despite mounting evidence to the contrary, DOJ continues to deny that Operation Fast and Furious was ill-conceived and had deadly consequences.

THE ATF POLICY ON INTERDICTION: "YOU DON'T GET TO GO HOME"

ATF's long-standing policy has been not to knowingly allow guns to "walk" into the hands of criminals. Yet DOJ and ATF used a 1989 ATF order to help justify allowing straw purchasers allegedly connected to Mexican drug cartels to illegally buy more than 1,800 weapons during Operation Fast and Furious. While this Order permits agents—at their discretion—to allow the illegal transfer of firearms to further an investigation, it does not go so far as to permit them to pull surveillance completely and allow the guns to walk.

A. The Justification for Operation Fast and Furious

FINDING: DOJ and ATF inappropriately and recklessly relied on a 20-year old ATF Order to allow guns to walk. DOJ and ATF knew from an early date that guns were being trafficked to the DTOs.

Released on February 8, 1989, ATF Order 3310.4(b) explains ATF's Firearms Enforcement Program. The Department of Justice and ATF relied on this Order to defend Operation Fast and Furious. ATF leadership in Phoenix believed a specific clause within the Order, section 148(a)(2), justified Operation Fast and Furious and its policy to allow guns to walk. The clause reads as follows:

148. "WEAPONS TRANSFERS"

a. Considerations. During the course of illegal firearms trafficking investigations, special agents may become aware of, observe, or encounter situations where an individual(s) will take delivery of firearms, or transfer firearm(s) to others. In these instances, the special agent may exercise the following options:

* * *

(2) In other cases, *immediate intervention* may not be needed or desirable, and the special agent may choose to allow the transfer of firearms to take place in order to further an investigation and allow for the identification of additional coconspirators who would have continued to operate and illegally traffic firearms in the future, potentially producing more armed crime.

ATF's reliance on this section of the Order is misguided. The phrase *"immediate intervention* may not be needed or desirable" does not justify a complete lack of intervention with regard to thousands of weapons illegally purchased by straw buyers allegedly linked to drug cartels. ATF cited this Order in an early briefing paper that contained the following paragraph:

> Currently our strategy is to **allow the transfer of firearms to continue to take place**, albeit at a much slower pace, in order to further the investigation and allow for the identification of co-conspirators who would continue to operate and **illegally traffic firearms to Mexican DTOs**

*which are perpetrating armed violence along the Southwest Border. This is all in compliance with ATF 3310.4(b) 148(a)(2). It should be noted that since early December efforts to "slow down" the pace of these firearms purchases have succeeded and will continue **but not to the detriment of the larger goal of the investigation.** It should also be noted that the pace of firearms procurement by this straw purchasing group from late September to early December, 2009 defied the "normal" pace of procurement by other firearms trafficking groups investigated by this and other field divisions. This "blitz" was extremely out of the ordinary and created a situation where measures had to be enacted in order to slow this pace down in order to perfect a criminal case.*

This statement leaves little doubt that ATF felt Operation Fast and Furious was compliant with existing ATF policy. Further, it shows that DOJ and ATF knew from an early date that the firearms were being illegally trafficked to Mexican drug cartels. Although senior ATF management cited the Order as justification for Fast and Furious, it did not pass muster with street agents. They believed that it did not permit a total lack of intervention. Agents believed they must interdict at some point if they have knowledge of an illegal firearms transfer. Yet senior management used the Order to justify the notion that ATF would completely drop surveillance of the weapons and then wait until receiving trace requests when the weapons were eventually recovered at crime scenes. Such traces would supposedly create a "nexus" between the drug cartels and the straw purchasers. The agents, however, did not agree with any interpretation of the order that would be consistent with that kind of strategy.

As Special Agent John Dodson testified:

Q. And just so we are clear on what your understanding of the order was, and we can all obtain it and read it and have our own understanding of it, but what were you taught about what that means?

A. That that implies when the straw purchaser makes the purchase at the counter, you don't have to land on them *right there at the counter or as soon as he walks out the door, that it is okay to allow it to happen, to allow him to go with that gun under your surveillance to the ultimate purchaser of it or whom he is delivering it to, or if he is taking it to a gang or a stash house or whomever, it is okay to allow it to happen, to go there, to be delivered. **But you don't get to go home.** You get the gun, is my understanding, what I have been taught and how in every other ATF office not only that I have been in but that I have gone like TDY to work at that that policy is implemented.*

Q. So, in other words, your understanding is that there is a temporal or time limitation on how long it can be allowed to continue on its course without you intervening.

A. I think it is not so much time as it is availability of eyes on. Like if I get an agent that's on the house and we know that gun is on the house, that's still okay . . . even if it is overnight, on to the next night, the gun and bad guy are still there. We are just waiting on the guy he is supposed to deliver it to to come by and pick it up.

Q. Well, the beginning of it said in other cases immediate intervention may not be needed or desirable.

A. Correct.

Q. So are you saying that, in other words, "intervention," that doesn't mean, "no intervention ever?"

A. Correct.

*Q. Just the intervention doesn't have to happen right now, **but intervention does need to occur**, that's your understanding?*

A. Yes, sir, that it is not as soon as the FFL hands the straw purchaser the gun, that's it, you can't let him leave the store with it.

Q. It is not a license to forego intervention at all?

A. Correct.

During Operation Fast and Furious, however, ATF agents *did* go home. They did *not* get the guns. ATF simply broke off surveillance of the weapons. Yet, as Agent Dodson explains it, the Order used to justify that practice actually anticipates interdiction at some point. It does not authorize what occurred under Fast and Furious:

More so, that line that says the agent has the discretion to allow the purchaser not – or the purchase to proceed or not, what it is trying to tell you is you don't have to effect the arrest or the interdiction right there in the store. It is telling you that you can allow it to happen until that guy leaves the store and meets with the person that he bought the gun for, then you can effect the arrest. **It is not telling you that you can watch this guy purchase thousands of firearms over 18 months and not do any follow-up on it.**

B. Trained to Interdict

FINDING: ATF agents are trained to "follow the gun" and interdict weapons whenever possible. Operation Fast and Furious required agents to abandon this training.

Interdiction v. Prosecution: Prior to their assignment with Operation Fast and Furious, ATF agents were trained to interdict guns and prevent criminals from obtaining them. Interdiction can be accomplished in many ways. While prosecutors focus on gathering proof "beyond a reasonable doubt" to be presented at trial, agents begin with a standard of "reasonable suspicion." If an agent can articulate a reasonable basis to suspect an illegal purchase, then the agent can take proactive steps to investigate, potentially develop probable cause to arrest, or prevent the illegal transfer of firearms some other way. From the agents' point of view, a prosecution isn't necessary in order to achieve the goal of preventing criminals from obtaining firearms. An arrest may not even be necessary. In fact, another portion of the ATF Order describes some of these other interdiction strategies:

b. Alternative Intervention Methods. In the event it is determined by the special agent that a weapons transfer should not take place, the special agent may consider *alternative methods of intervention* other than arrest and/or search warrants *that will prevent the culmination of the weapons transfer but allow the investigation to continue undetected*. These alternative methods are considered to be a course of action that must be approved by the RAC/GS or SAC as previously noted. These alternative interventions may include, but are not limited to:

> (1) A traffic stop (supported by probable cause to search or supported by a traffic violation allowing for plain view observations) by a State or local marked law enforcement vehicle that would culminate in the discovery and retention of the firearms. ***This would prevent the weapons transfer from fully occurring and may in turn produce new investigative leads.*** Should the occupants of the vehicle be new/unknown participants in the organization under investigation, they may be fully identified which in turn will yield additional information for follow-up investigation. Should the occupants of the vehicle be known participants in the investigation, requesting telephone tolls for these individuals (or if a Penn Register/T-III interception order is in use) for the period shortly after the traffic stop may show calls and yield identifying information relating to the intended receivers of the firearms.

Three of the special agents assigned to this operation had more than 50 years of law enforcement experience. Throughout their careers, ATF always taught them to get the guns away from criminals. When they observed signs of suspicious transactions, agents looked for ways to prevent weapons from falling into the wrong hands. Agent Dodson testified:

> *I can tell you this. We knew without a doubt at my old field division when someone had a case that said, hey, this guy is . . . supposed to be a straw and he is going to make this deal today, if he makes the deal, we were talking to them. I mean if we all left the office on an op for a suspected straw purchaser, that means we had, we suspected him of being a straw purchaser. Well, when he purchases, that adds to the suspicion. So he was getting talked to, either "knock and talk" or, depending on what happened or what he purchased might alter things and we might get to a higher level . . . that*

*reasonable suspicion or probable cause. **But we were\ doing something. If nothing else we were putting him on notice that we were watching him, all right, and that every time he went to the gun store, we were going to be there with him, or the minute one of those guns turned up in a crime somewhere, we were coming back to talk to him**, or even better, or maybe not better, but some point down the road we might be back to knock on your door and ask you, still got those guns or are you selling without a license, you better have a receipt or something to go with them to prove your point.*

*The bottom line, sir, whenever a walk situation with a gun occurred . . . **nobody went home until we found it, until we got it back.** There were no ifs, ands or buts, you didn't ask. Nobody said, "I got to make a soccer game," [or] "I have got to pick my dog up," nothing. Okay. If somebody said, "where is the gun," you knew it was an all-nighter until we found it.*

Fast and Furious employed the exact opposite practices. ATF agents rarely talked with straw purchasers, or conducted a "knock and talk." When guns recovered at crime scenes linked back to straw purchasers, ATF agents did not approach these straw purchasers. Agents did not ask them why did they did not still possess guns they had recently sworn on a federal form were for their personal use. Instead, ATF agents stood by and watched for months as the straw purchasers bought hundreds upon hundreds of additional AK-47 variants and Barrett .50 caliber sniper rifles. ATF failed to conduct proper surveillance of the walked guns. ATF leadership in Phoenix cannot account for the location of the walked guns until they turn up at a crime scene, which may be *after* they have been used to kill or maim innocent victims on both sides of the border. Untold numbers of these weapons likely reached the DTOs in Mexico.

To the extent that these walked weapons reached the DTOs, it is a direct result of the policy decision to no longer focus on interdicting weapons as soon as possible. From the agents' perspective, that decision was the polar opposite of their understanding of the previous policy. For example, Special Agent Olindo Casa testified:

> Q. And if you became aware that somebody purchased guns with the intent of transferring it to a third person, would it be your practice and experience to interdict those weapons right away?
>
> A. Yes, yes.
>
> Q. Is that your understanding of ATF policy?
>
> A. Yes.

However, under Fast and Furious in Phoenix, agents did not follow these methods. As Special Agent Lawrence Alt testified:

> Q. [I]s it fair to say that if you saw a suspect, a suspicious person . . . leaving an FFL with . . . an armful of boxes that appeared to be AK-47s or like weapons, that in your experience as an agent, I mean, would you be able to interdict that?
>
> A. That would be my normal course of action. I understand there is other strategies wherein you are trying to identify where those firearms are going to. So you might not interdict them until they are delivered, or if you have investigative measures in place to follow them, you might let them go to . . . what you believe is their ultimate destination.
>
> **But prior to my coming to Phoenix, Arizona, I had never witnessed a firearm not – I never witnessed a situation where there wasn't at least an attempt to interdict or take the firearm at some point.**
>
> Q. [Y]ou might allow the suspicious person to leave the FFL with a car full of weapons, you might make a decision not to do a traffic stop right then, but is it fair to say that you would want to follow that suspect?
>
> A. I have had experiences or been aware and involved either directly or indirectly in experiences where we knew there was illegal firearms purchases. Follow the gun was also the motto, follow the gun, stay with the gun. I am aware of a couple of instances in my past where people would sit on

houses all night long, days on end, waiting for the guns to go so that they could then follow it, satisfy the requirements of the investigation. . . . But I have never been involved in a situation where you would simply not do anything.

This changed when the Agent Alt arrived in Phoenix.

Agent Casa recounted a similar situation. He had also never heard of, nor seen, guns being allowed to walk until he got to Phoenix:

*. . . . But from the time I started as an ATF special agent . . . up until the time I got to Phoenix, that was my understanding, that **we do not let guns walk, absolutely, positively not**. And if we – if ever a case [where] we would do that, there better be a really good explanation why we did not grab that gun when we could.*
Q. But that changed when you came to Phoenix, I mean the practice at least changed, correct?
A. Yes.
Q. So that occurred while you were here?
A. Yes.

ATF policy is clear and unambiguous. As Agent Casa further explained:

Q. So could you – are you saying if you determine that somebody has acquired a firearm unlawfully –
A. Correct.
Q. – ATF's policies and procedures would be to interdict that weapon?
A. Yes. Yes.

Agent Dodson said it succinctly:

So my training and experience with ATF as well as with law enforcement prior to then essentially is you interdicted a gun whenever you could. Guns didn't go.

A third agent, Special Agent Peter Forcelli, spoke of the importance of interdicting these weapons:

Q. Did you have any kind of policy regarding gun trafficking, in other words . . . was your policy to interdict guns whenever possible?
A. Absolutely.

Every single agent on every single prior assignment adhered to a policy to interdict weapons as soon as possible, until Fast and Furious. As one agent put it, "It's like they grabbed the ATF rulebook and threw it out the window."

GUNWALKING DEFINED: ITS SEMANTICS

FINDING: DOJ relies on a narrow, untenable definition of gunwalking to claim that guns were never walked during Operation Fast and Furious. Agents disagree with this definition, acknowledging that hundreds or possibly thousands of guns were in fact walked. DOJ's misplaced reliance on this definition does not change the fact that it knew that ATF could have interdicted thousands of guns that were being trafficked to Mexico, yet chose to do nothing.

The Department of Justice has repeatedly and steadfastly denied that any guns were walked under Operation Fast and Furious. According to the narrowest possible interpretation, a gun is walked only when an ATF agent physically places an AK-47 into the hands of a straw purchaser and then lets that straw purchaser walk out of sight. Conversely, every single ATF field agent interviewed stated that guns are walked when ATF has the opportunity to interdict illegally purchased weapons, yet chooses not to even try.

DOJ officials must have known that straw purchasers were buying guns illegally and transferring them to third parties for trafficking across the border. This was clear, or at least should have been clear, from the following factors:

> (1) the sheer volume and frequency of the purchases,
>
> (2) ATF's and DOJ's communications with the cooperating gun dealers,
>
> (3) the contemporaneous notice dealers provided about hundreds of transactions with straw purchasers, and
>
> (4) notifications through the Suspect Gun Database that the firearms were being recovered in crime scenes in Mexico shortly after being purchased.

Yet, ATF failed to use this information to interdict future purchases and prevent guns from crossing the border.

Instead, ATF followed DOJ's new policy, and focused on simply trying to identify more and more members of the trafficking ring. It was a conscious decision to systematically avoid interdicting guns that normally should have been interdicted, according to the agents. Thus, the agents considered it to be gunwalking. Agent Dodson testified:

> My understanding of letting something walk or defining walk is, when it was in or could have been in and quite possibly should have been in law enforcement custody, a decision is made, a conscious decision is made to not take it into custody or to release it. Then it is walked. . . . [Y]ou are talking about walking dope, walking money, walking anything else. To walk a firearm was never taught. It was what we consider a no-brainer.

As the agent explained, ATF did not teach agents to walk firearms as such a practice was beyond comprehension. Agent Casa provided a similar understanding of gunwalking:

> Now, when I talk about walking guns, my understanding is that is when a person we suspect or have probable cause that a person illegally came across guns, whatever way they came across it, and we have knowledge of it and we are there and we do not interdict those guns, we do not take those guns, we do not do any warrantless seizure based on probable cause of those guns. That would be my understanding of letting guns walk.

Agent Forcelli defined gun walking as follows:

> . . . . If you can interdict it and you don't, in my opinion you have walked it. There are times . . . we do a car stop, the person maybe bought two guns, they would have a story that was reasonable. They had a pay stub . . . that indicated they had a salary or they had a – they can articulate why they bought it. A couple times it happened. Like I said, maybe twice they went on their way. Okay.

But again . . . walking guns, in my opinion, is if you can stop it and you don't. There are some whose definition is if ATF has the gun and gives it, then we are walking it.

Agent Alt also acknowledged two definitions of gunwalking:

So I call that the two versions of walking a gun. There is, it is a semantics issue. Some people will say that only the purest definition is walking a gun. Some people won't acknowledge that the other version is walking a gun. And I say potato, you say potato. I believe it is, my assessment, they are the same. That's it.

Regardless of which definition one subscribes to, the two situations both warrant action. Still, DOJ and some senior ATF officials maintain that federal agents did not sanction or knowingly allow the transfer of firearms to straw purchasers. Yet, the evidence demonstrates that DOJ and ATF *were well aware* of what was happening.

Phoenix Field Division leadership did not tolerate debate or dissent from agents over terminology or strategy. Agent Dodson testified:

Q. I believe you mentioned that there was some dispute about exactly what gun walking meant.

* * *

And can you describe what the difference was, difference of opinion was?

A. Well, yes, sir. . . . Again, as I said earlier, my understanding of gun walking . . . has been something was and/or should have been, could have been in law enforcement custody. When we should have done something and it wasn't, you have let it walk. There has to be an active decision . . . a choice is made to allow it to walk. It is not like something got away from you or you lost it. If a suspect beats you in a foot chase and he gets away, you didn't let him walk, you just lost the chase. So that's what walking is.

When [the Assistant Special Agent in Charge] came down to our office . . . we were told you don't know what walking is, we are not walking guns. And that's pretty much the extent of the debate, because in Phoenix there is very little debating one of the ASACs or the [Special Assistant in Charge]. So it was . . . a declaration, you don't know what walking guns is, we are not walking guns, this is all okay.

Regardless of whether it meets a technical definition of gunwalking, the strategy was clearly ill-conceived. Instead of candidly acknowledging the facts and working to correct the problem, DOJ has withheld critical information from Congress and the public, obfuscating the issue.

CONCERNS ABOUT GUNWALKING: "What the Hell is the Purpose of this?"

ATF special agents in Group VII expressed many concerns about the strategies employed during Fast and Furious. None of the agents had ever before allowed a gun to "walk." None of the agents had even heard of allowing a gun to be "walked." The ATF academy does not teach agents to walk weapons, and the practice is abhorrent. Yet, in this operation, veteran ATF agents acted against their training and well-established ATF practice in allowing guns to walk right out of their sight. In spite of the agents' frustration and dismay, ATF leadership from Phoenix to Washington refused to acknowledge the validity of their concerns.

A. Concerns fall on deaf ears and meet resistance

FINDING: ATF agents complained about the strategy of allowing guns to walk in Operation Fast and Furious. Leadership ignored their concerns. Instead, supervisors told the agents to "get with the program" because senior ATF officials had sanctioned the operation.

When agents learned that the tactics used in Fast and Furious required guns to be walked, many veteran special agents criticized and rebelled against the policy. These agents felt hamstrung, given that they could not use the training they had received throughout their careers.

As Agent Dodson testified:

Q. Based on our training and experience, what did you think about [walking guns]?

A. It was something I had never done before, sir. And quite frankly, I took great issue with it and concern. I felt like I understand the importance of going after the bigger target, but there is a way to do that. We did it successfully in the dope world all the time. And those skills and practices that we used there, a lot of them transfer over, and more than applicable in gun trafficking investigations, but we weren't allowed to use any of them.

Q. And did you ever have a recollection of sharing your frustration with Special Agent Casa?

A. Oh, yes, sir.

Q. And any other special agents that you can –

A. Yes, sir.

Q. And maybe you could just tell us what other agents you –

A. Pretty much everyone, sir. It was, I shared my reservations and concerns with Special Agent [L], with Dave Voth, with Special Agent [D] Special Agent [H], Special Agent Alt, Special Agent [P], several of the special agents that came on the GRIT, G-R-I-T. The gunrunner initiative is what it stands for. I shared them with or I voiced my concerns to other agents inside the Phoenix field division that was on other groups.

Agents felt compelled to speak up within days after joining Group VII. Agents complained to their superiors, to no avail. The agents, new to Phoenix, had to comply:

Q. So the special agents in Group 7 objected to this amongst themselves. And at what point did feedback start to get communicated up the chain, whether it was to the case agent, Special Agent [L], or Group Supervisor Voth?

A. Oh, it was almost immediately before we had . . . Special Agent Casa and I had taken it up with Special Agent [L], Special Agent [D], and as well as Group Supervisor Voth.

Having launched an innovative strategic plan, ATF senior leadership at Phoenix was excited at the prospect of a new way of combating drug cartel activity. ATF and DOJ leadership both approved of this plan. As such, ATF Phoenix leadership were loathe to let disgruntled field agents scuttle their signature achievement.

In this matter, a great divide developed between those who knew walking guns was a bad policy and vehemently spoke out against it, and those who believed walking guns was an effective policy.

A widely discussed e-mail from Group VII Supervisor David Voth best summarizes the divide that had emerged in Group VII, with senior special agents on one side, wanting to stop the operation, and those in the ATF chain of command on the other, wanting to continue the gun walking:

> It has been brought to my attention that there may be a schism developing amongst the group. This is the time we all need to pull together not drift apart. We are all entitled to our respective (albeit different) opinions however we all need to get along and realize that we have a mission to accomplish.
>
> I am thrilled and proud that our Group is the first ATF Southwest Border Group in the country to be going up on wire. On that note I thank everyone for their efforts thus far and applaud the results we have achieved in a short amount of time.
>
> Whether you care or not people of rank and authority at HQ are paying close attention to this case and they also believe we (Phoenix Group VII) are doing what they envisioned the Southwest Border Groups doing. It may sound cheesy but we are "The tip of the ATF spear" when it comes to Southwest Border Firearms Trafficking.
>
> We need to resolve our issues at this meeting. I will be damned if this case is going to suffer due to petty arguing, rumors or other adolescent behavior.
>
> I don't know what all the issues are but we are all adults, we are all professionals, and we have a exciting opportunity to use the biggest tool in our law enforcement tool box. **If you don't think this is fun you're in the wrong line of work — period!** This is the pinnacle of domestic U.S. law enforcement techniques. After this the tool box is empty. Maybe the Maricopa County Jail is hiring detention officers and you can get paid $30,000 (instead of $100,000) to serve lunch to inmates all day.

Despite this e-mail, agents continued to experience dismay and frustration as Operation Fast and Furious continued along its perilous path. As Agent Casa testified:

> Q. And is it fair to say that . . . the folks on your side of the schism wanted to do everything they could to interdict these weapons so they wouldn't get any farther down the street than they have to?
>
> A. Yes, sir. We were all sick to death when we realized that – when we realized what was going on or when we saw what was going on by the trends. We were all just, yes, we were all distraught.

The rift widened when the Assistant Special Agent in Charge (ASAC) authoritatively and unambiguously told Group VII that guns were not being walked, that the special agents were incorrect in their terminology, and that there would be no more discussion or dissension about this topic. Agent Dodson testified:

> A. Then we get an e-mail that . . . there is going to be a meeting. [the ASAC] is coming down, [the ASAC] comes into the Group 7 office and tells us essentially we better stand down with our complaints, that we didn't know what the definition of walking guns was, we weren't familiar with the Phoenix way of doing things, that **all of this was sanctioned** and we just needed to essentially shut up and get in line. That's not a quote, but that's the feel of the meeting, so ...
>
> Q. Do you remember approximately when that occurred?
>
> A. It was right after we went to the Group 7 building, so it had to be late February, early March 2010.

Even some - outside Group VII - with reservations about the practice, indicated that they gave them the benefit of the doubt because the case was being supervised by the U.S. Attorney's office.

Agent Forcelli testified:

> And I expressed concern . . . about that. And I believe some of those guns were purchased historically. It wasn't like 1200 were watched to go, but apparently they weren't interdicting either. And his response was . . . if you or I were running the group . . . it wouldn't be going down that way and that **the U.S. Attorney is on board, and it was Mr. [Emory] Hurley, and they say there is nothing illegal going on.**

B. Tragic, Yet Foreseeable Results

FINDING: Agents knew that given the large numbers of weapons being trafficked to Mexico, tragic results were a near certainty.

Since Group VII agents were instructed not to interdict as early and as often as they believed they should, the agents quickly grasped the likelihood of tragic results. Agent Alt testified:

> Q. At any point in time did you have communications that . . . this is going to end terribly, there is going to be deaths?

A. I know that was talked about . . . the probability of a bad situation arises with the number each – as the number of firearms increases, meaning firearms that are out and outside of our control in this environment with this type of a case, which we are talking about a firearms trafficking case, southwest border firearm trafficking case, I only hope the case agent knows where they are going. But they are out there and they are not accounted for by us, at least that I am aware of. So there is certainly a greater probability and a greater liability.

I can tell you that as early as June of last year I predicted to some of my peers in the office that we would be sitting right where we are today in this room.

Q. Speaking with Congressional investigators?

A. That this would be in front of a Congressional investigation. And I was in agreement with Agent Dodson that someone was going to die. And my observations in the office were there was an overwhelming concern, even amongst those persons on the other side of the schism, if I can use that term, that something bad was going to happen.

* * *

Q. And is it fair to say that anxiety is heightened because of the possibility of some of these guns getting into the hands of criminals and being used against your fellow law enforcement agents?

A. Yes. And it is not even the possibility, because we know that they were procured unlawfully. So if we know that from the beginning, they are already in the hands of criminals, so now we are simply dealing with what is the consequence of that.

The most frustrating aspect of the gunwalking policy for the agents was that they believed they *could* have interdicted and stopped the guns from walking.

When agents arrived in Phoenix in December 2009, they believed there was *already* enough information to arrest the straw purchasers, try to flip them, and begin working up the chain with an eye toward "bigger fish" in the organization. Yet, the fall of 2009 brought a remarkable departure from the normal practice of interdiction. ATF's strategy explicitly stated that it would allow straw purchasers to buy weapons, and that's exactly what happened.

Agent Dodson testified:

> Q. With the new resources in Group 7 in the fall of '09 . . . you talked about some of the special agents that were joined, if all of you had interdicted the weapons as you saw them, what percentage do you think you could have prevented from sort of entering the stream . . . if you read the press accounts of this, it is somewhere along the lines of 2,000 firearms have disappeared. How many do you think you and your colleagues would have been successful to interdict? Is it 10 percent, 50 percent?
>
> A. Well, the question is kind implausible, sir. . . . When we hit the ground in Phoenix, say, and the original 40 straw purchasers were identified, and I can't remember if it is 240 or 270 guns that they knew at that point that these guys were responsible for, you take, you minus that 270 from the estimate of 2,000, and whatever you have left is what we could have prevented. Because we should have landed on every one of those people the minute that we hit here. And the ones that we landed on that we couldn't make cases on, at least they would have been on notice that we were watching and they would have stopped buying, or every time they did, the flag went up and we could have been on them then. And of all the ones that we didn't land on, several of them would have spoken to us, a couple of them even maybe would have worked for us as a confidential informant or sources, which is how you climb the ladder in an investigation into an organization. Sitting back and watching isn't it. Okay? If you are watching a TV show at that point of the wire, you are not doing your job. Your job is to get out here and make a difference. And we could have done it when we hit the ground. So what are we talking? **1730, to answer your question**, is my opinion of how many of these firearms that we could have and should have prevented from ever being purchased by these individuals

and subsequently trafficked to known criminals or cartel elements south of the border and elsewhere.

Q. And is it fair to say if you started stopping these straw buyers as soon as they left [the gun dealers], is it fair to say that perhaps the drug trafficking organizations that they worked for would realize we got to get out of Phoenix, we have got to go to Dallas, we have got to go somewhere else, because Phoenix now has these new resources and they are catching us?

A. Right, if not, come up with an entirely new alternative way to get their weapons. If we shut down the whole straw purchasing scenario here in Phoenix, or significantly hurt it to the point where it is not advantageous for them to do so, you figure, if they are paying $600 for an AK or AK variant, all right, for every one that they buy we are taking off ten of them, okay, that's, I mean in any business sense that's not a good idea. Ultimately you are paying $6600 for one AK at that point. Am I correct?

Unfortunately, the agents' complaints fell on deaf ears. As one ASAC noted, the policy and Operation had been sanctioned. For many of the agents, the operation only fueled their outrage. According to the agents, the operation failed to use their investigative strengths, honed over dozens of years in law enforcement. Agents saw the whole operation as pointless, a poor way to operate, and above all, dangerous.

Agent Dodson testified:

Q. Can you be more specific about the instances in which you were told not to use those techniques?

A. Oh, certainly. Well, every time we voiced concerns, every time we asked the question. And this is so hard to convey because I understand you guys weren't there, you didn't live it. But every day being out here watching a guy go into the same gun store buying another 15 or 20 AK-47s or variants or . . . five or ten Draco pistols or FN Five-seveNs . . . guys that don't have a job, and he is walking in here spending $27,000 for three Barrett .50 calibers at . . . walks in with his little bag going in there to buy it, and you are sitting there every *day and you can't do anything, you have this conversation every day. You asked me ... a specific time where you voiced where you want to do this. Every day, all right? It was like are we taking this guy? No. Why not? Because it is not part of the plan, or it is not part of the case. [Agent L] said no, Dave said no, [Agent E] said no. **What are we doing here? I don't know. What the hell is the purpose of this? I have no idea.** This went on every day.*

DOJ and ATF determined that the goal of making the big case was worth the risk of letting hundreds and hundreds of guns go to criminals in the process. This conclusion was unacceptable to the agents on the ground carrying out these direct orders. The agents knew they were facilitating the sale of AK-47 variants to straw purchasers. Supervisors ignored complaints and retaliated against agents who did complain by transferring them out of ATF Phoenix Group VII.

As Agent Dodson recalled:

Q. [A]t any point in time do you have a recollection of commiserating with your colleagues, whether it was Special Agent Casa, whether it was Special Agent Alt, or some of the other special agents that were on sort of your side of the schism, for lack of a better word? Do you ever recall saying ... good grief, if we had just snatched these guns at the FFLs we wouldn't even be in this situation?

A. Oh, yes, sir, and not only with people on my side of the schism. I mean this was why I was, I mean I guess we will get to this later, but why I am no longer in Group 7, is because I addressed it with, or primarily with those on the other side of the schism.

* * *

Q. And is it fair to say at this point you are outraged?

A. Outraged and disgusted, however else you want to look at it.

Q. And is it fair to say that part of your outrage is because ... needless deaths are possibly occurring?

A. Oh, very much so, sir.

Q. That countless number of crimes are being perpetrated with these weapons that you and your colleagues may have facilitated –
A. Yes.

C. Catastrophe Becomes Reality

This agent's fear and outrage were realized by the death of Border Patrol Agent Brian Terry, a member of the U.S. Border Patrol Tactical Unit, as well as the almost certain deaths of countless Mexican citizens killed and the unknown amount of other crimes with weapons stemming from Fast and Furious. In Fast and Furious, ATF wanted to design a unique way to pursue the drug cartels. ATF and DOJ failed spectacularly to consider resulting negative outcomes.

As Agent Dodson noted:

*Well, sir, if I may, and first of all, please everyone understand, I am not on either, or either side of this political spectrum, nor do I want to be. And quite frankly, it is unfathomable to me how both sides or any person isn't completely livid about what we have been doing here. **I cannot see anyone who has one iota of concern for human life being okay with this**, and being willing to make this go away or not hold the people that made these decisions accountable. I don't understand it. And again, none of you owe me an explanation, that's just my personal opinion.*

WITNESSING GUNWALKING: "WE DID NOT STOP THEM"

Fast and Furious required agents to stand down, ignoring their training and professional instincts. Allowing guns to fall into the hands of the DTOs was the Operation's central goal.

Even when agents were able to interdict weapons, they received orders to stand down.

A. Watching Guns Walk

FINDING: Agents expected to interdict weapons, yet were told to stand down and "just surveil." Agents therefore did not act.

They watched straw purchasers buy hundreds of weapons illegally and transfer those weapons to unknown third parties and stash houses.

During their interviews, several agents offered detailed descriptions of their observations of suspected straw purchasers entering FFLs to purchase enormous quantities of assault rifles. Following orders, they did not intervene.

Agent Dodson remembered:

> Q. You got a guy that had purchased . . . **40 different AKs in the ast two months** and . . . five or ten of them had already returned in time to crime. **So I thought here we go, we are going to start interdicting people.** We – they would go in and buy another five or ten AK variants or . . . five or ten FN Five-seveN pistols at a time, and come out. We would see it. We would know . . . that whatever standard of reasonable suspicion or probable cause was met, and we were landing on somebody before the end of the day. **But that didn't happen.**
>
> Q. And that's something you realized how early in your fieldwork, first or second day?
>
> A. Oh, yes, sir. I mean first or second day you are starting to question why aren't we doing this. And then by the end of the week it was . . . frustration already as to how many guns have we watched these guys get away with.
>
> Q. In your first week, can you make an estimate of how many guns you saw get loaded into a vehicle and driven away? I mean, are we talking like 30 or one?
>
> A. Probably 30 or 50. It wasn't five. There were five at a time. These guys didn't go to the FFLs unless it was five or more. And the only exceptions to that are sometimes the Draco, which were the AK variant pistols, or the FN Five-seveN pistols, because a lot of FFLs just didn't have . . . 10 or 20 of those on hand.

Witnessing, but not contacting, straw purchasers buying weapons from FFLs became common practice for Group VII field agents in Phoenix. Agents sometimes conducted minimal surveillance following the purchases. Sometimes they conducted no surveillance.

As Agent Dodson testified:

> *We witnessed one of the individuals . . . the known straw purchasers arrive, go in. Sometimes one of us would actually be inside the FFL behind the counter. Sometimes if we had enough lead way we would go to the suspect's house and follow him from there to the FFL, or to a meeting . . . just prior to and see an exchange.*

Typically, agents ended surveillance of both the guns and the straw purchasers.

Agent Alt testified:

> *Watched and/or was aware – I shouldn't say watched – was aware that purchasers were routinely making purchases . . . at least in one case suspects who were known to be purchasing for other people were buying firearms with funds that were known to come from other people. And those firearms were not interdicted. Those firearms often went to a house or a place, and then surveillance was terminated there. So the disposition of the particular firearm may or may not have been known.*
> *Q. And did that happen frequently?*
> *A. Yes.*

B. Ordered to Stand Down

Superiors specifically ordered field agents to "stand down" despite establishing probable cause that a straw purchase had occurred. Agent Casa testified:

> *Q. And you were instructed or under orders from the case agent and group supervisor to do what, to do nothing?*
> *A. Well, when I would call out on surveillance, yes, I was advised do not – I would ask do we want to do a traffic stop, do we want to – I will throw another definition, you guys have probably heard this. I am sorry, guys. I don't know what you heard or didn't. It is called "rip." It is a slang for saying we are going to do a warrantless seizure of those firearms once we establish probable cause.*

*Yeah . . . one of those days I called the case agent on the Nextel, said, hey . . . our straw purchaser, one of our targets has transferred the guns, he is driving south. This unknown person that just got delivered the firearms probably . . . all intents and purposes gave the straw purchaser the money to buy the guns had all the guns and he is going north. Hey, why don't we go ahead and stop that vehicle, rip the guns, and you can do what you want, we can arrest them. We don't have to arrest them. But we will grab the guns. And they said no. And I said this person is an unknown person. Well, you got the license plate. Well, it can be, that car could be registered to anybody, we don't know who that person is, let's at least do a vehicle stop so we can ID the person so maybe later we could get the guns back. **No, just surveil.***

Agent Forcelli recounts that situation from a different point of view:

Well, as I said, there was that GRIT, people at command. And there was an instance where an agent was yelling over the radio. . . . There were a bunch of people milling around. And we heard an agent that sounded like he was in distress. And what happened was he was attempting to do a car stop. And we heard a female agent . . . telling him to stand down and not do the car stop. I later found out there were guns in the car and that the agent felt distressed because they had made him on the surveillance. So to let the guns go, it doesn't make any sense to me if you are burned.

Q. Do you know who the agent was?

A. Yes. It was Agent Casa.

Q. And so you specifically yourself heard him on the radio saying something to the effect I want to go get these guns now?

A. Yeah. And again, the reason, being a cop for so long you hear so many things on the radio, but you always can tell when somebody is in distress by the tone of their voice. As a cop you start racing to the scene before you actually hear the call. This was a similar instance, where you can tell by the tone of his voice something wasn't right.

Later on I spoke with him. And he said that a car had almost come at him. That's how aggressive they had become during the surveillance. And that's why he was so excited on the radio. But he was told to not stop the car with the guns in it, which to me makes no sense.

Agent Dodson described the situation:

I remember one time specifically we had been following this individual for so long to so many places that day . . . money pickups, gun drops, FFLs, and he got into an area of the city and he just started doing crazy [Ivans] . . . [like] unexplainable U-turns. He is doing heat runs, trying to burn surveillance, whatever cliché you want to use. So we knew we were made. Okay? We are made. He knows we are following. He knows we have been following him for awhile and we haven't done anything. We have to do something. I mean you have to do – we have to pull him over. We have to interact with him at some point. If not, he is always going to wonder, well, why are you following me. At least, for no other reason than a ruse, pull him over because . . . he did that illegal U-turn and whatever we need. We did it when I worked dope all the time. If they made surveillance, what did you do? Hey, there's an armed robbery back there, you guys match the description. No, you are not them. All right, later. And then we don't heat them up too bad. We weren't allowed to do that, not even for a ruse situation. **I mean there is a verbal screaming match over the radio about how . . . what are you talking about? There is no better time or reason to pull this guy over than right now.**

Q. So, in other words, whatever arguments might have been made before with regard to the specific instance that you are referring to about the utility of letting them continue their operations without knowing that you are onto them so that you can then follow and see where it goes, all those arguments go away at the point theymade the fact they are being surveilled, right?

A. Correct.

Unfortunately, ordering special agents to "stand down" when they planned to interdict guns became the norm. As Agent Dodson testified:

> Q. Can you recollect a time when you were conducting surveillance on an FFL and you saw firearms being loaded into a car when you said to your colleague we got to go, we got to go seize this now, I understand the direction we have been given, but this is bad stuff, these are bad people, we need to go just –
>
> A. Yes, sir.
>
> Q. And did you ever do that?
>
> A. No, sir. We were, at the time, one of the incidents that I recall specifically, Special Agent [D] was in the wire room at the time. We had been directed by both case agent and group supervisor that absent both of them, she is in charge. When we were communicating the interdiction that we were going to make over the radio, she, monitoring the radio traffic in the wire room, came back over and ordered us to stand down. I debated this with her, probably far more lengthy than I should have over the radio, and again ultimately was just ordered to stand down. There were actually more than one of these discussions with her and Group Supervisor Voth, as well as with Special Agent [L], when I thought we had a duty to act, that that was nonfeasance on our part by not doing so. And each time I was . . . told to stand down and somewhat reprimanded afterwards for voicing it.

Other agents had similar experiences in being told to stand down. Agent Casa remembered:

> And a situation would arise where a known individual, a suspected straw purchaser, purchased firearms and immediately transferred them or shortly after, not immediately, shortly after they had transferred them to an unknown male. And at that point I asked the case agent to, if we can intervene and seize those firearms, and I was told no.

These were not isolated incidents. Group VII members discussed, debated, and lamented walking guns on a daily basis, but the practice continued. Agent Casa testified:

> Q. And what did you observe during your surveillance?
>
> A. [I] observed suspected straw purchasers go to area federal firearms licensees, FFLs, go into the store, walk out with a large number of weapons, get into a vehicle, drive off.

C. "We Were Walking Guns. It was Our Decision"

As all of the accounts from numerous ATF agents demonstrate, ATF intentionally and knowingly walked guns. One of the ASACs in Phoenix reported that this policy was "sanctioned." To allow these guns to be bought and transferred illegally was a conscious and deliberate decision, not merely by failing to take action to interdict, but also by giving the green light to gun dealers to sell to known straw purchasers. By sanctioning the purchases even after dealers expressed concerns, ATF agents said they were actually facilitating the transactions:

Q. And essentially you witnessed guns walk; that was not consistent with your training and experience?

A. Sir . . . by the very definition of allowing them to walk, if I witnessed guns walk, that means it is another agency's operations. If I go help another agency and this is their op, then I witnessed guns walk. **We were walking guns. It was our decision.** We had the information. **We had the duty and the responsibility to act, and we didn't do so.** So it was us walking those guns. We didn't watch them walk, we walked.39

Agent Dodson later explains the consequences:

> Q. That countless number of crimes are being perpetrated with these weapons that you and your colleagues may have facilitated --
>
> A. Yes.
>
> Q. -- moving into the hands of the bad guys?
>
> A. Yes, sir. **I would argue that it wasn't a "may have facilitated." It was facilitated.** These FFLs wouldn't have made these purchases. I mean they addressed their concerns to, I mean to ATF

both formally as well as to us when we were inside getting copies of the forms, that this whole – The genesis of this case was when they were calling in these people that they knew. **This guy comes in, buys 10, 15, 20 AKs or . . . a 22-year-old girl walks in and dumps $10,000 on . . . AK-47s in a day, when she is driving a beat up car that doesn't have enough metal to hold hubcaps on it. They knew what was going on.** *The "may have facilitated" to me is kind of erroneous. We did facilitate it. How are we not responsible for the ultimate outcome of these [g]uns?*

COLLATERAL DAMAGE: A FAST AND FURIOUS INEVITABILITY

An increase of crimes and deaths in Mexico caused an increase in the recovery of weapons at crime scenes. When these weapons traced back through the Suspect Gun Database to weapons that were walked under Fast and Furious, supervisors in Phoenix were giddy at the success of their operation.

A. Increasing Volume Equals Increasing Success

FINDING: Operation Fast and Furious contributed to the increasing violence and deaths in Mexico. This result was regarded with giddy optimism by ATF supervisors hoping that guns recovered at crime scenes in Mexico would provide the nexus to straw purchasers in Phoenix.!

Since ATF supervisors regarded violence and deaths in Mexico as inevitable collateral damage, they were not overly concerned about this effect of the Operation. Quite the opposite, they viewed the appearance of Fast and Furious guns at Mexican crime scenes with *satisfaction*, because such appearances proved the connection between straw purchasers under surveillance and the DTOs. For example,

Group VII Supervisor David Voth eagerly reported how many weapons their "subjects" purchased and the immense caliber of some of these guns during the month of March alone:

MEXICO STATS

958 killed in March 2010 (Most violent month since 2005)

937 killed in January 2010

842 killed in December 2009

SINALOA - MARCH STATISTICS

187 murders in March, including 11 policemen

I hope this e-mail is well received in that it is not intended to imply anything other than that the violence in Mexico is severe and without being dramatic we have a sense of urgency with regards to this investigation. Our subjects purchased 359 firearms during the month of March alone, to include numerous Barrett .50 caliber rifles. I believe we are righteous in our plan to dismantle this entire organization and to rush in to arrest any one person without taking in to account the entire scope of the conspiracy would be ill advised to the overall good of the mission. I acknowledge that we are all in agreement that to do so properly requires patience and planning. In the event however that there is anything we can do to facilitate a timely response or turnaround by others we should communicate our sense of urgency with regard to this matter.

Thanks for everyone's continued support in this endeavor,

David Voth
Group Supervisor
Phoenix Group VII

The agents within Group VII described Voth's reaction to all this gun violence in Mexico as "giddy." In addition to this e-mail, private conversations they had with Voth gave them the impression that Voth was excited about guns at Mexican crime scenes subsequently traced back to Fast and Furious. Agent Dodson explains:

Q. Then there is an e-mail that was on CBS news that I made notes about written on April 2, 2010 by Group Supervisor Voth?

A. Yes, sir.

Q. And he reported that our subjects purchased 359 firearms during March alone.

A. Yes, sir.

Q. That there were 958 people killed in March of 2010.

A. Yes, sir.

Q. And he was . . . he was essentially trumpeting up the violence that was occurring as a result of an ATF sanctioned program, is that correct?

A. Agent or Group Supervisor Voth took that, or the way that he presented that to us was look here, this is proof that we are working a cartel, the guns that our guys are buying that we are looking at are being found, are coming back with very short time to crime rates in Mexico in known cartel related violence, and the violence is going through the roof down there, we are onto a good thing here.

Q. The e-mail further goes on and says there was 937 killed in January 2010, 842 killed in December, 2009. The numbers are increasing?

A. Yes, sir.

This evidence established a nexus between straw purchasers in the United States and the DTOs in Mexico, bringing ATF one step closer to catching the "bigger fish." This strategy of letting the "little fish" go in order to capture the "bigger fish" was the ultimate goal of Phoenix Group VII. As Agent Dodson explained:

Q. Okay. So earlier we were discussing an e-mail that . . . was describing from Mr. Voth where he appears to present the crimes in Mexico. You said something to the effect that he was, he was presenting the guns being recovered in Mexico as proof that you were watching the right people.

A. Correct.

Q. And that the increasing levels of violence were proof you were on the right track, essentially. I just wanted to clarify. Is that, when you were saying those things, was that your reading of his e-mail, or do you recall other conversations that you had with him outside of the e-mail that . . . this was evidence that you were on the right track?

A. Well, both. I get that impression from reading his e-mail, but perhaps I get that impression because of knowing him how well I did.

There were several instances. Whenever he would get a trace report back . . . **he was jovial, if not, not giddy, but just delighted about that, hey, 20 of our guns were recovered with 350 pounds** *of dope in Mexico last night. And it was exciting.* To them it proved the nexus to the drug cartels. It validated that . . . we were really working the cartel case here.

Agent Alt described in great detail his disgust at the self-satisfaction of ATF leadership for sending guns into what they knew to be a war zone. He also expounded on his view that the Group Supervisor should have been more concerned with those deaths in Mexico rather than with motivating his team. He testified:

> *Why then do we stand by and try to motivate agents to do something more to stem the homicides . . . with no further mention on the homicides and correlate that with the number of guns recovered in Mexico in a given month, when we should be saying how many of those guns left this state that we knew about in relationship to our cases in conjunction with these murders? That didn't happen.*

B. "You Need to Scramble Some Eggs"

According to the ATF agents, their supervisors in Phoenix were sometimes shockingly insensitive to the possibility the policy could lead to loss of life. Agent Dodson explained:

> *Q. [S]omebody in management . . . used the terminology "scramble some eggs."*
> *A. Yes, sir.*
> *Q. If you are going to make an omelette you have got to scramble some eggs. Do you remember the context of that?*
> *A. Yes, sir. It was – there was a prevailing attitude amongst the group and outside of the group in the ATF chain of command, and that was the attitude. . . . I had heard that . . . sentiment from Special Agent [E] Special Agent [L], and Special Agent Voth. And the time referenced in the interview was, I want to say, in May as the GRIT team or gunrunner initiative team was coming out. I was having a conversation with Special Agent [L] about the case in which the conversation ended with me asking her are you prepared to go to a border agent's funeral over this or a Cochise County deputy's over this, because that's going to happen. And the sentiment that was given back to me by both her, the group*

supervisor, was that . . . if you are going to make an omelette, you need to scramble some eggs.

C. An Inevitable and Horrible Outcome

The increasing number of deaths along with the increasing number of Fast and Furious guns found at Mexican crime scenes evoked a very different reaction among the line agents. They had great anxiety about the killings across the border. Their concern focused on reports of shootings and assaults of law enforcement officials. They worried openly of the consequences of walked weapons used to shoot a police officer. This worst-case scenario came to fruition when United States Border Patrol Agent Brian Terry was murdered and two "walked" AK-47 rifles were found at the scene of the murder. Agent Forcelli described the mood following the Terry murder:

> *Q. Do you recall any specific conversations that you had about after, after learning that . . . two of the guns at the scene had been traced back to the Fast and Furious case?*
> *A. [T]here was kind of a thing like deja vu, hey, we have been saying this was going to happen. The agents were pretty livid and saying exactly that. We knew. How many people were saying this was going to happen a long time before it did happen? And then there was a sense like every other time, **even with Ms. Giffords' shooting, there was a state of panic**, like, oh, God, let's hope this is not a weapon from that case. And the shooting of Mr. [Zapata] down in Mexico, I know that, again, that state of panic that they had, like please let this not come back. This was an embarrassment . . . that this happened to the agent, tragic. I mean my heart goes out to this family. I lost colleagues, and I couldn't imagine the pain they were going through. And it made it painful for us, even those not involved in the case, to think ATF now has this stain.*

Agent Alt explained the process by which ATF learned that weapons were being trafficked into Mexico.

> *Q. But how would you identify that they ended up in Mexico?*

A. Well, there is a variety of ways. One . . . you would identify where they are going by virtue of recoveries that are happening in crimes or interdictions. . . . So you identify that they are going south. And I think then the strategy, if I understand it, is that the firearms are then, once . . . they are going south, you try and follow them and figure out where they are going and to who they are going to tie to a greater organization and more people, identify the hierarchy of the organization. That's the strategy. And I don't know how you perfect a case doing that when you don't have the guns. . . . But the strategy to me would have to be that there has got to be some measure of accounting or follow-up as to where they end up.

The notion that these guns moved into Mexico and aided the drug war distressed the ATF field agents, including Agent Casa:

Q. It was a likely consequence of the policy of walking guns that some of those guns would wind up at crime scenes in Mexico?
A. Yeah.
Q. And is it fair to say that some, if not many, of these crime scenes would be where people would be seriously injured or possibly killed?
A. Of course.
*Q. **So is it a fair, predictable outcome of the policy that there would be essentially collateral damage in terms of human lives?***
*A. **Sure**.*

Agent Casa also emphasized that those who planned and approved Operation Fast and Furious could have predicted the ensuing collateral violence:

I feel for the family of Agent Terry, I feel for his death. . . . I don't know how some of the people I work with could not see this was going to be an inevitable outcome, something like this happening. And I don't know why they don't think that six months from now this won't happen again, or a year from now, a year and a half from now.

But I don't know the exact number of guns that were put out into the streets as a result of this investigation. But they are not going to disintegrate once they are used once. They are going to keep popping up over and over and over.

D. The Pucker Factor

FINDING: Every time a law enforcement official in Arizona was assaulted or shot by a firearm, ATF agents in Group VII had great anxiety that guns used to perpetrate the crimes may trace back to Operation Fast and Furious.!

The design defect of Fast and Furious was its failure to include sufficient safeguards to keep track of thousands of heavy-duty weapons sold to straw purchasers for the DTOs. ATF agents did not maintain surveillance of either the guns or the straw purchasers. The guns were therefore lost. The next time law enforcement would encounter those guns was at crime scenes in Mexico and in the United States. However, because ATF had contemporaneous notice of the sales from the gun dealers and entered the serial numbers into the Suspect Gun Database, agents were notified whenever a trace request was submitted for one of those walked guns. As Agent Alt testified:

Q. [A] little bit earlier you talked about a level of anxiety, the nxiety among the agents, perhaps even the supervisors, relating to weapons that are found at crime scenes. There was a death, there is a murder scene in Mexico. There is a trace that comes in of some kind, and the weapon is then connected to a weapon that may have been one of the weapons that were walked. . . . Is that accurate?

A. **Yes. I used the word anxiety. The term I used amongst my peers is pucker factor.**

* * *

> Q. Pucker factor, precisely. But that's what it is relating to? I am saying that correctly, right?
> A. Yes.
> Q. And this pucker factor, in your view, is related to a gun showing up at a crime scene, right, a murder scene, someone gets killed, et cetera?

A. Absolutely.

Q. [B]ut isn't that crime scene also the reason or the place that permits us to trace the gun? In other words, once the gun is walked, let's say it walks south, isn't the only other information we are ever going to get about that gun, isn't that going to come from a crime scene?

A. Most likely, unless we have some resource in place down there, whether it be an informant or an undercover or an agent or something telling us where those guns end up.

* * *

Q. So assuming for a second that that does not exist because we don't have any evidence to speak of, the only way we are going to see this firearm that was let go --

A. Is a crime recovery.

Q. Crime gun recovery --

A. That's correct.

Q. -- which would be either in the pocket of a person caught for some other offense or very likely at a shooting?

A. Most of the Mexican recoveries are related to an act of violence.

* * *

Q. But so typically the recovery will have evolved around a serious injury or gun related?

A. Or about drug related.

Q. But someone is either dead or hurt or both or something frequently?

A. Yes . . . there is a lot of violence, and guns are recovered with respect to the violence. A lot of your big seizures of the guns, though, the big seizures of the guns, mass is usually in conjunction of seizures of other things.

* * *

*My opinion is the last portion of your statement is spot on, you have to accept that there is going to be collateral damage with regard to that strategy. **You can't allow thousands of guns to go south of the border without an expectation that they are going to be recovered eventually in crimes and people are going to die.***

THE TRAGIC DEATH OF US BORDER PATROL AGENT BRIAN TERRY

FINDING: Jaime Avila was entered as a suspect in the investigation by ATF on November 25, 2009, after purchasing weapons alongside Uriel Patino, who had been identified as a suspect in October 2009. Over the next month and a half, Avila purchased 13 more weapons, each recordedby the ATF in its database within days of the purchase. Then on January 16, 2010, Avila purchased three AK-47 style rifles, two of which ended up being found at the murder scene of U.S. BorderPatrol Agent Brian Terry. The death of Border Agent Brian Terry was likely a preventable tragedy.

Fast and Furious has claimed the life of an American federal agent. Late in the evening of December 14, 2010, Border Patrol Agent Brian Terry, a native of Michigan, was on patrol with three other agents in Peck Canyon, near Rio Rico, Arizona. One of the agents spotted a group of five suspected illegal aliens; at least two were carrying rifles. Although one of the border patrol agents identified the group as federal agents, the suspected aliens did not drop their weapons. At least one of the suspected aliens fired at the agents, who returned fire. Agent Terry was struck by on bullet that proved to be fatal.51 Most of the suspected aliens fled the scene, though one of them, Manual Osorio- Arellanes, had been wounded and was unable to flee. A slew of federal agents from a variety of agencies arrived at the scene and the authorities' recovered three weapons from the suspects, who had dropped their rifles in order to flee the scene faster. Two of those recovered weapons were AK-47 variant rifles that had been bought on January 16, 2010 by straw purchaser Jaime Avila during Operation Fast and Furious. Avila was entered as a suspect in the investigation by

ATF on November 25, 2009. This occurred after he purchased weapons with Uriel Patino, a straw buyer who had previously been identified as a suspect in October 2009. On November 24, 2009, agents rushed to the FFL to surveil Avila and Patino, but arrived too late. Over the next month and a half, Avila purchased 13 more weapons, each recorded by the ATF in its database within days of the purchase. Avila bought the weapons recovered at the scene of

Agent Terry's murder almost two months after ATF knew he was working with Patino. Avila's purchases would eventually total fifty two under Fast and Furious.52 Patino's purchases would eventually top 660. As with all the Fast and Furious suspects, gun dealers provided contemporaneous notice of each sale to the ATF.53

The day after the Terry shooting, law enforcement agents located and arrested Avila in Phoenix. The U.S. Attorney's Office in Arizona later indicted him. Avila's indictment, however, is typical of the indictments that have resulted thus far from Fast and Furious. Avila was indicted on three counts of "lying and buying"—including false statements on ATF Form 4473, a prerequisite to the purchase of any firearm. These three indictments, however, do not stem from the weapons purchased on January 16, 2010, that eventually ended up at the Terry murder scene. Instead, Avila was indicted with respect to rifles he bought *six months later* and which also turned up at a crime scene.

On May 6, 2011, DOJ unsealed an indictment of Manuel Osorio-Arellanes for the murder of Brian Terry.54 Federal authorities, led by the FBI, are pursuing his co-conspirators, including the gunman suspected of firing the fatal shot and fleeing the scene.

In Phoenix, the news of Agent Terry's death deeply saddened, but did not surprise, Group VII agents. They had agonized over the possibility of this event, and they ruefully contemplated future similar incidents resulting from the abundance of illegal guns.

During their transcribed interviews, the ATF agents shared their reactions to Agent Brian Terry's murder. Agent Dodson testified:
> *Q. Along those lines, when did you find out that Agent Terry was killed?*
> *A. I found out December 16th, 2010.*
> *Q. And what can you tell us about your recollections that information?*
>
> *   * * ***
>
> *A. Well, I was called by another agent and was told that – or asked if I had heard about Agent Terry's death. I told him that I had. And then he confirmed for me what I already*

thought when he called, which was that it was one of the guns from Fast and Furious. And then later that day, I was speaking to my acting supervisor, Marge Zicha, and she had made a comment to me that they were very busy because two of the Fast and Furious guns were found at the scene of Agent Terry's homicide.

Agent Dodson also detailed ATF's awareness of and its multiple contacts with the accused murderer, Jaime Avila, for months prior to Agent Terry's murder.

*So essentially in January 2010, or December when I got there, **we knew Jaime Avila was a straw purchaser**, had him identified as a known straw purchaser supplying weapons to the cartel. Shortly thereafter, we had previous weapons recovered from Mexico with very short time to crime rates purchased by Jaime Avila, as I recall.*

*And then in May we had a recovery where Border Patrol encounters an armed group of bandits and recovered an AK variant rifle purchased by Jaime Avila, and we still did not – **purchased during the time we were watching Jaime Avila, had him under surveillance, and we did nothing**.*

Then on December 14th, 2010 Agent Brian Terry is killed in Rio Rico, Arizona. Two weapons recovered from the scene . . . two AK variant weapons purchased by Jaime Avila on January 16th, 2010 while we had him under surveillance, after we knew him to be a straw purchaser, after we identified him as purchasing firearms for a known Mexican drug cartel.

Although the ATF agents' worst fears were confirmed, they did not feel good about being right. In the wake of Agent Terry's death, they were even more upset, saddened, and embarrassed. Agent Alt explained:

I have loved working for ATF since I have been hired here. I came here to retire from ATF. I could be doing any number of things, as you all are aware. . . . I could be whatever I chose to be, and I chose to be here. I am not -- I am embarrassed here. I regret the day that I set foot into this field division because of some of the things that a few people have done and the impact that it has had on our agency, and not the least of, not the least, though, is the impact it has had on the public and safety and Agent Terry. While I don't know that guns in any of these cases are directly responsible for his death, I am appalled that there would be in any way associated with his death.

A December 15, 2010 e-mail exchange among ATF agents details the aftermath of Agent Terry's death. ATF, fearing the worst, conducted an "urgent firearms trace" of the firearms, recovered on the afternoon of the murder. By 7:45 p.m. that evening, the trace confirmed these fears:

From: █████████████████
To: █████████████████
Cc: █████████████████
Sent: Wed Dec 15 19:45:03 2010
Subject: U.S. Border Patrol Agent killed in the line of duty - Two firearms recovered by ATF
The two firearms recovered by ATF this afternoon near Rio Rico, Arizona, in conjunction with the shooting death of U.S. Border Patrol agent Terry were identified as 'Suspect Guns' in the Fast and Furious investigation █████████████████

The firearms are identified as follows:

     Romarm/CUGIR, 762 rifle, Model GP WASR 10/63, serial number 1971CZ3775
     Romarm/CUGIR, 762 rifle, Model GP WASR 10/63, serial number 1983AH3977

█████████contact me late this afternoon requesting Intel assistance in the tracing of two recovered firearms.

I initiated an urgent firearms trace requests on both of the firearms and then contacted the NTC to ensure the traces were conducted today.

I was advised by the NTC that the firearms were entered into ATF Suspect Gun database by SA Medina and associated to the Fast and Furious investigation. The NTC further advised that on 01/16/10 Jaime AVILA purchased three Romarm 7.62 rifles from Lone Wolf Trading Company, two of these firearms are the recovered firearms cited above.

No trace has been submitted on the third firearm purchased by AVILA (serial number 1979IS1530). I am researching the trace status of the firearms recovered earlier today by the FBI.

Agent Terry did not die in vain. His passing exposed the practice of knowingly allowing the transfer of guns to suspected straw purchasers. ATF now maintains it no longer condones this dangerous technique. The cessation of this practice will likely save lives on both sides of the border. Tragically, however, we will be seeing the ramifications of the policy to allow guns from Fast and

Furious be transferred into the hands of suspected criminals for years to come. These weapons will continue to be found at crime scenes in the United States and Mexico.

THE BEGINIING OF DOJs DENIALS "HELL, NO"

FINDING: Phoenix ATF Special Agent in Charge (SAC) William Newell's statement that the indictments represent the take-down of a firearms trafficking ring from top to bottom, and his statement that ATF never allowed guns to walk are incredible, false, and a source of much frustration to the agents.

On January 25, 2011, Phoenix SAC William Newell gave a press conference announcing the indictment of 20 individuals as a result of Fast and Furious. Most of the indictment involves "lying and buying" – paper transgressions that carry much lighter sentences than felonies relating to actual firearms trafficking. Under "lying and buying," a straw purchaser improperly fills out ATF Form 4473, required before the purchase of any firearm, by submitting false information. A comparison of the indictment with the goals of Fast and Furious reveals the Operation's utter failure. According to the agents, the Department could have indicted all 20 defendants far sooner than January 2011. Instead, the timing of the indictment appears to coincide with the outrage following the killing of Border Agent Brian Terry. Agent Dodson testified:

> A. Essentially, the indictments looked very similar in January 2011, when they were finally served, as they did in December 2009 when I first got here. The only difference is the number of purchases that were made. Some of the names of people are new, some have been added and some taken out, but no major players at all.
>
> Q. So the publicly announced indictments, they are all for straw purchasers, right?
>
> A. Yes, sir, which we could have rounded up . . . a year and a half ago.
>
> Q. You could have arrested them the day you saw this stuff happening?
>
> A. And saved those 1730 guns from being trafficked.

At the press conference announcing the indictments, SAC Newell made two notable comments. Newell claimed that the indictments represented a take-down of a firearms trafficking ring from top to bottom. Yet virtually all of the indicted defendants were mere straw purchasers—not key players of a criminal syndicate by any stretch of the imagination.

Newell's second notable comment was equally negligent and inaccurate. When asked whether or not ATF ever allowed guns to walk, Newell emphatically exclaimed **"Hell, no!"**

His denial was shocking to those who knew the truth, like Agent Alt:

> *Q. And why is that engrained in your memory?*
> *A. Candidly, my mouth fell open. I was asked later by the public information officer for our division . . . and I told him that I thought that – I was just astounded that he made that statement and it struck me and I don't know how he could make that statement.*
>
> * * *
>
> *Q. When SAC Newell made those statements at the press conference and you said something along the lines – did your jaw drop?*
> *A. Literally my mouth fell open. I am not being figurative about that. I couldn't believe it.*
> *Q. Is it fair to say that his statements that caused your mouth to drop, that's a spectacular lie, isn't it?*
> *A. Yes. My mouth fell open because I thought, I perceived it as being either completely ignorant or untruthful. But also a person in that position I don't really – I don't know that I would have made – the statement was unnecessary to make. He did not need to make the statement. If I am in a position like that and I have gotten involved or have knowledge of an investigation, me personally, I probably would have avoided comment. I certainly would have avoided making a comment like that.*

Agent Casa also expressed similar astonishment at Newell's inaccurate comment following the press conference:

Q. At the press conference I believe he was asked whether or not guns were walked, and his response was hell no. Do you remember that?

A. Yes, I do.

Q. What was your reaction to that statement?

A. I can't believe he just answered the question that way.

Q. And why can't you believe that?

A. Because we, in my definition of walking guns, we had walked a bunch of guns. When I say we, Group 7. And under this case that we are discussing, a bunch of firearms were walked against the objections o f some senior agents.

Q. So Newell's statement was inaccurate?

A. I would say it was very inaccurate.

Agent Forcelli shared similar sentiments over Newell's remarkable statements during the press conference.

Q. Right. Did you attend that press conference that SAC Newell came down to do, or did?

A. No. I was involved in the command post that day. I wasn't there. I heard about it. I was appalled.

Q. Tell us about your reaction. What were you appalled by?

A. My understanding is somebody asked him if guns walked, and his response was hell no.

Q. How did you feel about that?

A. Insulted. Because I know that they were saying that this was a technique that was like a great new technique we were using. . . . And it just amazes me. But he knew what was going on. He is the SAC. And agents knew that guns were not being interdicted.64 None of the agents interviewed believed Newell's dramatic comment to be truthful. His denial of the existing policy sought to end questioning on this topic once and for all. Instead, it only engendered more attention and interest.

DOJs CONTINUED DENIALS: "THAT IS FALSE"

FINDING: Despite mounting evidence to the contrary, DOJ continues to deny that Operation Fast and Furious was ill-conceived and had deadly consequences.

The denials of gunwalking became more sensational as they continued. Presented with an opportunity to set the record straight, the Department of Justice instead chose a path of denial.

A. "Of Course Not"

In a February 4, 2011 letter to Senator Charles Grassley, Ranking Member of the Senate Judiciary Committee, DOJ's Assistant Attorney General for Legislative Affairs wrote:

> At the outset, the allegation described in your January 27 letter – that ATF "sanctioned" or otherwise knowingly allowed the sale of assault weapons to a straw purchaser who then transported them into Mexico – **is false**.
>
> ATF makes every effort to interdict weapons that have been purchased illegally and prevent their transportation to Mexico.

When asked in later meetings and letters how this statement could be true in light of all the evidence to the contrary, DOJ officially stood by it. The argument that it is true relies on the fine distinction that it was not the *straw purchasers themselves* who physically crossed the border with the weapons, but rather the unknown third parties to whom they transferred the firearms. DOJ offered no specific defense of the second sentence.

Of course, this statement misses the point entirely. ATF permitted known straw purchasers to obtain these deadly weapons and traffic them to third parties. Then, at some point after ATF broke off surveillance, the weapons were transported to Mexico. ATF was definitely aware that these guns were ending up in Mexico, being transported through Arizona and Texas Points of Entry.

The second part of this statement is also patently false. Numerous ATF agents have gone on the record with stories that directly contradict it. During interviews with, these agents had the chance to respond directly to DOJ's position. Not surprisingly, they uniformly rejected it. Agent Alt testified:

> Q. And I will just read a portion of that into the record. The second paragraph of the letter said, the second sentence of the second paragraph says, "ATF makes every effort to interdict weapons that have been purchased illegally and

> prevent their transportation to Mexico," period. Is that
> sentence, based on your knowledge of what was going on
> here in Phoenix, true or not true?
> A. **No, it is not true.**

Agent Forcelli agreed:

> Q. [The] second sentence of the second paragraph of the
> letter says: ATF makes every effort to interdict weapons
> that have been purchased illegally to prevent their
> transportation to Mexico," period. Have you heard that
> before, that that representation was made to Congress?
> A. I was unaware of that. And I will tell you based on what I
> know has occurred that that is false.

Agent Forcelli reiterated, "Based on my conversations in regards to
that meeting between Mr. Hurley and the ATF's agents and the two
gun dealers, no. *It is false.*" And when asked if the DOJ's statement
was true, given what he had personally witnessed in Phoenix,
Agent Casa replied, "I think you already know the answer to that.
Of course not."

B. More Denials

Even after the U.S. Congress presented it with evidence that the
statements in the February 4, 2011 letter were false, the
Department of Justice *still* stood by its initial position. In a May 2,
2011 response to a letter from Senator Grassley, the Department
maintained its original position:

> It remains our understanding that ATF's Operation Fast and
> Furious did not knowingly permit straw buyers to take guns
> into Mexico. You have provided to us documents, including
> internal ATF emails, which you believe support your
> allegation. . . . [W]e have referred these documents and all
> correspondence and materials received from you related to
> Operation Fast and Furious to the Acting Inspector General,
> so that she may conduct a thorough review and resolve your
> allegations.

The Justice Department also notes that the Attorney General has "made clear . . . that the Department should never knowingly permit firearms to cross the border." Although the Department issued this directive in early-March, well after the congressional investigation of Operation Fast and Furious had begun, it is a welcome affirmation of what the ATF whistleblowers had been trying to tell their bosses for over a year before Agent Brian Terry was killed.

CONCLUSION

We will persist in seeking documents and testimony from Justice Department officials and other sources to thoroughly examine all the key questions. The Department should avail itself of the opportunity to come clean and provide complete answers. It should also reverse its position and choose to fully cooperate with the investigation.

Appendix B: Congressional Oversight Report, July 2011

The Department of Justice's Operation Fast and Furious: Fueling Cartel Violence

JOINT STAFF REPORT

Prepared for Rep. Darrell E. Issa, Chairman

United States House of Representatives

Committee on Oversight and Government Reform

& Senator Charles E. Grassley, Ranking Member

United States Senate Committee on the Judiciary

112th Congress

July 26, 2011

Table of Contents

JOINT STAFF REPORT (cont'd)

"That is, I mean, this is the perfect storm of idiocy."

–Carlos Canino, Acting ATF Attaché in Mexico

Executive Summary

The previous joint staff report entitled The Department of Justice's Operation Fast and Furious: Accounts of ATF Agents chronicled Operation Fast and Furious, a reckless program conducted by the Bureau of Alcohol, Tobacco, Firearms, and Explosives (ATF), and the courageous ATF agents who came forward to expose it. Operation Fast and Furious made unprecedented use of a dangerous investigative technique known as "gunwalking." Rather than intervene and seize the illegally purchased firearms, ATF's Phoenix Field Division allowed known straw purchasers to walk away with the guns, over and over again. As a result, the weapons were transferred to criminals and Mexican Drug Cartels. This report explores the effect of Operation Fast and Furious on Mexico. Its lethal drug cartels obtained AK-47 variants, Barrett .50 caliber sniper rifles, .38 caliber revolvers, and FN Five-seveNs from Arizona gun dealers who were cooperating with the ATF by continuing to sell to straw purchasers identified in Operation Fast and Furious.

In late 2009, ATF officials stationed in Mexico began to notice a large volume of guns appearing there that were traced to the ATF's Phoenix Field Division. These weapons were increasingly recovered in great numbers from violent crime scenes. ATF intelligence analysts alerted Darren Gil, Attaché to Mexico, and Carlos Canino, Deputy Attaché, about the abnormal number of weapons. Gil and Canino communicated their worries to leadership in Phoenix and Washington, D.C., only to be brushed aside. Furthermore, ATF personnel in Arizona denied ATF personnel in Mexico access to crucial information about the case, even though the operation directly involved their job duties and affected their host country.

Rather than share information, senior leadership within both ATF and the Department of Justice (DOJ) assured their representatives in Mexico that everything was "under control." The growing number of weapons recovered in Mexico, however, indicated otherwise. Two recoveries of large numbers of weapons in November and December 2009 definitively demonstrated that Operation Fast and Furious weapons were heading to Mexico. In fact, to date, there have been 48 different recoveries of weapons in Mexico linked to Operation Fast and Furious.

ATF officials in Mexico continued to raise the alarm over the burgeoning number of weapons. By October 2010, the amount of seized and recovered weapons had "maxed out" space in the Phoenix Field Division evidence vault.1 Nevertheless, ATF and DOJ failed to share crucial details of Operation Fast and Furious with either their own employees stationed in Mexico or representatives of the Government of Mexico. ATF senior leadership allegedly feared that any such disclosure would compromise their investigation. Instead, ATF and DOJ leadership's reluctance to share information may have only prolonged the flow of weapons from this straw purchasing ring into Mexico.

ATF leadership finally informed the Mexican office that the investigation would be shut down as early as July 2010. Operation Fast and Furious, however, continued through the rest of 2010. It ended only after U.S. Border Patrol Agent Brian Terry was murdered in December 2010 with weapons linked to this investigation. Only then did the ATF officials in Mexico discover the true nature of Operation Fast and Furious. Unfortunately, Mexico and the United States will have to live with the consequences of this program for years to come.

See E-mail from [ATF Evidence Vault Employee] to Hope MacAllister October 12, 2010 (HOGR ATF – 002131- 32).

Findings

- In the fall of 2009, ATF officials in Mexico began noticing a spike in guns recovered at Mexican crime scenes. Many of those guns traced directly to an ongoing investigation out of ATF's Phoenix Field Division.

- As Operation Fast and Furious progressed, there were numerous recoveries of large weapons caches in Mexico. These heavy-duty weapons included AK-47s, AR-15s, and even Barrett .50 caliber rifles – the preferred weapons of drug cartels.

- At a March 5, 2010 briefing, ATF intelligence analysts told ATF and DOJ leadership that the number of firearms bought by known straw purchasers had exceeded the 1,000 mark. The briefing also made clear these weapons were ending up in Mexico.

- ATF and DOJ leadership kept their own personnel in Mexico and Mexican government officials totally in the dark about all aspects of Fast and Furious. Meanwhile, ATF officials in Mexico grew increasingly worried about the number of weapons recovered in Mexico that traced back to an ongoing investigation out of ATF's Phoenix Field Division.

- ATF officials in Mexico raised their concerns about the number of weapons recovered up the chain of command to ATF leadership in Washington, D.C. Instead of acting decisively to end Fast and Furious, the senior leadership at both ATF and DOJ praised the investigation and the positive results it had produced. Frustrations reached a boiling point, leading former ATF Attaché Darren Gil to engage in screaming matches with his supervisor,

International Affairs Chief Daniel Kumor, about the need to shut down the Phoenix-based investigation.

- Despite assurances that the program would be shut down as early as March 2010, it took the murder of a U.S. Border Patrol Agent in December 2010 to actually bring the program to a close.

- ATF officials in Mexico finally realized the truth: ATF allowed guns to walk. By withholding this critical information from its own personnel in Mexico, ATF jeopardized relations between the U.S. and Mexico.

- The high-risk tactics of cessation of surveillance, gunwalking, and non-interdiction of weapons that ATF used in Operation Fast and Furious went against the core of ATF's mission, as well as the training and field experience of its agents. These flaws inherent in Operation Fast and Furious made its tragic consequences inevitable.

Weapons Traced to the ATF Phoenix Field Division

FINDING: In the fall of 2009, ATF officials in Mexico began noticing a spike in guns recovered at Mexican crime scenes. Many of those guns traced directly to an ongoing investigation out of ATF's Phoenix Field Division. Starting in late 2009, ATF officials in Mexico noticed a growing number of weapons appearing in Mexico that were traced to the ATF's Phoenix Field Division. Completely unaware of Operation Fast and Furious at the time, Carlos Canino, then Deputy Attaché to Mexico, was surprised when he learned of the number of weapons seized in Mexico that were connected to this one case in Phoenix. Canino explained:

> *"Either late October, early November, mid November, 2009, I was informed about the large number of guns that have made it on to the suspect gun database relating to this investigation [Operation Fast and Furious]. That is when I*

became aware, okay they just opened up this case in October of '09, and I thought, wow, look at all these guns. I thought two things: I thought, okay, all these guns, the reason all these guns are here is because we are finally on to these guys, and we went back and did our due diligence and found out that these guys had already beaten us for 900 guns. That was one of the things I thought."

Canino informed his boss, then ATF Attaché to Mexico, Darren Gil, about an unusual amount of weapons being seized in Mexico. Gil stated:

"I remember the event that my chief analyst and my deputy came in and said, hey, we're getting this abnormal number of weapons that are being seized in Mexico and they're all coming back to the Phoenix field division. So that was my first awareness of this regarding anything to do with this case."

ATF officials in Mexico never received any notice or warning from ATF in Phoenix or Washington, D.C. about the possibility of a spike in guns showing up in their host country. Instead, they began to suspect something was amiss as an inordinate number of weapons recovered in Mexico traced back to the Phoenix Field Division. The weapons were being seized from violent crime scenes involving Mexican drug cartels. One of the early seizures occurred after a shoot-out between warring cartels. Canino described learning about this incident:

Q. When was the next time that you got some information about Operation Fast and Furious after October, 2009?
A. I need to go back and check, but I was approached by an ICE agent at the U.S. embassy, and he showed me some pictures of a shoot up between the Sinaloa cartel and the La Familia cartel in a small town up in the mountains of Sonora. He asked – I saw the picture a lot of dead bodies he told me that the Sinaloa cartel had come into the area to try to push out the La Familia cartel, the La Familia cartel had ambushed the Sinaloans up in the mountains, and literally decimated the group. There was some firearms recovered on

the scene. He asked if we could trace the guns, and we did. When we got the traces back, I believe two or three guns had come back to the case number that is now known as Operation Fast and Furious. I believe I reached out to ATF Group VII special agent Tonya English via e mail and I notified her that some of the firearms in her case had been recovered as a homicide, what were they planning, what were they planning to do, what is going on with this case?

According to Canino, he did not receive any information about the operation's future plans or an explanation for the growing number of weapons being recovered at Mexican crime scenes linked to Operation Fast and Furious.5 However, these seizures were only the beginning. Over the next several months, an alarming number of weapons would be seized in Mexico and traced to Phoenix.

Fast and Furious Weapons Recovered at Crime Scenes

- FINDING: As Operation Fast and Furious progressed, there were numerous recoveries of large weapons caches in Mexico. These heavy-duty weapons included AK-47s, AR-15s, and even Barrett .50 caliber rifles – the preferred weapons of drug cartels. The following chart represents a list of recoveries in Mexico where weapons found were traced back to Operation Fast and Furious. Despite its length, this list is not complete. Rather, this list is compiled solely from information the Justice Department has provided to date. Many more recoveries may have occurred and will continue to occur in the future, but it is impossible to determine precisely how many weapons recoveries in Mexico trace back to Operation Fast and Furious. So far, the Justice Department has provided documents that reference at least 48 separate recoveries involving 122 weapons connected to Operation Fast and Furious.

Recovery #	Date	Location	Notes on Recovery	# of Fast and Furious Guns Recovered
1	11/15/2009	Costa Grande, Guerrero	15 AK-47s, 30 guns, 9 guns traced to Operation Fast and Furious[6]	9
2	11/20/2009	Naco, Sonora	41 AK-47s and 1 50 caliber. "Time-to-crime," the period between the purchase date and the recovery date, of 1 day. Two multiple sales summaries linked to this seizure[7]	42
3	11/26/2009	Agua Prieta, Sonora	15 rifles, 8 pistols, traced to [SP 1][8]	1
4	12/9/2009	Mexicali, Baja	$2 million US, $1 million Mexican, 421 kilos cocaine, 60 kilos meth, 41 AK-47s, 5 traced to Operation Fast and Furious[9]	5
5	12/18/2009	Tijuana, Baja	"El Teo" link, 5 AK-47 type rifles recovered and 1 linked to [SP 2][10]	1
6	12/18/2009	Tijuana, Baja	Traced to weapons bought 11/13/09[11]	1
7	1/8/2010	Tijuana, Baja	"El Teo" link, 2 guns traced to F&F, bought by [SP 2] on 12/13/09 and [SP 1][12]	2
8	1/11/2010	Guasave, Sinaloa	2,700 rounds of ammo, 3 belts of rounds, 9 rifles, 2 grenade launchers, 1 gun traced to Operation Fast and Furious[13]	1

Recovery #	Date	Location	Notes on Recovery	# of Fast and Furious Guns Recovered
9	2/8/2010	La Paz, Baja	4th recovery related to "El Teo" organization[14]	1
10	2/21/2010	Sinaloa, Mexico	15 rifles, 5 handguns, 11,624 rounds of ammunition. At least 4 weapons traced to [SP 1] [15]	4
11	2/25/2010	Tijuana, Baja	"El Teo" link, attempted State Police Chief assassination, guns traced to [SP 4] [16]	1
12	3/14/2010	Juarez, Chihuahua	5 weapons traced back to Operation Fast and Furious purchased by [SP 2], [SP 3], and [SP 2][17]	5
13	6/15/2010	Acapulco, Guerrero	6 rifles, 1,377 rounds of ammo, 1 traced back to Operation Fast and Furious[18]	1
14	6/24/2010	Tijuana, Baja	6 AK-47 type firearms, 5 traced back to [SP 2][19]	5
15	7/1/2010	Tubutama, Sonora	DTO battle, 15 firearms seized, 12 rifles, 3 pistols, 1 traced to Operation Fast Furious[20]	1
16	7/4/2010	Navajoa, Sonora	25 AK-47 rifles, 78 magazines, over 8,000 rounds of ammo, 1 AK-47 traced to [SP 1] 3/2/10 purchase[21]	1
17	7/8/2010	Culiacan, Sinaloa	Grenade launcher, 2 submachine guns, 8 rifles, 3 shotguns, 1,278	1

Recovery #	Date	Location	Notes on Recovery	# of Fast and Furious Guns Recovered
			rounds of ammo, 1 rifle traced to Operation Fast and Furious[22]	
18	7/21/2010	El Roble, Durango	5 handguns, 15 rifles, 70 armored vests, night vision goggles, 1 traced to [SP 1] 3/22/10 purchase[23]	1
19	7/27/2010	Durango, Durango	Barrett 50 caliber traced to [SP 1] purchase on 3/22/10[24]	1
20	8/1/2010	Chihuahua, Chihuahua	Romarm 762s traced to 12/17/09 purchase[25]	1
21	8/1/2010	Sinaloa de Leyva, Sinaloa	Barrett 50 caliber traced to Operation Fast and Furious, bought 6/8/10[26]	1
22	8/11/2010	Santiago, Durango	16 rifles, 110 magazines, 36 bullet-proof vests, 1 rifle traced to Operation Fast and Furious[27]	1
23	8/13/2010	Santiago Papasquiaro, Durango	Romarm/Cugir 762 traced to Operation Fast and Furious[28]	1
24	8/14/2010	El Naranjo, Sinaloa	16 firearms including Barrett 50 caliber, 69 magazines, 2,060 rounds of ammo, 1 weapon traced to Operation Fast and Furious[29]	1
25	8/24/2010	Nogales, Sonora	Romarm/Cugir 762 traced to Operation Fast and Furious, bought 12/14/09[30]	1
26	9/8/2010	San Luis, Sonora	Romarm/Cugir 762 traced to Operation Fast and Furious, bought 12/14/09[31]	1

Recovery #	Date	Location	Notes on Recovery	# of Fast and Furious Guns Recovered
27	9/9/2010	Nogales, Sonora	Guns traced to Operation Fast and Furious, bought on 11/27/09[32]	1
28	9/10/2010	Tijuana, Baja	6 firearms recovered, 6 firearms traced to Operation Fast and Furious purchases on 8/6/10 and 8/11/10[33]	6
29	9/14/2010	Nogales, Sonora	Romarm/Cugir 762 traced to Operation Fast and Furious[34]	1
30	9/18/2010	Colonia Granjas, Chihuahua	Romarm/Cugir 762 traced to Operation Fast and Furious[35]	1
31	9/22/2010	Saric, Sonora	18 AK-47 rifles and 1 Barrett 50 caliber, 1 firearm traced to Operation Fast and Furious[36]	1
32	9/24/2010	Saric, Sonora	Guns bought on 2/16/10 traced to [SP 3] and [SP 1][37]	1
33	9/26/2010	Reynosa, Tamaulipas	Traced guns to Operation Fast and Furious bought 3/18/10[38]	1
34	9/28/2010	Juarez, Chihuahua	Romarm/Cugir 762 traced to Operation Fast and Furious, bought 1/7/10[39]	1
35	10/11/2010	Saric, Sonora	Firearm traced to 11/17/09 purchase[40]	1
36	10/12/2010	Tepic, Nayarit	Barrett 50 caliber traced to Operation Fast and Furious, bought 2/17/10[41]	1

Recovery #	Date	Location	Notes on Recovery	# of Fast and Furious Guns Recovered
37	10/12/2010	Juarez, Chihuahua	Romarm/Cugir 762 traced to Operation Fast and Furious bought 1/7/10[42]	1
38	10/19/2010	Reynosa, Tamaulipas	Romarm/Cugir 762 traced to Operation Fast and Furious[43]	1
39	10/28/2010	Acapulco, Guerrero	Romarm/Cugir 762 traced to Operation Fast and Furious[44]	1
40	11/4/2010	Chihuahua, Chihuahua	16 guns, 2 traced to Operation Fast and Furious, Used in the murder of Mario Gonzalez[45]	1
41	11/22/2010	Nogales, Sonora	Traced to guns bought 11/27/09[46]	1
42	12/14/2010	Puerto Penasco, Sonora	5 guns traced to Operation Fast and Furious, bought 12/11/09, 12/14/09, 6/8/10, and 6/15/10[47]	5
43	12/17/2010	Zumu Rucapio, MC	Traced to Operation Fast and Furious, bought 11/27/09[48]	1
44	12/28/2010	Obregon, Sonora	12 total firearms, 1 firearm traced to Operation Fast and Furious, bought 4/12/10[49]	1
45	1/9/2011	Chihuahua, Chihuahua	6 rifles and magazines seized, 1 firearm traced to Operation Fast and Furious[50]	1
46	1/25/2011	Culiacan, Sinaloa	Romarm/Cugir 762 traced to Operation Fast and Furious, bought 3/8/10[51]	1

Recovery #	Date	Location	Notes on Recovery	# of Fast and Furious Guns Recovered
47	2/4/2011	Juarez, Chihuahua	Barrett 50 caliber traced to Operation Fast and Furious, bought 2/2/10[52]	1
48	2/19/2011	Navajoa, Sonora	37 rifles, 3 grenade launchers, 16,000 rounds of ammo, 1 Firearm traced to Operation Fast and Furious, purchased on 3/8/10[53]	1
			TOTAL	122[54]

These documented recoveries indicate that a significant number of Operation Fast and Furious guns ended up in Mexico. However, there are indications that the numbers could be larger. For example, within 24 hours of the murder of Border Patrol Agent Brian Terry, Special Agent in Charge (SAC) Bill Newell asked for the total number of Operation Fast and Furious firearms recovered to date in Mexico and the U.S.55 Five days later, on December 21, 2010, Newell forwarded the totals to his boss, Deputy Assistant Director William McMahon, indicating that he had the numbers compiled because, "I don't like the perception that we allowed guns to „walk.'"56 According to the tally Newell received on December 16, 2010, approximately 241 firearms had been recovered in Mexico and 350 in the U.S.57 The number reported to Newell as recovered in Mexico as of the day after Agent Terry's death is twice what can be verified through documents produced by the Department of Justice as outlined in the table above.

Furthermore, this number is much higher than the 96 firearms reported by the Department of Justice as recovered in Mexico in answers to questions for the record received on July 22, 2011

More troubling, several of these recoveries highlight the deadly consequences of Operation Fast and Furious.

From: McMahon, William G.
Sent: Tuesday, December 21, 2010 11:21 AM
To: Newell, William D.
Subject: RE: simple numbers on F&F recoveries

10-4 thanks.

William G. McMahon
Deputy Assistant Director (West)
Office of Field Operations

From: Newell, William D.
Sent: Tuesday, December 21, 2010 11:21 AM
To: McMahon, William G.
Subject: Fw: simple numbers on F&F recoveries

For what it's worth and since I don't like the perception that we allowed guns to "walk", I had David Voth pull the numbers of the guns recovered in Mexico as well as those we had a direct role in taking off here in the US. Almost all of the 350 seized in the US were done based on our info and in such a way to not burn the wire or compromise the bigger case. The guns purchased early on in the case we couldn't have stopped mainly because we weren't fully aware of all the players at that time and people buying multiple firearms in Arizona is a very common thing.

***

NOTICE: This electronic transmission is confidential and intended only for the person(s) to whom it is addressed. If you have received this transmission in error, please notify the sender by return e-mail and destroy this message in its entirety (including all attachments).

From: Voth, David J.
To: Newell, William D.
Sent: Thu Dec 16 19:22:42 2010
Subject: simple numbers on F&F recoveries
Sir,

I can make this more grand tomorrow if you wish but right now by my count;

* Firearms recovered in Mexico = 241
* Firearms recovered in the USA = 350

Thanks,

David Voth
Group Supervisor
Phoenix Group VII

A. Tracing the Recoveries

ATF officials in Mexico learned about many of these recoveries through open sourcing, such as articles in local newspapers or internet searches. After learning of these recoveries, however, it was incumbent on ATF employees in Mexico to attempt to view the weapons recovered as soon as possible in order to see if any link existed between the weapon and the United States. Mexican authorities transported the seized weapons to local police stations for processing. Once processed, the authorities turned the weapons over to the Mexican military, which stored them in vaults indefinitely. Once the Mexican military acquired these weapons, they were considered to be for the exclusive use of the military, and viewing them required a court order. It was therefore imperative for ATF agents in Mexico attempt to view the weapons as soon as possible after a recovery.

When ATF agents in Mexico were able to view these recovered weapons, they could also enter the serial numbers of the weapons into an online internal tracing system known as e-Trace. ATF has a procedure for tracing weapons. This initiates a manual tracing process which involves notifying the National Tracing Center (NTC), located in Martinsburg, WV, of the recovery. NTC then identifies the purchaser as well as the date of purchase. The process can take several days. ATF also maintains a Suspect Gun Database (SGD). This database is a list of all the guns purchased that ATF believes might turn up at crime scenes. Since no specific criteria exist for entering a gun into the SGD, it is usually up to the case agent's discretion.

During Operation Fast and Furious, Group VII case agents entered over 1,900 guns into the SGD, usually within days of the purchase. Since these weapons were already in the SGD, the case agent would receive notice the trace request was submitted and the full manual trace process was unnecessary.

Starting in late 2009, ATF officials in Mexico began to notice that many of the weapon recoveries in Mexico traced back to the same Phoenix investigation. ATF personnel in Mexico called the Phoenix Field Division to notify them of what was occurring. The response from Phoenix was that everything was under control and not to worry about the investigation. Because the guns were in the SGD, the case agent in Phoenix received notice of trace requests.

The case agent could limit the information that other ATF officials would receive to merely a notice that the trace results were "delayed," which effectively kept ATF personnel in Mexico out of the loop.

For example, in June 2010, Hope MacAllister, the Operation Fast and Furious case agent asked an NTC employee to postpone the completion of several traces for guns recovered in Mexico. With the subject line "RE: Suspect Gun Notification – DO NOT Trace ?," the employee writes, "Good morning, as case agent you advised ,do not trace', [t]race will be held pending upon your instructions."60 In her response, MacAllister asks, "Can we postpone completing that trace as well? Thanks!"61 These holds prevented ATF personnel in Mexico from discovering the origin of the recovered guns.

To make matters worse, ATF officials in Mexico did not even know that their fellow agents were shutting them out of the investigation. With reassurances from ATF Phoenix and ATF Headquarters in Washington D.C. that things were under control, ATF officials in Mexico remained unaware that ATF was implementing a strategy of allowing straw purchasers to continue to transfer firearms to traffickers. Even though large recoveries were taking place in

Mexico, with the awareness of senior ATF officials in both Phoenix and Washington D.C, ATF officials in Mexico did not have the full picture. What they were able to piece together based on several large weapons seizures made them extremely nervous.

B. The Naco, Mexico Recovery

The first large recovery of weapons in Mexico linked to Operation Fast and Furious occurred on November 20, 2009, in Naco, Sonora – located on the U.S./Mexico border. All of the 42 weapons recovered in Naco traced back to Operation Fast and Furious straw purchasers.

Forty-one of these weapons were AK-47 rifles and one was a Beowulf .50 caliber rifle. Twenty of the weapons in this recovery were reported on multiple sales summaries by ATF, and these weapons had a "time-to-crime" of just one day.62 Within a span of 24 hours, a straw purchaser bought guns at a gun store in Arizona and facilitated their transport to Naco, Mexico with the intent of delivering the guns to the Sinaloa cartel. Mexican authorities arrested the person transporting these weapons, a 21-year old female. Mexican authorities interviewed her along with her brother, who was also in the vehicle.

According to an official in ATF's Office of Strategic Information and Intelligence (OSII), the female suspect told law enforcement that she intended to transport the weapons straight to the Sinaloa cartel.63 From the very first recovery of weapons ATF officials knew that drug trafficking organizations (DTOs) were using these straw purchasers.

C. The Mexicali Recovery

Nearly three weeks after the Naco recovery, an even bigger weapons seizure occurred in Mexicali, the capital of the state of Baja California, located near the border. The seizure included the following weapons:

- 41 AK-47 rifles
- 1 AR-15 rifle
- 1 FN 5.7

In addition, Mexican authorities seized the following items:

- 421 kilograms of cocaine
- 60 kilograms of methamphetamine
- 392 rounds of ammunition
- $2 million U.S. dollars
- $1 million Mexican pesos

Of the twelve suspects detained, all were from the state of Sinaloa.64 Several were identified members of the Sinaloa cartel.65 The guns recovered at the scene traced back to straw purchasers being monitored under ATFs Operation Fast and Furious.66 With a second large recovery tracing to the same case in Phoenix in less than three weeks, there was little doubt to ATF officials monitoring Operation Fast and Furious what was happening. As one ATF Special Agent wrote to Fast and Furious Case Agent Hope MacAllister, "[the head of the Sinaloa cartel] is arming for a war."

D. The El Paso, Texas Recovery

On January 13, 2010, the ATF Dallas Field Division seized 40 rifles traced to Operation Fast and Furious suspect [SP 2].68 This seizure connected Operation Fast and Furious suspects with a specific high-level "plaza boss" in the Sinaloa DTO.69 Additionally, this seizure may have represented a shift in the movement of Operation Fast and Furious weapons in order to provide the necessary firearms for the Sinaloa Cartel's battle for control of the Juarez drug smuggling corridor.

This possible shift of Operation Fast and Furious weapons may have been a result of the death of Arturo Beltrán-Leyva in December 2009. Mexican authorities killed Beltrán-Leyva, the leader of the Beltrán-Leyva DTO, effectively crippling his family's DTO. The resulting decreased competition in Sonora between the Sinaloa DTO and the Beltrán-Leyva DTO may have contributed to the shift in Operation Fast and Furious weapons transported to Juarez. The map below, created by the Drug Enforcement Administration (DEA), reflects the areas of DTO influence in Mexico:

AREAS OF CARTEL INFLUENCES IN MEXICO

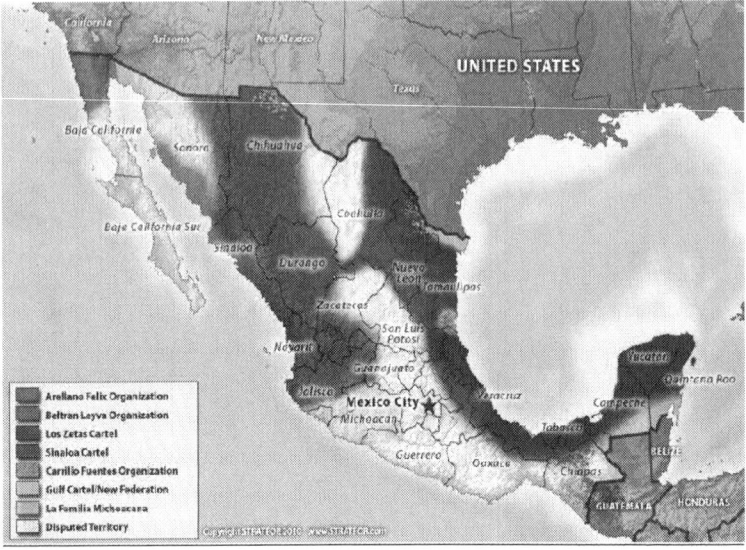

E. Tuesday Briefings at ATF Headquarters

These weapons recoveries did not occur in a vacuum. Upon learning of the recoveries, analysts in ATF's Office of Strategic Information and Intelligence (OSII) in Washington, D.C. attempted to piece together fragments of information to report up the chain of command.

According to ATF personnel, every Tuesday morning OSII holds a briefing for the field operations staff to share and discuss information about ongoing ATF cases.73 Typically, the four Deputy Assistant Directors for Field Operations attend. Additionally, Mark Chait, the Assistant Director for Field Operations, often attends. Occasionally, Deputy Director William Hoover and Acting Director Kenneth Melson attend these briefings. OSII first briefed on Operation Fast and Furious on Tuesday December 8, 2009, including the Naco recovery. The following week, OSII briefed the Mexicali recovery.

Subsequent briefings covered other recoveries that had occurred in the United States. The magnitude of the Operation Fast and Furious investigation quickly became apparent to senior ATF officials.

F. January 5, 2010 Briefing

Assistant Director Mark Chait, Deputy Assistant Director Bill McMahon, International Affairs Chief Daniel Kumor, Southwest Border Czar Ray Rowley, and Assistant Director James McDermond all attended the January 5, 2010, field-ops briefing led by Intelligence Operations Specialist Lorren Leadmon.74 At this briefing, the participants expressed concerns about Operation Fast and Furious. Though the briefing included the normal updates of weapons seizures linked to Operation Fast and Furious provided every Tuesday, the January 5, 2010, briefing also included a key addition.

OSII had compiled a summary of all of the weapons that could be linked to known straw purchasers under Operation Fast and Furious to date and presented this information to the group.

The total number of guns purchased in just two months was 685.75 Steve Martin, an ATF Deputy Assistant Director for OSII, took extensive notes during the briefing. Examining the locations where the weapons ended up in Mexico, he outlined potential investigative steps that could be taken to address the problem.

Due to the sheer volume of weapons that had already moved south to Mexico, he had a hunch that guns were being walked:

> A. So I made – they were talking about – I had [SP 1] in there, I had [SP 2] who were major purchasers. And I had numbers by them about how many guns they had purchased from the PowerPoint. I had a little picture drawn, with Phoenix at the top and then guns going two ways, one down to Naco and then over to Mexicali.
> Q. Uh huh.

A. And that was because we said . . . it's the same distance to go from Phoenix to these two places. So they don't all have to go to here to arm the Sinaloa Cartel; they can go over to Mexicali and bring them that way-same distance. So that's one thing I wrote as I was being briefed. I also wrote down guns, I think, guns walking into Mexico. Because that's just, kind of, what's going through my head. And I had, if yes into Mexico, then some things to do; if no into Mexico, things to do. Then I put a list of a whole list of stuff that you could do investigative wise: interview straw purchasers, put trackers on the guns, put pole cams up, mobile surveillance, aerial surveillance, a number of stuff.

Hoping to draw from his experience as a former Assistant Special Agent in Charge (ASAC) and Special Agent in Charge (SAC), Martin wanted to offer suggestions on a plan for the case – specifically, how to track weapons, conduct surveillance, and eventually bring Operation Fast and Furious to a close. Those in field operations – the chain of command responsible for overseeing and implementing Operation Fast and Furious – responded to his suggestions with complete silence. ATF personnel within field operations felt free to ignore OSII's suggestions and complaints because OSII's role was to support field operations:

A. From my notes, I asked Mr. Chait and Mr. McMahon, I said, what's your plan? I said, what's your plan? And I said, hearing none, and I don't know if they had one. I said . . . there are some things that we can do. Ray Rowley, who was the southwest border czar at the time, asked, how long are you going to let this go on?
Q. This is in January 2010?
A. January 5th, that meeting, that's correct. Ray has since retired. So I said, well, here are some things that . . . we might think of doing. And we had talked about this before, we'd brainstormed stuff, too, with Lorren. Lorren even talked about it. Kevin talked about it. Kevin O'Keefe had done a lot of trafficking investigations in south Florida – about identifying some weak straw purchasers, let's see who

the weak links are, maybe the super young ones, the super old ones. Pole cameras . . . put them up to see who is coming and going, to help you with surveillance. The aerial surveillance, the mobile surveillance, trackers. I said . . one of the first things I would do is think about putting trackers, to help me keep track of where they're going. And I said, as far as going into Mexico, I said, have we thought about putting trackers on them and let them - - follow them into Mexico? Dan Kumor said, the Ambassador would never go for that. I said, okay, fine. I said, I'm not going to pursue that anymore, assuming that. Had we thought about putting trackers on them and following them down to see where they're going across, to see where they go, who they're in contact with, and where they cross the border, we might find out something new and then . . . interdict. And I got no response. And I wasn't asking for one. I was just . . . throwing this stuff out.

Q. You said this to who again, Mr. Chait?

A. Mr. Chait, Mr. McMahon, Mr. Kumor. My boss was there, Jim McDermond, who agreed with me because we talked probably daily.

Q. Did any of those folks step up at that time and say, "Oh, no, no, no. We've got another great plan in place"?

A. No. No.

Q. They were silent?

A. Yes. And I don't know if they had one. I mean, they could have. I don't know.

Q. Do you remember if they were nodding their head, giving you any nonverbal cues that . . . this sounds like a bright idea that you're suggesting?

A. Not that I recall, no.

Q. Or was it just like a blank look on their face?

A. Just listening.

Whether Mr. Chait or Mr. McMahon had a plan for Operation Fast and Furious is unclear. What is clear is that they did not take kindly to suggestions from OSII about the operation. They were not inclined to discuss the operation at all, choosing instead to excuse themselves from the conversation:

> A. Somewhere during the meeting, Mr. Chait said that he had to go to another meeting, and he left. Mr. McMahon said that he had to go check some E-mails in a classified system, and he left. And then it was just the rest of us talking.
>
> Q. Do you feel that the other meeting, checking the E-mails on a classified system, was that an indication to you that they just didn't want to talk about this topic?
>
> A. You know, I'm not going to go into their brain on that one.
>
> Q. Okay. Well . . . sitting in a room with them, was that your perception?
>
> A. Well, I would like – it would have been nice to have some interaction. . . .
>
> Q. So it was a one-way conversation of suggestions from you, from Mr. McDermond, to how to effectively limit –
>
> A. Pretty much from me and the others to the field officers.

G. March 5, 2010 Briefing

FINDING: At a March 5, 2010 briefing, ATF intelligence analysts told ATF and DOJ leadership that the number of firearms bought by known straw purchasers had exceeded the 1,000 mark. The briefing also made clear these weapons were ending up in Mexico.

Two months after the January 5, 2010 briefing, ATF headquarters hosted a larger, more detailed briefing on Operation Fast and Furious. Not part of the normal Tuesday field ops briefings, this special briefing only covered Operation Fast and Furious. David Voth, the Phoenix Group VII Supervisor who oversaw Operation Fast and Furious, traveled from Phoenix to give the presentation. On videoconference were the four southwest border ATF SACs: Bill Newell in Phoenix, Robert Champion in Dallas, J. Dewey Webb in Houston, and John Torres in Los Angeles.

In addition to the usual attendees of the Tuesday morning field ops briefings (the Deputy Assistant Directors for Field Operations, including Bill McMahon, and Mark Chait, Assistant Director for Field Operations), Deputy Director William Hoover also attended. Joe Cooley, a trial attorney from the gang unit at Main Justice, also joined. After a suggestion from Acting ATF Director Ken Melson in December 2009, Assistant Attorney General Lanny Breuer personally assigned Cooley as a DOJ representative for Operation Fast and Furious. Kevin Carwile, chief of the Capital Case Unit at Main Justice, may have also been present. According to Steve Martin, the inclusion of Main Justice representatives was unusual. An extremely detailed synopsis of the current details of the investigation ensued, including the number of guns purchased, specific details of all Operation Fast and Furious weapons seizures to date, money spent by straw purchasers, and organizational charts of the straw purchasers and their relationship not only to each other, but also to members of the Sinaloa DTO. At that point, there had been 15 related weapons seizures over a four to five month period.

Total Costs of Firearms Purchased as of February 27, 2010			
Name	Gun Purchases	Invoice Total	Notes
	$8,189.50	$8,880.81	
	11,984.00	13,002.64	
			Need Receipts
	2,589.60	3,125.57	
	36,959.75	38,823.33	
	36,541.75	39,663.33	
	3,199.60	3,466.77	
	6,487.00	7,038.39	
	3,999.50	4,333.46	
	22,719.80	23,781.91	
			Need Receipts
	8,789.50	9,530.91	
	849.98	849.98	
	4,494.75	4,873.80	
	100.00	100.00	
	7,445.97	7,731.27	
	59,663.40	64,929.98	
	1,999.75	2,166.73	
	1,999.80	2,158.78	
	204,110.59	213,756.87	
	3,992.00	4,331.32	
	1,799.00	1,951.92	
			Need Receipts
	134,638.84	140,034.36	
	19,963.75	21,657.66	
	7,984.00	8,662.63	
	24,892.25	24,892.25	Ammunition
TOTAL PURCHASES	$615,394.08	$649,745.32	

The next set of slides at the briefing detailed the fifteen recoveries of weapons that had already taken place during Operation Fast and Furious [sic]. Following a map indicating the locations in both the United States and Mexico of these recoveries were detailed slides for each recovery, including the number of guns recovered, the purchaser, the transporter, and the intended recipient in the Sinaloa cartel.

Two of the first slides in the March 5, 2010 presentation detailed the number of weapons bought as of February 27, 2010 -1,026 -

and the amount of money spent, in cash, to purchase these weapons - nearly $650,000:

Total Firearms Purchased as of February 27, 2010	
Name	**Total of Firearms**
███	313
███	241
███	116
███	68
███	55
███	30
███	25
███	22
███	20
███	20
███	18
███	17
███	13
███	10
███	10
███	8
███	8
███	8
███	5
███	5
███	3
███	2
███	1
███	1
███	1
███	1
███	1
███	1
███	1
███	1
███	1
TOTAL	**1026**

For example, the slide pertaining to the Mexicali seizure indicated that the 12 detained suspects were all from Sinaloa, Mexico, "Confirmed Sinaloa cartel."83 The slide also catalogs the full recovery: "41 AK-47s, 1 AR-15 rifle, 1 FN 5.7 pistol, 421 kilograms of cocaine, 60 kilograms of meth, 392 miscellaneous rounds of ammunition, $2 million U.S., and $1 million Mexican pesos."84 In addition, the slide graphically depicts the relationships between the straw purchasers and the weapons seized. And finally, the slide on the El Paso recovery links Operation Fast and Furious to a Texas investigation and to the "plaza boss" in the Sinaloa cartel that Fast and Furious ultimately targeted.

Given the rich detail in the presentation, it is clear that the guns bought during Operation Fast and Furious were headed to the Sinaloa cartel. As Martin testified:

> Q. The guns are up to 1,026 at this point?
> A. That's correct.
> Q. I know you had expressed some complaints earlier when it was only at 685. So there's no doubt after this briefing that the guns in this case were being linked with the Sinaloa cartel, based on the -
> A. Based on the information presented, I'd say yes.
> Q. And that was presumably very apparent to everybody in the room?
> A. Based on this one, it says the people are connected with the Sinaloa cartel, I would say that's correct. The volume of guns purchased and the short time-to-crime for many of these guns clearly signaled that the Sinaloa cartel received the guns shortly after their purchase in Arizona. If ATF had attempted to interdict the weapons, it is likely that hundreds of these weapons would not have ended up with this dangerous cartel or entered Mexico.87 Martin agreed that was clear:
> Q. But whether the guns were walking, whether they were flying, whether they just disappeared, based on all the evidence that

you've collected to this point, it was pretty clear that the guns were going almost linearly from the FFLs to the DTOs? A. They were headed that way.

Several individuals, such as Ray Rowley and those in OSII, had already expressed their concerns, only to have them fall on deaf ears. Others, however, remained silent, despite the ominous consequences:

Q. Was there any concern ever expressed about the guns being....essentially just bee lined right to the drug trafficking organizations about what the DTOs might actually do with the guns?

A. I think it was common knowledge that they were going down there to be crime guns to use in the battle against the DTOs to shoot each other.

Q. So these guns, in a way, are murder weapons? A. Potentially.

The only person that did speak up during the March 5, 2010 presentation was Robert Champion, SAC for the Dallas Field Division participating by videoconference, who asked "What are we doing about this?"90 According to Lorren Leadmon, in response, Joe Cooley from Main Justice simply said that the movement of so many guns to Mexico was "an acceptable practice."

Shortly after the March 5, 2010 presentation on Operation Fast and Furious, OSII stopped giving briefings on the program to ATF management during the weekly Tuesday meetings. OSII personnel felt that nobody in field operations heeded their warnings, and OSII no longer saw the point of continuing to brief the program.

V. Kept in the Dark

FINDING: ATF and DOJ leadership kept their own personnel in Mexico and Mexican government officials totally in the dark about all aspects of Fast and Furious. Meanwhile, ATF officials in Mexico grew increasingly worried about the number of weapons recovered in Mexico that traced back to an ongoing investigation out of ATF's Phoenix Field Division.

Not surprisingly, ATF officials in Mexico grew increasingly alarmed about the growing number of weapons showing up in Mexico that traced back to the Phoenix Field Division. Yet, when they raised those concerns, ATF senior leadership both in Phoenix and Washington, D.C. reassured them that the Phoenix investigation was under control. No one informed them about the details of Operation Fast and Furious. No one informed them that ATF was knowingly allowing guns to be sold to straw buyers and then transferred into Mexico.

> *A. Volume of Weapons Raises Eyebrows in Mexico*
> *ATF leadership in Mexico started noticing an "abnormal" number of weapons flowing from Phoenix into Mexico as early as the end of 2009. Former ATF Attaché Darren Gil explained:*
> *Q. Now, at some point you mentioned that in late 2009, early 2010, your analysts made you aware of an increase in the number of recoveries, firearm recoveries being traced back to Phoenix; is that right?*
> *A. Correct.*
> *Q. And I think the word you used was abnormal. Can you explain for us what exactly -- what was normal?*
> *A. Normal was – there's, I want to say there's at least 1,000 FFLs along the border. And . . . some people use the trail of ants terminology, some people use the river of iron terminology, but generally you'll get a handful of traces to this FFL, handful of traces to this FFL, Federal Firearms Licensee, all along the border.*

> ** * **

> *I asked my analyst, because I was fairly new. I said, why is this abnormal. He says, look, Darren, we have all these trace results and they come from a variety of FFLs, but then you have a high correlation here with this one particular investigation coming out of Phoenix where we're getting this way and above the number of recoveries we get from all*

these other Federal Firearms Licensees. So it stuck out to my analyst who presented that to me that it was an abnormal, his terminology actually, abnormal number of recoveries.

The "abnormal number of recoveries" concerned Gil and his agents in Mexico. Gil sought answers:

Q. And when your analyst made you aware of this uptick, what was the next step that you took?

A. Pretty much a review, show me what you're talking about, which he did. And then the phone call to Phoenix. And then after the phone call to Phoenix, which I spoke of, throughout the rest of the time it was primarily dealing with ATF headquarters, primarily with the chief of international affairs, Dan [Kumor].

B. Reassurances from Phoenix and Washington, D.C.

Attaché Gil initially reached out directly to the Phoenix Field Division to express his concerns about the growing number of weapons. Gil explained:

Q. So when your staff in Mexico determined that a particular weapon was tracked back to Phoenix, did they try or did you try to make contact with some of the ATF staff in the Phoenix field office?

A. I did. I called the division, tried to make contact with the SAC. I don't believe I spoke with the SAC, but I got a returned call and spoke with the ASAC there, George [Gillett]. I identified my concerns, hey, we're getting an abnormal number of traces. From what I recall his response was, yes, we're aware of it. We have an ongoing investigation. We have a ton of resources on it. We're looking at it. We're working at it, and thanks for calling and making us aware and then we'll follow it up from there. Yet the seizures continued unabated, and the answers Gil received failed to better explain the underlying cause. Gil continued:

Q. So your discussions with Mr. [Gillett] in early January, is it fair to say you weren't satisfied with the results of that call?

A. I was satisfied with the first response, sure. They're working a case, they're trying to identify what the problem is, how these weapons are getting there, they're aware of it.

That's a normal response, okay, good, we're on the job. But . . . unfortunately, my chief analyst and my deputy would come back and say, Darren, these are – we're getting more and more and more of these seizures. And I would make inquiries with the Phoenix field division and I wasn't getting any responses back. And I may have gotten two more phone calls, yeah, we're working on it, we're working on it.

Despite these reassurances, the volume of weapons flowing from Phoenix into Mexico continued to grow. Further, no one at ATF provided Gil or his staff any explanation as to why the volume continued to grow. When Gil and his staff tried to access the trace data on their E-Trace system to find out for themselves, they learned they did not have access. As Gil explained:

And at that point, with the number of seizures we were receiving in Mexico, that wasn't – that connected to the fact that my analyst didn't have access to the trace data in E-Trace, where we entered the data, normally we . . . would get that information back regarding the trace.

Unfortunately, my . . . deputy advised me that we were entering the data but we weren't getting the trace results back, all we were getting was "trace information delayed". And what that generally means is, there's been a hold placed on it by either the tracing center or by a field division because they didn't want that information released for some particular reason.

Members of Phoenix Field Division Group VII, including its case agent with support from the Group supervisor, actively shut out their colleagues in Mexico. As a result, Attaché Gil decided to seek answers from senior leadership in Washington, D.C.: "Ultimately I made phone calls to the chief of international affairs, Dan [Kumor], to try and get responses because I wasn't getting responses from Phoenix like I thought I should."97 In early 2010, Attaché Gil shared his concerns with Kumor about the increasing number of gun recoveries in Mexico linked to Phoenix:

Q. At some point I understand you had some conversations with your boss back in Washington, Mr. [Kumor]. Was he the first person in Washington that you spoke to about the abnormal number of weapons that you were recovering?
A. Yes.

Q. And do you remember when the first time you raised this issue with Mr. [Kumor] was?
A. Again, it would be early 2010, probably around – probably January, about the same time. We talked almost certainly weekly and almost daily basis, so he would have been notified at that time.

Q. And do you remember what his reaction was when you first raised the issue with him?
A. Certainly, yeah, okay, let me check on it, it's an ongoing investigation, let me make some inquiries and I'll get back with you.

Q. And did he ever get back with you?
A. Yes.

Q. And what did he say?
A. Again, he said an on-going investigation, they're looking at straw purchasers, they have cooperative Federal Firearms Licensees and it sounds like a significant investigation. And . . . he didn't have access to the trace information either but . . . the Phoenix field division is aware of the investigation. The chain up to him is aware of the investigation, so everybody is aware of it and it looks like they have it under control.

Gil found it insufficient to hear the investigation was "under control." In the meantime, guns from a known straw purchasing ring continued to flow into Mexico from Arizona. Although Gil and his agents in Mexico remained in the dark about the tactics and strategy of Operation Fast and Furious, they realized something was wrong. Gil continued to express his concerns:

Q. And did you ever raise any issues with Mr. [Kumor] that while they . . . may think they have it under control, it may not be under control because we are recovering an abnormal number of firearms?

A. Again, spring time it got to the point of at what point are we going to . . . to close this investigation down? I mean, after 500 or so seizures I think you should have had enough data collection on what you're trying to show or prove. It was my position, it was Chief [Kumor's] position as well. He says, yeah, you're right. And he goes, so when are they going to close this down. And we were both on the same position there that this thing needed to be shut down. So there was a number of ongoing – you saw my CBS interview, screaming matches . . . it was a very frustrated – high frustration level. And that was one of the reasons for...being frustrated.

Understandably, Gil was frustrated. Hundreds of weapons appeared suddenly in Mexico – traced to Phoenix – without explanation. Gil and his agents struggled to get answers from their own agency. Although ATF officials in Phoenix and Washington, D.C. acknowledged that an investigation was underway, they refused to share the details of the strategy and operation with the agents in Mexico. Gil took their silence as suggesting that his colleagues did not trust him to keep the information confidential:

Q. Did you have any idea why you weren't being made aware of the specific details of this investigation?

A. I can tell you what I was told and they were afraid that I was going to either brief the ambassador on it or brief the Government of Mexico officials on it.

Q. And it was your understanding that individuals within ATF higher than Chief [Kumor] didn't want the ambassador to know about the investigations?

A. I couldn't say that . . . specifically they didn't want the ambassador to know. I know I asked...why can't I be briefed on this. Well, they're afraid that you would brief the GOM officials, Government of Mexico officials or . . . brief the ambassador. They were just worried about somebody leaking whatever was unique about this investigation.

VI. More Complaints and More Reassurances

ATF officials in Mexico constantly worried about the number of guns flowing from Phoenix to Mexico in connection with the

Phoenix Field Division's investigation. Mexican authorizes continued to seize guns at violent crime scenes involving Mexican DTOs. Without being privy to the particular tactics utilized by Operation Fast and Furious, ATF's representatives in Mexico suspected something was terribly amiss. Because initial contacts with Phoenix provided few answers, ATF officials in Mexico continued to report their concerns up the chain of command to ATF leadership in Washington, D.C. Instead of acting on their complaints, senior leadership at both ATF and the Department of Justice praised the investigation. However, ATF agents in Mexico kept sounding the alarm. In July 2010, Gil and his agents received notification that the Phoenix Field Division's investigation would be ending and shut down.101 In reality, ATF agents in Phoenix closed the investigative stage of Operation Fast and Furious in January 2011, only after the tragic death of Border Patrol Agent Brian Terry in December 2010.

A. Concerns Raised up the Chain of Command

- FINDING: ATF officials in Mexico raised their concerns about the number of weapons recovered up the chain of command to ATF leadership in Washington, D.C. Instead of acting decisively to end Fast and Furious, the senior leadership at both ATF and DOJ praised the investigation and the positive results it had produced. Frustrations reached a boiling point, leading former ATF Attaché Darren Gil to engage in screaming matches with his supervisor, International Affairs Chief Daniel Kumor, about the need to shut down the Phoenix-based investigation.

Without knowing of possible gunwalking tactics used in Operation Fast and Furious, Gil and other ATF officials in Mexico knew the investigation needed to be shut down based on the empirical data. As Gil testified:

Q. And the number of firearms recovered in Mexico, you said it was about 500 in the spring, did that number continue to rise?

A. Yes, it did. I want to say by the time I left I think it was up to, which was in October, I think it was up to – the last data I think I was quoted was like 700 or so.

Q. And that continued to alarm you?

A. It was a topic of discussion every time – pretty much every time we spoke about when this thing was going to be shut down. And the general – the origin of it was, again, because it worried my folks. My chief analyst, who would see the data every day. He'd put in the trace results, he'd get information back, data – "trace results not available", which means ATF put a hold on it somewhere.

So number one, we were submitting our information and we weren't getting our own trace data back, so that was an issue. The number was an issue. The fact that these guns were found in crime scenes, which we could not notify the GOM, the Government of Mexico, was an issue.

The fact that this brought pressure on us from the GOM because they're saying, why are we using – we're spending – ATF is spending extraordinary number of resources to train them on the Spanish E-Trace. And in the same breath they're saying, look, we're not getting anything back so why should we use this Spanish E-Trace, it's a waste of our time. And we have to say, no, it gives you this, this, and this. And they go, yeah, but we're not getting anything back.

So it became a big event that we're not getting this trace data back and it frustrated my folks, they in turn notified me. And we had meetings on it and then I'd make my calls to headquarters, again, primarily Chief [Kumor], and voiced our concerns. And it got to the point I would have my staff, on conference calls that we have, speak with Chief [Kumor] trying to – what the heck is going on here.

Gil and his staff struggled to deal with this growing crisis. Despite the increasing number of guns from Phoenix showing up at violent crime scenes in Mexico, ATF agents in Phoenix continually denied the ATF agents in Mexico the relevant information explaining this spike. Gil was so passionate about his and his staff's concerns that he had yelling matches with his boss:

> Q. Who were those screaming matches with?
> A. Primarily with Chief [Kumor]. And it wasn't just on this, all right, keep that in mind.... However, this was also part of it and at some point screaming, yelling . . . hey, when are they going to shut this, to put it bluntly, damn investigation down, we're getting hurt down here.
> When, again, I think I mentioned in my CBS interview, when the Mexicans find out about this. And this was not even knowing of the potential for gun walking. This was just . . . not shutting this investigation down and letting another 300 weapons come into the country after the first 300 weapons. Because, again, it's inconceivable to me to even allow weapons to knowingly cross an international border.

* * *

> Q. So it was clear to you that this ongoing case based out of Phoenix was proceeding, they weren't shutting it down, you disagreed with that because you saw too many weapons showing up in Mexico?
> A. That's a fair assessment.
> Deputy Attaché Canino shared Gil's concerns about the number of guns entering Mexico and that something needed to be done:
> Q. What discussions did you have about the weapons from the Phoenix case in Mexico with Mr. Gil, Mr. Darren Gil?
> A. We were very concerned . . . with that amount of guns and short period of time on a suspect gun data and they kept climbing.

* * *

> I said, Darren, this is a problem . . . these many guns coming down here is a problem. We made that known to Danny Kumor . . . Danny was in agreement he pushed it up the

chain and we were told yeah it is a case out of Phoenix and it is going great.

Gil and Canino prevailed upon their direct supervisor, Daniel Kumor, ATF's Chief of International Affairs, to take their concerns about the volume of weapons in Mexico up the chain of command:

Q. When you say pushed it up the chain, what do you mean exactly?

A. He told his superior.

Q. That would have been who?

A. That would have been deputy assistant director Bill McMahon.

Gil also testified that Kumor spoke to his superior, Deputy Assistant Director McMahon, about this matter:

Q. And do you know if [Kumor] had any conversations with Mr. [McMahon], did he ever relate to you that he's had these conversations with Mr. [McMahon]?

A. Sure. He would say, I'll – I'm going to go meet with . . . Bill [McMahon], the deputy assistant director. And he would – and then in our conversations he would respond and, hey, I've spoken with Bill and he's going to send notification out or contact Phoenix and see what's going on, sure.

Gil also discussed his concerns with McMahon during trips to Washington:

Q. Did you take any trips to Washington during this time period of –

A. Sure.

Q. - January 2010 to before you left October 2010?

A. Yes.

* * *

Q. You said, might have discussed it with Mr. [McMahon]. If you did, it wasn't something that you remember in detail?

A. Yeah, would have been, hey . . . . is this thing still going on, and when is it going to be shut down. And something to the effect they're either working on it – again, their general response was they're working on it, they're going to close it down as soon as they can, and we'll let you know.

While Phoenix was "working on it," guns continued to flow unabated into Mexico. Gil, Canino, and other ATF agents in Mexico raised legitimate concerns, but leadership told them to stand down. According to ATF leadership, not only was everything "under control," but everyone in ATF and DOJ were well aware of the investigation in Phoenix:

> *Q. And at any point during those conversations was it made clear to you that the director is aware of this program?*
> *A. Yes. At one point, I mean, again, probably during one of the final screaming matches was . . . I think I threw the question out there, hey, is DOJ aware of this investigation? Are they aware of what's going on, and are they approving this. And then the chief's response was, yes, not only is . . . the director aware of it, Billy, William Hoover is aware of it, DOJ is aware of it. And then . . . through that fact – they have a Title 3, so DOJ must be aware of it certainly for that aspect. And certainly the US Attorney's office in Phoenix is aware of it because they had to approve the investigation. But – so it wasn't just is the direct link aware of it . . . if the acting director is aware you assume everybody is aware of it. And then, okay, they don't want me to know something for some reason that's fine, they have their reasons and . . . you got to defer to your executive staff.*

Senior leadership in Phoenix and Washington, D.C. continued to provide reassurances without answers during their visits to Mexico. Canino recalled several visits by both Mark Chait and Bill McMahon:

> *Q. Did senior officials from DOJ and ATF visit Mexico with regard to*
> *this case?*
> *A. This case specifically?*
> *Q. Did they make any visits to Mexico?*
> *A. Sure, yeah. Mmh hmm.*

Q. Would this case have been one of the things that got discussed during their visits?

A. We talked about it, but we said . . . hey what is going on with this case out of Phoenix, we are starting to see a lot of guns in the suspect gun database, kind of alarming, so many guns. They said hey . . . we've got it handled, we are working, it is a good case out of Phoenix.

Q. Who would those officials have been?

A. Well, the director had come down, the deputy director had come down, the deputy associate director had come down.

Q. Who is that?

A. Bill McMahon. This assistant director for field operations, that is the guy who is in charge of all agents.

Q. Mark Chait?

A. Mark Chait came down. Bill Newell came down. So, yeah these guys have come down.

Q. Multiple visits?

A. Yeah. Some of them, multi visits and they talked, hey, yeah, we got a big case out of Phoenix.

As Gil later stated, "[a]t that point . . . you just got to say, fine, these guys, they're the leaders of this agency and they have some plan that I'm not aware of, but hopefully they have a good one."

B. A "Good Investigation"

The Phoenix Field Division and ATF headquarters extolled the virtues of the investigation to ATF personnel in Mexico. For example, during Acting ATF Director Kenneth Melson's 2010 spring visit, Gil's staff asked about the Phoenix case. Gil detailed Acting Director Melson's response:

Q. And do you recall what Mr. Melson said?

A. Generally his response was, he's aware of it, it's an ongoing investigation, it's providing some good intelligence . . . [A]ll positive as far as the investigation, it looks good. And I remember, I think Deputy Director Hoover was there. I think he turned to the deputy director and said, yeah, we'll check on it when we get back but I think it's providing some good results and we'll check on when it's going to be closed down, but my understanding it should be closed down fairly soon.

Canino confirmed Gil's recollection:

> *Q. And when any of the ATF officials came to Mexico, whether it is Melson or Hoover, do you recall briefing them? Or maybe briefing is the wrong word.*
> *A. Mentioning it? Sure.*
> *Q. Do you remember mentioning that there's a lot of firearms being tracked back to Phoenix?*
> *A. Mmh-hmm.*
> *Q. Do you remember what their response was?*
> *A. It was like, yeah . . . we got a case. We got a good case going on in Phoenix.*

* * *

> *Q. Senior people in headquarters were aware of the case and they were not as alarmed?*
> *A. Right.*
> *Q. They thought it was under control, or they thought it was a great case, about to come to fruition?*
> *A. Correct.*

C. Lanny Breuer and the Department of Justice

Gil and Canino received the same message of support for Operation Fast and Furious from the Department of Justice. During a visit to Mexico, Lanny Breuer, the Assistant Attorney General for the Criminal Division demonstrated his awareness of the case:

> *Mr. [Breuer] kind of summed up his take on everything at the end, and one of them was that there's an investigation that ATF is conducting that looks like it's going to generate some good results and it will be a good positive case that we can present to the Government of Mexico as efforts that the US Government is taking to try and interdict weapons going into Mexico. And that was about – that was it. That was just a general statement. Myself and my deputy I believe were in the room and we kind of looked at each other. We're aware*

of this case, and so we assumed that's what he was mentioning. And we just wanted to make sure – we look at each other going, hope the ambassador [Carlos Pascual] doesn't ask any questions because we really don't know anything about the case. And luckily the ambassador did not.

Canino also remembered a visit from Breuer where Breuer touted the Phoenix case:

Q. And during meetings with Mr. Breuer, did this subject come up?

A. I mean, I was in a meeting, it was a country team meeting, or it might have been a law enforcement team meeting . . . Ambassador, Mr. Breuer was there, Darren was there, Mr. Breuer . . . the Ambassador was saying hey, you know what . . . we need a big win we need some positive, some positive [firearms trafficking] cases. And Lanny Breuer says, yeah, there is a good case, there is a good case out of Phoenix. And that is all he said.

* * *

Q. But do you remember the specific incident with the Ambassador talking about the success stories?

A. Right.

Q. And that is when Breuer mentioned this large case in Phoenix?

A. Yeah. He said we got, there is a good case out of Phoenix.

Q. And is it your impression that the case he was referring to is what now what you now know to be Fast and Furious?

A. Yeah, when he said, I thought, oh, okay . . . he knows. He knows about this case.

The Department of Justice, and more specifically, Assistant Attorney General Lanny Breuer, clearly knew about Operation Fast and Furious. Further, the Department of Justice's Office of Enforcement Operations (OEO) approved numerous of the wiretap applications in this case. These applications were signed on behalf of Assistant Attorney General Breuer in the spring of 2010. Instead of stemming the flow of firearms to Mexico,

Operation Fast and Furious arguably contributed to an increase in weapons and violence.

Additionally, the United States Attorney's office in Arizona – another DOJ component – was inextricably involved in supervising Operation Fast and Furious as the office was part of a prosecutor-led and OCDETF funded strike force.

According to many agents, the U.S. Attorney's office's intimate day-to-day involvement was to the detriment of ATF's Phoenix Field Division. Furthermore, although DOJ knew about the operation, it kept key people who needed this information in the dark.

D. Still in the Dark

By their own accounts, members of the senior leadership of both ATF and DOJ wanted a big firearms trafficking case to demonstrate success in combatting [sic] Mexican cartels. Despite this goal, they failed to provide specifics of the case to both Mexican officials and ATF personnel stationed in Mexico. As the chief ATF advisor in Mexico, Gil found this lapse of information sharing embarrassing.

As Attaché in Mexico, Gil needed to be aware of ATF operations that impacted Mexico. Nevertheless, his own agency intentionally withheld critical details of the tactics and strategy behind Operation Fast and Furious. Gil did not even know the name of the operation until January 2011:

> *Q. And generally, it would have been your job to approve operations that involved Mexico given your position as the attaché?*
> *A. Correct. Any activity regarding certain ATF in Mexico should have come through the ATF attaché's office in Mexico, and certainly any investigative activity should have been brought to the attention of the office.*

* * *

A. Again, I was aware there was an investigation, but I wasn't aware of the particulars of the investigation.

According to Gil, ATF leadership withheld information from him and other ATF agents in Mexico because of a fear that they would brief the Government of Mexico on the investigation and would jeopardize Operation Fast and Furious:

Q. Did anyone ever tell you, this is sensitive and we can't let the Government of Mexico know about this case?

A. Yeah, in one of my conversations – it was probably more than one, but certainly one that I recall, because it was so out of character, but . . . what our impression was in Mexico was it's a high level investigation. We understand the security issues of it. There's a Title 3 going on. So we all assume it's probably a corrupt Federal Firearms Licensee or more or others, and maybe they do have a connection that's flowing weapons there and they're working on it. But at some point, okay, you haven't gotten the information by this time . . . you need to shut it down just for safety and security reasons. So that was the assumption we had.

* * *

Well, they're worried the Mexicans are going to get – the Government of Mexico would get it and it would ruin their investigation. All right, so let us know. Well . . . they're afraid that you'll either willingly or unknowingly release this information to your GOM counterparts.

Okay, well, how about letting me know as the attaché. Well, they're afraid that you'll do the same. And at that point . . . I called my folks and I said, look, they say they have it under control, all we can do is continue our mission down here and work towards our objectives and hopefully this investigation will bear fruit down the road that everybody is going to be happy with.

But the problem we had, and I noted in my interview, was that these weapons are being recovered in violent crime scenes of Mexican law enforcement interacting with cartels or Mexican military officials interacting with cartels. And these guns are going to come back in the murder of some of these officials and we're going to have some explaining to do.

Ultimately, ATF leadership's withholding of information worked against its own representatives in Mexico. This realization was a source of major irritation and frustration for Gil:

Q. Is it inconceivable to you that you were not a part of these discussions?

A. Again, I've repeatedly said I was very frustrated down there. And so that answer is, yes, I was very frustrated because I was not part of the ongoing investigation.

Q. So when you're told about a bigger picture, when you're told about a more sophisticated case, you hear [Lanny Breuer] referencing an ATF case, which is presumably this case. . . . At any point in time did you say, why am I not read into this case? Why am I not a party to these conversations?

A. Sure. Myself, my deputy, my staff, we were all frustrated. We didn't understand it. We understand the concept to keep secret investigations, that if you leak something potentially that it could get corrupt the case or get somebody . . . unfortunately get somebody hurt or killed. We understand that, but as I said, one of my screaming matches was over this issue that, okay, you don't want us to -- okay, if you tell me I'm not going to release anything to the Government of Mexico then I won't release it, but let me know.

When you tell me, well, we don't want to let you know because

we're afraid you'll notify the ambassador or ultimately somehow the Government of Mexico is going to find out, yes, that irritates me. And you can see why the voice level went up and the vulgar language probably came out on certain occasion because it is very, very irritating.

Q. And you were trying to help them understand these guns are being recovered at crime scenes, these guns are in the possession of cartels, people are dying?

A. Correct.

Q. Is that part of your –

A. Myself, the deputy, I mean, it's like ground-hog day and – that's the best way to put it. Every time the event came up for whatever reason, maybe it was a new seizure, I was notified again, hey, when is this going to be shut down. And it's the same response that, hey, we're still working on it, it's still ongoing, we're getting some good information and we'll shut it down as soon as we can.

E. Told Operation Fast and Furious Being Shut Down

FINDING: Despite assurances that the program would be shut down as early as March 2010, it took the murder of a U.S. Border Patrol Agent in December 2010 to actually bring the program to a close. As the ATF officials in Mexico continued to express concerns throughout 2010, ATF leadership told them the investigation would be shut down as soon as possible. Gil explained:

I queried Chief [Kumor] again . . . and that – and the ongoing discussion continued, they're aware of it, they're going to close it down as soon as they possibly can, but there's still – they think the investigation is not to the point where they can close it yet. And the discussions went on and on. It went to the point I departed Mexico.

Gil left his position as Attaché to Mexico in October 2010 and retired from the ATF just a few months later. At the time of his retirement, Operation Fast and Furious remained ongoing. Several months before Gil retired, Deputy Attaché Canino wrote to Dan Kumor with disturbing statistics:

Like I said, this is a problem. I sent an e-mail, I think it was July of 2010...letting Dan Kumor know that approximately . . . the count was up to 1,900 guns in suspect gun data, 34 of which were, 34 of which were .50 caliber rifles. And I, my opinion was that these many .50 caliber rifles in the hands of one of these cartels is going to change the outcome of a battle. Dan pushed it forward. He was told, yeah, we are taking the case off in August of 2010. The case doesn't get taken off until January 25, 2011.

Kumor's response led Canino to believe that arrests were imminent in Operation Fast and Furious:

> *Q. So anyway let's talk about Danny Kumor telling you it is going to be closed down. You send him in the e-mail in July?*
>
> *A. He says, hey, I talked to Bill McMahon, Bill McMahon said they are taking the case down in August.*
>
> *Q. What did that mean to you? What was your understanding?*
>
> *A. That they were going to shut the case down and make arrests.*
>
> *Q. Now, at that point you still didn't know that they were gun walking?*
>
> *A. I never knew, I never believed it until this past April. Even after I ... talked to other guys in intel.*
>
> *Q. Just to go back to this. So when they said they are going to close the case down, what did you interpret that to mean? What was they were shutting down?*
>
> *A. They were going to start making arrests. Now ... through the fall, late fall, and I have been talking to Bill.*
>
> *Q. Bill Newell?*
>
> *A. Bill Newell, and Bill told me, hey, Carlos, we are going to probably take this down you know we are trying to take it down, I think he said December or so ... Novemberish. ... This is right around October ... November, December we are going to take this*
>
> *down ... then, the Terry murder happens.*

The first arrest finally came in December 2010, immediately after Agent Terry's murder. More followed a few weeks later in January 2011. Prior to these arrests, Canino and the other ATF agents in Mexico continued to urge ATF leaders to shut down Operation Fast and Furious to no avail. Canino testified:

> *Like I said, right around after somebody told me the figure was 1,200 guns ... there's a case out of Phoenix. ... They'll take it off when they take it off. We're concerned. ... I've made my concerns up the chain ... sent that e-mail in July. I'm told they're going take it off in August. From September nothing, October .... October, November, Bill Newell says,*

I'm going to start taking this off. . . . October, November. December comes around, Agent Terry happens. They take it off in January, end of January.

Kumor testified about his conversation with Deputy Assistant Director William McMahon about shutting down Operation Fast and Furious:

Q. But he did suggest to us in an interview we did that at least in part he was telling you we've got to shut that case down, we've got to shut that case down?

A. Oh, yeah, we've had those discussions.

Q. But that got heated as well. He was very animated about needing to shut this case down?

A. And if we did which is very possible and I'd say I agree with you a hundred percent but it's not my call, and I've already made those concerns known . . . to Bill [McMahon], and it's not – I don't have the authority to do it. And I said, matter of fact, whoever comes down or if you want to pick up the phone, you can tell them and see if you get anywhere with them. But the bottom line is that they're saying that the U.S. attorney's office is not going to authorize them to arrest these people. And, again, they're up on a wire and they're trying to put this case together.

Q. And when you say "Bill," you mean McMahon?

A. Yes.

F. Concerns Communicated to Deputy Assistant Director McMahon

Despite Dan Kumor's testimony to the Committees' investigators, Deputy Assistant Director for Field Operations William McMahon tried to minimize his knowledge of the concerns expressed by ATF agents in Mexico to their supervisors at Headquarters during his testimony to the Committees:

Q. What about Mr. Kumor? Did he express any concerns about this case?

A. Not that I remember.

Q. Essentially you were having two direct reports –
A. Uh huh.
Q. Expressing major concerns about this case to you.
A. I did?
Q. Yes, Mr. Kumor and Mr. Rowley. That doesn't ring a bell?
A. No, it doesn't. Them expressing concerns?128
A December 17, 2009 e-mail from Bill Newell indicates that he intended to brief McMahon about Ray Rowley's concerns regarding weapons showing up in Mexico in great numbers:

From:	Newell, William D.
Sent:	Thursday, December 17, 2009 11:45 AM
To:	Gillett, George T. Jr.
Cc:	Voth, David J.
Subject:	Re:

Well done, thank you. I will address Ray's concerns with McMahon.
Bill Newell
Special Agent In Charge
ATF Phoenix Field Division (AZ and NM)

███████

NOTICE: This electronic transmission is confidential and intended only for the person(s) to whom it is addressed. If you have received this transmission in error, please notify the sender by return e-mail and destroy this message in its entirety (including all attachments).

From: Gillett, George T. Jr.
To: Newell, William D.
Cc: Voth, David J.
Sent: Thu Dec 17 13:27:49 2009
Subject:
Bill-

OSII has not yet finished a link diagram on this investigation. Therefore, there is no "chart" in existence diagramming this investigation. Lorren Leadmon and crew are currently working on such a link-diagram chart, but it is not yet complete. Mr. Leadmon did have a power point that gave an overview of the case and that has been forwarded to GS Voth. However, that power point is about 1 week old, so the info is already a bit dated. GS Voth and Mr. Leadmon are speaking on a regular basis, so the lines of communication are now the equivalent of the proverbial fire hose. During one of their conversations, Lorren told Voth that Ray Rowley received a briefing on the investigation this week and mentioned the possibility of needing to shut the investigation down due to the large number of guns that have already been trafficked. Therefore, I spoke with Ray Rowley today and explained that even though the identified straw-purchasers bought approximately 175 guns last week alone, we have slowed down the FFL on future purchases and are obtaining intelligence directly related to this investigation from the current DEA wire tap. Ray did express some concern regarding the total number of guns that have been purchased by this straw-purchase scheme. I cautioned Ray on not doing any type of informal calculations on purchase numbers as that likely will result in double counting of firearms (counting purchased guns as well as recovered guns). I have also advised that we will slow the purchasers down as much as possible, but we have not identified the network yet. The result will be that the responsible conspirators will have new straw-purchasers operational before we complete the booking paperwork. I have asked Ray to consider me his direct point of contact on any future questions and/or concerns and I will do the same with him. I have also spoken with Kevin O'Keefe today and maintain those lines of communication.

As for plans to proceed, I have asked Mr. Voth to begin preparing a white paper that outlines progress to date as well as a plans for proceeding with the investigation. I know that he wants to take the information from the DEA wire and spin it off on a wire involving these subjects. I have also asked Mr. Voth to prepare a list of resources that HQ can provide (personnel and equipment) to support this investigation. I will keep you posted as things arise.

George T. Gillett
Assistant Special Agent In Charge
ATF - Phoenix Field Division

In his testimony, Kumor noted that he lacked the authority to shut down this investigation, but he reiterated that he raised the concerns expressed to him by A TF agents in Mexico with McMahon:

> Q. And you and Gil were in agreement that this was concerning, and you supported him in his view that something ought to be done -
> A. Yes, once they started showing up, absolutely.
> Q. But you didn't have the authority to do it?
> A. No.
> Q. However, you did raise those concerns with Bill McMahon?
> A. Yes.

Kumor specifically refuted McMahon's testimony to the Committees' investigators about these events:

> Q. So if McMahon said to us that you never raised these concerns with him, that wouldn't be completely honest; right?
> A. That I never raised them?
> Q. Right.
> A. That's false. That's not true.
> Q. So you did raise these concerns on multiple occasions with Mr. McMahon?
> A. I did. I raised the issue of the fact that these weapons had been had started showing up and . . . what are we going to do? What's going on? Obviously if they're showing up in Mexico, that's a problem.
> Q. How early did you raise that with him as far as the best you can recall?
> A. When this thing first started. When this case first started that you're going to have . . . I know in March when they were showing the screen and how many guns were involved.
> Q. March of 2010?
> A. March of 2010, yes.
> Q. And McMahon was at that meeting?
> A. I believe he was.
> Q. So he saw all these guns?

A. Right.

Q. Did he ever express to you that's a concern of his?

A. Yeah, I think we've had – we had discussions where he was concerned as well. But, again, it kind of came back to . . . our hands are tied. The U.S. attorneys' office is not going to charge these guys . . . . [T]hey want to go up on a wire, so they're going up on a wire, and they're going to do the case that way. So from my standpoint, I was like, well . . . the U.S. attorney's office is involved. . . . Newell is running the case. You're aware of it.

VII. Reaction of ATF Officials in Mexico

- FINDING: ATF officials in Mexico finally realized the truth: ATF allowed guns to walk. By withholding this critical information from its own personnel in Mexico, ATF jeopardized relations between the U.S. and Mexico. When Special Agent John Dodson and the other ATF whistleblowers first came forward with allegations that guns were walked across the Mexican border during Operation Fast and Furious, Canino and Gil refused to believe them. Gil and Canino could not believe that the ATF would actually utilize a tactic that contravened the training and field experience of every ATF agent. Gil and Canino, the top two ATF officials in Mexico, could not even conceive that ATF would employ a strategy of allowing weapons transfers to straw purchasers. As Canino testified:

Q. So at no time did you think [gunwalking] was a deliberate effort or part of a strategy?

A. No. That was, like I said, in 21 years as an ATF agent, as a guy who teaches surveillance techniques, as a guy who teaches agents how to conduct field operations, never in my wildest dreams ever would I have thought that this was a technique. Never. Ever. It just, it is inconceivable to me.

Q And that is because of the dangers involved?

A. Just – you don't do it. You don't wa[lk] guns. You don't wa[lk] guns. . . . You don't lose guns. You don't walk guns.

You don't let guns get out of your sight. You have all these undercover techniques, all these safety measures in place so guns do not get out of your custody or control. I mean, I mean, you could follow, you could do a surveillance for 1,000 miles . . . either use planes, trackers, you use everything under the sun, but at the end of the day, those guns do not leave your control. At some point those guns do not get into the streets.

Gil felt the same way as Canino:

...And so the – to me, when I first heard this going on in the media about the potential for ATF letting guns walk, it was inconceivable. I didn't want to believe it. It just – it would never happen. Everybody knows the consequences on the other end of . . . these guns aren't going for a positive cause, they're going for a negative cause. The term "guns walking" didn't exist in my vocabulary.

In fact, Canino – an instructor for field operations and undercover operations for ATF since 1998, and a founding member and teacher of the ATF enhanced undercover training program – felt so confident that these allegations were false, that he began assuring people that the allegations had no merit:

Never, it is just, you don't do that. It is not – what these guys did was basically grab the ATF rule book on trafficking and threw it out the window. This is indefensible. It is indefensible. The ATF does not do this. . . . I owe people apologies because when this first came out, I did not believe it.

* * *

[W]hen this first broke, I said there is no way this happened...[M]y boss told me, hey, Carlos don't be so vocal about this...wait, wait to see what happens. I told him, I said, boss, we didn't do this. He said how are you so sure? I said because we don't teach this, this is not how we are taught.

Dan Kumor remembers cautioning Canino about being too quick to deny the allegations. As Canino's supervisor, Kumor did not want him to potentially have to retract false and misleading comments made to his Mexican counterparts. As somebody stationed in ATF headquarters, Kumor may have known there could be some merit to the allegations:

> And I said . . . but I told Carlos, I said . . . until we find out what's going on, I wouldn't be – if we get questions about what happened, we're going to have to direct all that to the Phoenix field division or field ops because we don't know. And the last thing I want to do is represent or have you guys represent to the Mexicans or anybody else that, hey . . . there's no issues with any of this case.
>
> We don't know, and I don't want that coming back later because that would certainly be an issue with them as far as their reputations and their ability to be able to operate in the future down there.

As more information came to light, however, Gil and Canino concluded that hundreds and hundreds of guns had been walked. These guns ended up in at crime scenes in Mexico, about which Gil and Canino received extensive briefings. Gil and Canino became incensed when they finally began to learn about the full scope of Operation Fast and Furious and the investigative techniques involved:

> Q. When you first got the impression that this was part of a strategy to let guns walk into Mexico, what was your reaction to that strategy?
>
> A. I wasn't convinced that this happened until this past April after all the allegations were made, and I talked to different people. I was beyond shocked. Embarrassed. I was angry. I'm still angry. Because this is not what we do.

* * *

> That is, I mean, this is the perfect storm of idiocy. That is the only way I could put it. This is, I mean, this is inconceivable to me. This is group think gone awry. You know what General George Patton says, if we are all thinking alike, then nobody is thinking. Right? Nobody was thinking here. How

*could anybody think, hey, let's follow, I mean there is a guy
in this case that bought over 600 guns. At what point do you
think you might want to pull him aside and say, hey, come
here for a second.*

When Canino himself uncovered hard evidence that ATF had
allowed the guns to disappear from their surveillance he
understood the whistleblower allegations were true:

Q. Okay, and take us through what happened in April.
A. I was here on a visit to headquarters.
Q. Alcohol, Tobacco and Firearms headquarters?
*A. Alcohol, Tobacco and Firearms headquarters, and I was, I
was looking at a, the management log on this case. And the
first two pages, if I'm not mistaken, there are entries there
that chronicle us walking away on three separate occasions
from stash houses.*
Q. And did that sound to you incredible?
A. I stopped reading.
*Q. So you only got through two pages of this management
log?*
A. Yeah.
Q. And then you couldn't read it any longer?
A. Didn't want to.
Q. Because you were so upset?
A. Yes.
*Q. And you were upset because walking away from three
stash houses struck you as so outrageous?*
*A. Walking away from one, walking away from one gun
when you know that that gun is going to be used in a crime
when you, I mean, there is no, there was no gray area here
guys. There was no gray area here. We knew that these guys
were trafficking guns into Mexico. There is no gray area.
They weren't trafficking, [the] guys weren't going out and
buying two Larson pistols. These guys were buying 7.62,
223's, .50 caliber rifles, okay, there was no mistake about
this. This is no gray area.*

Gil realized the full scope of Operation Fast and Furious only
after he retired from ATF. It took the public allegations of the

whistleblowers and contacts with his former colleagues for Gil to fully comprehend the tactics used in Operation Fast and Furious:

> Q. Now, when you were speaking with [a Congressional investigator] you indicated that you learned about the specific tactics of operation Fast and Furious. Can you remind us when that was?
>
> A. It was after I retired. It was after the shooting of Border Patrol Agent Terry. I started getting phone calls saying, hey, this is – there is something to this thing, these guns were knowingly allowed into Mexico. And so that was the first knowledge that I had about the potential allowing guns to go into Mexico.
>
> Q. And how did you become aware of that?
>
> A. Several phone calls from agents, speaking to my deputy or my former deputy, Carlos [Canino], who I remained in contact with. Seeing Agent Dodson on TV and getting phone calls primarily. And then I was contacted by several media sources including CBS.

After realizing that ATF had let guns walk, Gil's concerns turned to the safety of ATF agents in Mexico:

> Q. And I believe you mentioned that in the aftermath of Agent Dodson's interview on CBS, you had concerns about your former agents in Mexico. What were – what were the concerns you had for them?
>
> A. I had spoken to my deputy primarily and he mentioned that, obviously, the Government of Mexico, our counterparts are not happy with this situation. It made it tough for them that . . . didn't want to work with them. It's like, hey, we can't trust you, you guys are allowing these guns to come in. Inside the embassy because the Government of Mexico was irritated with us, they held that against the other agencies within the embassy, maybe slowing down Visas to allow personnel to come in and work in Mexico. . .Obviously the ambassador probably, I didn't speak -- I haven't spoken to him since I left the country, but my understanding is he wasn't happy about it. And so there might have been some friction there between the acting attaché', Carlos [Canino],

and him. And so it was several conflicts going on. And, again, they just started looking at the articles and the bloggers and some of the media reports in Mexico that the ATF was corrupt, and we were taking kickbacks to allow these weapons to come in, which puts a big zero – crossbar on my guys' backs down there.
Q. When you say crossbar?
A. I'm sorry, I should clarify that.
Q. Sure.
A. Puts a mark on their back, for instance, targets for not only corrupt cartel members to find out who they are and kidnap or kill, which is some of the unfortunate areas I had to deal with down there. And then – or Government of Mexico officials not happy and... they may arrest you, indict you, take away your Visa and throw you out of the country. So there's all these things going on down there amongst my former crew.

VIII. Persistent Consequences of Operation Fast and Furious

FINDING: The high-risk tactics of cessation of surveillance, gunwalking, and noninterdiction [sic] of weapons that ATF used in Fast and Furious went against the core of ATF's mission, as well as the training and field experience of its agents. These flaws inherent in Operation Fast and Furious made tragic consequences inevitable.

A. The Murder of Mario Gonzalez Rodriguez

On October 21, 2010, drug cartel members kidnapped Mario Gonzalez Rodriguez from his office. At the time of the kidnapping, his sister Patricia Gonzalez Rodriguez was the Attorney General of the state of Chihuahua in northwestern Mexico. A few days after the kidnapping, a video surfaced on the Internet in which Mario Gonzalez Rodriguez sat handcuffed, surrounded by five heavily armed men wearing masks, dressed in camouflage and bullet-proof vests. Apparently under duress, Rodriguez alleged that his sister had ordered killings at the behest of the Juarez cartel, located in Chihuahua. The video quickly went viral, instantly becoming a major news story in Mexico.

Patricia Gonzalez Rodriguez denied her brother's allegations, claiming the armed men holding him hostage coerced Mario into making his statements. Patricia Gonzalez Rodriguez asserted her brother's kidnapping was payback for the prosecutions of members of the Sinaloa cartel and corrupt Mexican law enforcement officers. Ms. Rodriguez left her post as attorney general later that month.

On November 5, 2010, Mexican authorities found Mario Gonzalez Rodriguez's body in a shallow grave.142 Shortly after this grisly discovery, the Mexican federal police engaged in a shootout with drug cartel members, which resulted in the arrest of eight suspects. Police seized sixteen weapons from the scene of the shootout. Two of these weapons traced back to Operation Fast and Furious.

E-mails obtained by the Committees indicate that ATF knew about the link to Operation Fast and Furious almost immediately after the trace results came back. A November 15, 2010 email from ATF's OSII to the Phoenix Field Division alerted Phoenix that two of the recovered AK-47s weapons traced back to Operation Fast and Furious. A number of employees from OSII contacted their colleagues in Phoenix to alert them of this connection. OSII agents also told ATF personnel in Mexico. Carlos Canino informed ATF headquarters about the link between the Gonzalez murder and the subsequent shootout to Fast and Furious. However, no one authorized Canino to inform the Mexican government about the connection.

> Q. Who did you mention it to?
> A. I mentioned it to the Director.
> Q. That's Acting Director Melson?
> A. Yes. I mentioned it to Billy Hoover, I mentioned it to Mark Chait, I mentioned it to Bill McMahon, I mentioned it to my boss Danny Kumor.

* * *

A. I remember at least two times when I mentioned it to them. I said one of us – look, here's what happened. Okay, this woman is a prominent politician.
Q. This is Miss Patricia Gonzalez?
A. Right.
Q. She's no longer a –
A. No longer, right. . . . [T]his is front page news for days in Mexico, we need to tell them this, because if we don't tell them this, and this gets out, it was my opinion that the Mexicans would never trust us again because we were holding back this type of information. And every time I mentioned it... guys started looking at their cell phones, silence in the room, let's move on to the next subject. . . . I wasn't told, yea, tell her, but I was never told, no, you can't tell her. I was never told that. It was just indecision.
Q. So you were getting no instructions at all?
A. Zero instructions.

Acting Attaché Canino continued to feel strongly that the Mexican government should be informed of the link between the Mario Gonzalez murderers and Operation Fast and Furious. He also believed that, given the seriousness of the information and the negative fallout that would likely ensue, ATF headquarters should share this information with the U.S. Ambassador to Mexico.

The rapidly escalating media scrutiny would eventually expose the connection between the Mario Gonzalez Rodriguez murderers and Operation Fast and Furious. In Canino's view, sharing this information directly with Mexican officials before the press exposed it was of paramount importance to preserve U.S.-Mexico relations and the ability of ATF personnel to operate in Mexico. Not until June 2011, nearly eight months after ATF became aware of the link between Operation Fast and Furious and the guns recovered following the shootout, did Canino notify the Mexican government:

Q. And why did you do that [tell Ms. Morales]?

A. I communicated that to the Mexican Attorney General Maricela Morales because I did not want her to find out through media reports where these guns had come from. I wanted her to find out from me, because she is an ally of the U.S. Government. She is committed to fighting these cartels, she is a personal friend, and I owe her that.

Q. That courtesy?

A. I owe her that courtesy, absolutely.

* * *

Q. And even though you really didn't get permission – well, I guess Mr. Kumor sort of approved, but no one else really did?

A. Right.

Q. But you still decided that it was important for you to disclose that information?

A. If I hadn't told the Attorney General this, and this had come out in the news media, I would never be able to work with her ever again, and we would be done in Mexico. We just might as well pack up the office and go home.

Q. So the fact that these guns traced back to this program Fast and Furious has the potential, perhaps even did, to create an international incident?

A. This has already created an international incident.

Q. But this is even more personal?

A. When the Mexican media gets a hold of this, it's going to go crazy.

Q. By "this" you're talking about the tracing to the death of Mario Gonzalez?

A. Absolutely.

* * *

Q. Now, what was her reaction when you told her?

A. She was shocked.

Q. Did she say anything, exclaim anything?

A. She said, "Hijole," which translates basically into, "Oh, my."

Q. Oh, my God? Oh, my?

A. Yeah.

The failure to inform the Mexican government earlier risked possible international implications. This failure to inform is another example of ATF leadership withholding essential information related to Operation Fast and Furious.

B. The Mexican Helicopter Incident

A May 2011 shootout between Mexican police and cartel members demonstrates the broadening impact of Operation Fast and Furious. On May 24, 2011, La Familia DTO gunmen forced a Federal Police helicopter to make an emergency landing in the state of Michoacán, located in western Mexico.149 The gunmen attacked the helicopter, wounding two officers on board and forcing the aircraft to land near the scene of the attack.150 Canino described the event:

> *A. I think it was on May 24th the Mexican Federal Police mounted an operation against members of La Familia.*
> *Q. That's a drug cartel?*
> *A. Right. In the State of Michoacán. When the Mexican Federal Police was deploying its troops via helicopter, they came under fire from members of La Familia. I believe in the May 24th incident two crewmen were hit.*
> *Q. These were soldiers or policemen?*
> *A. Policemen, Federal policemen. They were hit. The helicopter flew off. My understanding is that that helicopter could have made it back to the base under its own power; however, it landed to render aid to the injured people on board.*

On May 29, 2011, the federal police launched a massive raid on the La Familia DTO. During the raid, cartel gunmen again attacked Federal Police helicopters and wounded two more officers:

> *A. Fast forward to May 29th. Again, the Mexican Federal Police mount another operation. I believe this time it was in*

the State of - - I need to look at a map. Anyway, it was a bordering State.

Q. Okay.

A. They were coming in. Members of La Familia cartel engaged – there were four helicopters – engaged them. I believe all four helicopters were struck by fire. Mexican Federal Police returned fire from the helicopters; able to suppress the fire coming in, offloaded, and the helicopters all flew back, and they were back in service within a few days.

Q. Now, was there any people hurt on the ground, any deaths?

A. I believe in the second operation, I believe ... Mexican Federal Police killed, I believe either 11 or 14 people.

The raid resulted in the deaths of 11 cartel members and the arrest of 36 cartel members, including those suspected of firing on the helicopter several days earlier. Authorities also found a cache of more than 70 rifles at the scene, including a Barrett .50 caliber rifle. Some of these weapons traced back to Operation Fast and Furious. Mexican police also found a stash of heavy-duty body armor belonging to the cartels. This was the first time ATF in Mexico had seen such body armor in the hands of the cartels. Along with the Barrett .50 caliber rifles, these vests symbolized a new level of sophistication in cartel weaponry.

During a trip to Mexico City on June 25, 2011, Members and staff from the U.S. House of Representatives Committee on Oversight and Government had an opportunity to visually inspect the damaged helicopter.155 Several bullet holes were evident on the body of the aircraft, and one round from a .50-caliber rifle penetrated the thick "bullet proof" glass windshield.

The downed helicopter incident and subsequent police raid resulted in the recovery of Operation Fast and Furious weapons that may have been used against the Mexican police. Barrett .50 caliber rifles provide a significant upgrade to the cartels' ability to inflict serious damage and casualties on their enemies. As Canino testified:

[T]he count was up to 1,900 guns [associated with Fast and Furious] in suspect gun data, 34 of which were, 34 of which were .50 caliber rifles. And I, my opinion was that these many .50 caliber rifles in the hands of one of these cartels is going to change the outcome of a battle.

Previously, weapons had been linked back to the Sinaloa cartel and members of the El Teo organization, an off-shoot from the Beltrán -Leyva cartel. La Familia DTO is the third cartel connected to Operation Fast and Furious weapons. The May 24, 2011 shooting shows that Operation Fast and Furious weapons may be found in a broader geographic area than the territory controlled by the Sinaloa DTO.157 This spread of Operation Fast and Furious weapons may place an even greater number of Mexican citizens in harm's way.

IX. Conclusion

According to the Justice Department's July 22, 2011 response to Questions for the Record posed by Senator Grassley, Fast and Furious suspects purchased 1,418 weapons after becoming known to the ATF.158 Of those weapons, 1,048 remain unaccounted for, since the Department's response indicates that the guns have not yet been recovered and traced.159 U.S and Mexican law enforcement officials continue to seize weapons connected to the operation and recover weapons at crime scenes on both sides of the border. Given the vast amount of

Operation Fast and Furious weapons possibly still in the hands of cartel members, law enforcement officials should expect more seizures and recoveries at crime scenes. According to several agents involved in Operation Fast and Furious, ATF agents will have to deal with these guns for years to come.160

Some aspects of Operation Fast and Furious may ultimately escape scrutiny given the difficulties of tracing weapons recovered in Mexico. The possibility remains for more high profile deaths linked to Operation Fast and Furious. Canino bluntly described his reaction to that possibility:

> Q. When you first got the impression that this was part of a strategy to let guns walk into Mexico, what was your reaction to that strategy?
>
> A. The guys in Mexico will trace those . . . I'm beyond angry. Brian Terry is not the last guy, okay, guys? Let's put it out there right now. Nobody wants to talk about that. Brian Terry is not the last guy unfortunately. . . . Unfortunately, there are hundreds of Brian Terrys probably in Mexico . . . we ATF armed the [Sinaloa] cartel. It is disgusting.

The faulty design of Operation Fast and Furious led to tragic consequences. Countless United States and Mexican citizens suffered as a result. The lessons learned from exposing the risky tactics used during Operation Fast and Furious will hopefully be a catalyst for better leadership and better internal law enforcement procedures. Any strategy or tactic other than interdiction of illegally purchased firearms at the first lawful opportunity should be subject to strict operational controls. These controls are essential to ensure that no government agency ever again allows guns to knowingly flow from American gun stores to intermediaries to Mexican drug cartels.

Appendix C: US v. Vicente Jesus Zambada-Niebla

UNITED STATES DISTRICT COURT

NORTHERN DISTRICT OF ILLINOIS

EASTERN DIVISION

UNITED STATES OF AMERICA,) Case No. 09 CR 383

Judge Ruben Castillo

VICENTE JESUS ZAMBADA-NIEBLA

MEMORANDUM OF LAW IN SUPPORT OF MOTION FOR <u>DISCOVERY REGARDING DEFENSE OF PUBLIC AUTHORITY</u>

Defendant, Vicente Jesus Zambada-Niebla, submitted his initial discovery request on the United States government on September 24, 2010. The Government objected to many of the discovery requests as not being "relevant" in its response dated November 8, 2010, particularly as they related to the requests set forth in the attached motion for discovery regarding the defense of public authority. Mr. Zambada-Niebla has filed his notice of the defense of public authority pursuant to Fed. R. Crim. P. 12.3, thereby making his discovery requests relevant and exculpatory as set forth below.

In that notice, Mr. Zambada-Niebla asserts the defense of actual and/or believed public authority, for acts that began from at least on or about January 1, 2004 and continued to and included on or about March 19, 2009, and or entrapment by estoppel, on behalf of the United States Department of Justice, Drug Enforcement Administration, and the Federal Bureau of Investigation. The discovery requested herein is necessary for the investigation and preparation of that defense.

BACKGROUND

Humberto Loya-Castro (Loya) is a high ranking member of the leadership of the Sinaloa Cartel and is a close confidante of Joaquin Guzman Loera (Chapo) and Ismael Zambada-Garcia (Mayo), the father of Mr. Zambada-Niebla, who are also charged in the indictment and are named as the heads of the Sinaloa Cartel. The Sinaloa Cartel has been described as one of the largest drug trafficking organizations in the world. Both Chapo and Mayo have been the subject of several federal indictments in the United States and have been the subject of extradition requests from the United States to Mexico. It has been reported that the United Stated government has offered a five million dollar reward for the apprehension of both Chapo and Mayo. Loya, who is a Mexican attorney, is not only a principal advisor to Chapo and Mayo in their alleged drug trafficking operations, but is also involved in their alleged drug trafficking operations.

Loya was indicted along with Chapo and Mayo in 1995 in the Southern District of California and charged with participation in a massive narcotics trafficking conspiracy (Case No. 95CR0973). That case was dismissed on the prosecution's own motion in 2008 after Loya became an informant for the United States government and had provided information for a period of over ten years.

Sometime prior to 2004, and continuing through the time period covered in the indictment, the United States government entered into an agreement with Loya and the leadership of the Sinaloa Cartel, including Mayo and Chapo. Under that agreement, the

Sinaloa Cartel, through Loya, was to provide information accumulated by Mayo, Chapo, and others, against rival Mexican Drug Trafficking Organizations to the United States government. In return, the United States government agreed to dismiss the prosecution of the pending case against Loya, not to interfere with his drug trafficking activities and those of the Sinaloa Cartel, to not actively prosecute him, Chapo, Mayo, and the leadership of the Sinaloa Cartel, and to not apprehend them. The Defendant is alleged in the indictment to be a high ranking member of the Sinaloa Cartel.

United States government agents in Mexico, including but limited to the DEA and ICE, were told by Loya that Mayo and Chapo and other alleged members of the Sinaloa Cartel, and Mr. Zambada-Niebla, were providing information to the United States government under the agreement with Loya, who would then pass along the information to the agents. Loya told United States government agents when he was going to meet with Chapo and Mayo and was told that they would not follow him to and from his meetings with Mayo and Chapo so that Mayo and Chapo could be assured that their whereabouts would not be known to government agents. The relationship between Loya and the leadership of the Sinaloa Cartel was such that Loya was permitted to sit in on meetings and discussions that the DEA was having regarding the Sinaloa Cartel, without regard to the likelihood that Loya would pass that information along to Mayo and Chapo. In addition, the defense has evidence that from time to time, the leadership of the Sinaloa Cartel was informed by agents of the DEA through Loya that United States government agents and/or Mexican authorities were conducting investigations near the home territories of cartel leaders so that the cartel leaders could take appropriate actions to evade investigators-even though the United States government had indictments, extradition requests, and rewards for the apprehension of Mayo, Chapo, and other alleged leaders, as well as Mr. Zambada-Niebla.

In addition, Mayo and Chapo were informed through Loya that the United States government would not share any of the information they had about the Sinaloa Cartel and/or the leadership of the Sinaloa Cartel with the Mexican government in order to better assure that they would not be apprehended and so that their operations would not be interfered with. Mr. Zambada-Niebla was a party to the agreement between the United States government and the Sinaloa Cartel and provided information to the United States government through Loya pursuant to the agreement. Loya himself continued his drug trafficking activities with the knowledge of the United States government without being arrested or prosecuted.

Mr. Zambada-Niebla was aware that Mr. Loya-Castro was permitted to continue his drug trafficking activities so long as Mr. Loya-Castro and the leadership of the Sinaloa Cartel provided information to the United States government. The DEA was aware that Mr. Zambada-Niebla was providing information to Loya pursuant to the agreement because Loya told them. Representatives of the DEA told Loya that they were grateful for the information provided by Mr. Zambada-Niebla.

Pursuant to the agreement, Loya arranged for Mr. Zambada-Niebla to meet with United States government agents at the Sheraton Hotel in Mexico City in March of 2009 for the purpose of introducing Mr. Zambada-Niebla to the agents and for the purpose of his continuing to provide information to the DEA and the United States government personally, rather than through Loya. Loya's federal case had been dismissed in 2008 and the DEA representative told Mr. Loya-Castro that they wanted to establish a more personal relationship with Mr. Zambada-Niebla so that they could deal with him directly under the agreement. Mr. Zambada-Niebla believed that under the prior agreement, any activities of the Sinaloa Cartel, including the kind described in the indictment, were covered by the agreement, and that he was immune from arrest or prosecution. Loya was told by United

States government agents, and told Mr. Zambada-Niebla, that Mr. Zambada-Niebla would not be arrested if he met personally with the DEA agents, even though the DEA agents knew that there was an extradition warrant outstanding for his arrest. DEA agents told Mr. Loya-Castro to tell Mr. Zambada-Niebla that they wanted to continue the same arrangement with him as they had with Mr. Loya-Castro. Mr. Loya-Castro relayed that message to Mr. Zambada-Niebla. When Mr. Zambada-Niebla met voluntarily with the government agents in Mexico City in the presence of Mr. Loya-Castro, the aforementioned assurances were repeated to Mr. Zambada-Niebla. Mr. Zambada-Niebla was told he would not be arrested, that the agents knew of his prior cooperation through Loya, and that they just wanted to continue receiving information from him. Mr. Zambada-Niebla was also told that the arrangements with him had been approved at the highest levels of the United States government. Mr. Zambada-Niebla was told that a Washington, D.C. indictment would be dismissed and that he would be immune from further prosecution. There is also evidence that at the hotel, Mr. Zambada-Niebla did accept the agreement and thereafter in reliance on that agreement, provided further information regarding rival drug cartels. Mr. Zambada-Niebla was told that the government agents were satisfied with the information he had provided to them and that arrangements would be made to meet with him again. Mr. Zambada-Niebla then left the meeting. Approximately five hours after the meeting, Mr. Zambada-Niebla was arrested by Mexican authorities.

Based on the above, Mr. Zambada-Niebla is entitled to discovery of documents and other files in the possession, custody, or control of the United States government that relate in any way, shape, or form to the circumstances surrounding the above-outlined activities. The defense has information that indicates that the government has in its possession documents, files, recordings, notes, and additional forms of evidence that are exculpatory and would tend to support the allegations set forth above in his defense of public authority. The defendant herein incorporates by reference the points and authorities submitted in support of his motion for the production of exculpatory evidence.

ARGUMENT

The United States government and its various agencies have a long history of providing benefits, permission, and immunity to criminals and their organizations to commit crimes, including murder, in return for receiving information against other criminals and other criminal organizations. Perhaps no better example is the celebrated case of Whitey Bulger, the Boston crime boss and murderer, who along with other members of criminal organizations, were given carte blanche by the FBI to commit murders in order to receive information in return about the Italian mafia and other criminal organizations in the New England area (*See New York Times Editorial June 29, 2011*). This tactic has been used extensively by the justice department and its various agencies in the "war on drugs" without concern for the loss of lives in both Mexico and the United States and without concern for the continued smuggling of illicit drugs into the United States or ending their consumption.

As Robert C. Bonner, the former head of the DEA and Commissioner of the United States Customs Department pointed out in his recent article in Foreign Affairs magazine titled "The New Cocaine Cowboys, How to Defeat Mexico's Drug Cartels" (July/August 2010, p.25), the United States government's plan to destroy the Cali and Medellin drug cartels in Colombia was based (as in this case) on giving carte blanche to rival cartels to continue their drug smuggling operations in the United States without concern for its associated death and destruction in both countries, in return for their assistance against the Cali and Medellin cartels. He makes it clear that in Colombia, "the objective was to dismantle and destroy the Cali and Medellin cartels-not to prevent drugs from being smuggled into the United States or to end their consumption" (p.42). He goes on to say "the United States must accept that the goal in Mexico is similar; the destruction of the large Mexican cartels, nothing more and nothing else" (p.42, 43) (emphasis added).

This strategy, which he calls "Divide & Conquer," using one drug organization to help against others, is exactly what the Justice Department and its various agencies have implemented in Mexico. In this case, they entered into an agreement with the leadership of the Sinaloa Cartel through, among others, Humberto Loya-Castro, to receive their help in the United States government's efforts to destroy other cartels. Under that agreement, the Sinaloa Cartel under the leadership of defendant's father, Ismael Zambada-Niebla and "Chapo" Guzman, were given carte blanche to continue to smuggle tons of illicit drugs into Chicago and the rest of the United States and were also protected by the United States government from arrest and prosecution in return for providing information against rival cartels which helped Mexican and United States authorities capture or kill thousands of rival cartel members. Indeed, United States government agents aided the leaders of the Sinaloa Cartel.

Among other benefits received by the leadership of the Sinaloa Cartel was that United States government agents did not share any of the information they received relating to the Sinaloa Cartel with the Mexican government and the leadership of the Sinaloa Cartel was kept informed of both Mexican and United States government operations in areas near their location. Indeed, Mr. Loya-Castro was permitted to be present while government agents were discussing strategies regarding operations they were conducting in Mexico. Moreover, no effort was made by United States government agents to apprehend Ismael Zambada-Niebla or "Chapo" Guzman, who had been indicted several times in the United States and were subjects of extradition requests by the United States government.

In addition, Mr. Loya-Castro, who had been providing information to the United States government for over ten years, had his indictment in the United States District Court in San Diego, California, dismissed on government motion in 2008 and was knowingly permitted by United States government agents to continue his participation in drug trafficking activities in both the United States and Mexico. He had been told by government officials that he was immune from prosecution and the United States lived up to its agreement with him.

Mr. Zambada-Niebla was a party to Mr. Loya-Castro's agreement, and was a party to the agreement reached with the Sinaloa Cartel leadership, and received the same assurances. There is also evidence that Mr. Zambada-Niebla acted in accordance with and reliance upon that agreement and provided information regarding rival drug cartels through Mr. Loya-Castro to the United States government for several years before he voluntarily met with United States government agents in Mexico City on or about March 17, 2009. United States government agents were told by Mr. Loya-Castro and knew that Mr. Zambada-Niebla had been providing information against rival drug cartels through him for a substantial period of time prior to the meeting. That meeting was arranged through Mr. Loya-Castro and Mr. Zambada-Niebla was assured that he would not be arrested or prosecuted even though there was a United States indictment against Mr. Zambada-Niebla out of the United States District Court in Washington D.C. (Case No. 03-CR-00034), and even though he had been for at least eight months the subject of an investigation which resulted in the indictment in this case. In addition, these assurances were made even though the United States had petitioned the Mexican government for extradition of Mr. Zambada-Niebla on the Washington, D.C. case. Moreover, Mr. Zambada-Niebla was assured by United States government representatives that Mexican authorities would not be informed that the Mexico City meeting on or about March 17, 2009 was going to take place. There is also evidence that Mr. Zambada-Niebla went to the hotel pursuant to the previous agreement and was assured by government agents that the agreement would remain in effect if he continued to provide information against rival drug cartels. Mr. Zambada-Niebla was told by government agents that with the approval and authorization of the United States Justice Department in Washington D.C., the Washington, D.C. indictment would be dismissed and he would have immunity from arrest, prosecution, and any further charges, so long as he continued to provide information against rival drug cartels. In reliance on that agreement, Mr. Zambada-Niebla provided further information that evening regarding rival drug cartels.

After the meeting, Mr. Zambada-Niebla was permitted to leave and arrangements were made for him to meet again with United States government representatives. However, the next morning, Mr. Zambada-Niebla was arrested by Mexican government authorities.

The thrust of the majority of the requests for information to be provided in Mr. Zambada-Niebla's motion for discovery regarding his public authority defense, are focused on obtaining information from the United States government relating to the facts and circumstances surrounding the United States government's agreements with Mr. Loya-Castro, the Sinaloa Cartel leadership, and Mr. Zambada-Niebla, and the related interactions between the United States government, Mr. Loya-Castro, the Sinaloa Cartel leadership, and Mr. Zambada-Niebla as a result of those agreements and relationships. Mr. Zambada-Niebla has evidence that the materials requested exist, are exculpatory, and support the public authority defense.

The United States government considered the arrangements with the Sinaloa Cartel an acceptable price to pay, because the principal objective was the destruction and dismantling of rival cartels by using the assistance of the Sinaloa Cartel-without regard for the fact that tons of illicit drugs continued to be smuggled into Chicago and other parts of the United States and consumption continued virtually unabated.

Essentially, the theory of the United States government in waging its "war on drugs" has been and continues to be that the "end justifies the means" and that it is more important to receive information about rival drug cartels' activities from the Sinaloa Cartel in return for being allowed to continue their criminal activities, including and not limited to their smuggling of tons of illegal narcotics into the United States. This is confirmed by recent disclosures by the Congressional Committee's investigation of the latest Department of Justice, DEA, FBI, and ATF's "war on drugs" operation known as "Fast & Furious."

Mr. Zambada-Niebla in requests #48-51, seeks to obtain information regarding Operation "Fast & Furious" and the findings regarding that operation in the Joint Staff Report prepared for Darrell R. Issa, Chairman of the United States House of Representatives Committee on Oversight and Government Reform and Senator Charles E. Grassley, the ranking member of the United States Committee on the Judiciary, because the materials requested are relevant to his defense of public authority and are exculpatory.

The Joint Staff Report revealed that the operation known and authorized at the highest levels of the Justice Department and which included agents from ATF, DEA, FBI, ICE, and the IRS, allowed guns to be illegally purchased in the United States and transported to Mexico to end up in the hands of members of drug cartels. This chain of events inevitably placed the guns in the hands of violent criminals which the Department of Justice not only was aware of, but sponsored and supported. The Department of Justice and its agency partners knew that the foreseeable result of this strategy was that death and destruction would occur in Mexico. Indeed, as confirmed in the report, violence and death did occur in Mexico and the result was not only approved but regarded with "giddy optimism by ATF supervisors" (*See Congressional Committee Report on Fast & Furious*). Not only was Congress and the public not informed about what was going on, but more importantly, as is true in this case, the Mexican government and the intended victims of such actions were not informed, thereby preventing them from being able to take any precautionary measures. It is estimated that approximately three thousand people were killed in Mexico as a result of "Operation Fast & Furious," including law enforcement officers in the state of Sinaloa, Mexico, the headquarters of the Sinaloa Cartel. The Department of Justice's leadership apparently saw this as an ingenious way of combating drug cartel activities.

It has recently been disclosed that in addition to the above-referenced problems with "Operation Fast & Furious," the DOJ, DEA, and the FBI knew that some of the people who were receiving the weapons that were being allowed to be transported to Mexico, were in fact informants working for those organizations and included some of the leaders of the cartels. The evidence seems to indicate that the Justice Department not only allowed criminals to smuggle weapons, but that tax payers' dollars in the form of informant payments, may have financed those engaging in such activities. Neither the ATF or Congress were apparently informed of that situation.

Only July 5, 2011, representative Issa and Senator Grassley sent a letter to United States Attorney General Eric Holder suggesting that multiple United States agencies were employing as informants members of Mexican drug organizations who were responsible for importing into their nation thousands of weapons from the United States, leading to more than forty thousand homicides in Mexico's drug war since late 2006. Acting Director of the ATF Kenneth Melson has also asserted that cartel leaders were paid informants of the DEA and FBI and were among the individuals who knowingly received weapons pursuant to "Operation Fast & Furious." Several of the requests in Mr. Zambada-Niebla's request for discovery re public authority defense are focused on obtaining government information to determine whether leaders and/or members of the Sinaloa Cartel were among the individuals who received the weapons and to determine whether their receiving of the weapons was pursuant to the agreement that was originally entered into between the United States government and Mr. Loya-Castro and the leaders of the Sinaloa Cartel, which is still in effect.

Director Melson confirms what Mr. Zambada-Niebla is asserting in the matter before this Court; i.e. that the United States government at its highest levels entered into agreements with cartel leaders to act as informants against rival cartels and received benefits in return, including, but not limited to, access to thousands of weapons which helped them continue their business of smuggling drugs into Chicago and throughout the United States, and to continue wreaking havoc on the citizens and law enforcement in Mexico. It is clear that some of the weapons were deliberately allowed by the FBI and other government representatives to end up in the hands of the Sinaloa Cartel and that among the people killed by those weapons were law enforcement officers.

Mr. Zambada-Niebla believes that the documentation that he requests will confirm that the weapons received by Sinaloa Cartel members and its leaders in Operation "Fast & Furious" were provided under the agreement entered into between the United States government and Mr. Loya-Castro on behalf of the Sinaloa Cartel that is the subject of his defense re public authority. Mr. Zambada-Niebla believes that the documentation will also provide evidence showing that the United States government has a policy and pattern of providing benefits, including immunity, to cartel leaders, including the Sinaloa Cartel and their members, who are willing to provide information against rival drug cartels, as is alleged by Mr. Zambada-Niebla herein.

Mr. Zambada-Niebla also requests in #42 that the United States government produce material relating to the 2003 "House of

Death" murders, which took place in Juarez, Mexico, and were committed by United States government informants. As confirmed in the Joint Assessment Report prepared by government authorities investigating those murders, agents of the United States government had prior knowledge that murders were going to be committed by their informants but did not take any measures to either inform the Mexican government or the intended victims, because government representatives determined it was more important to protect the identity of their informants. The informants were assisting the United States government in the investigations of major drug traffickers and the government determined that the killings of over a hundred Mexican citizens was an acceptable price to pay for enabling them to continue their narcotics investigations.

Mr. Zambada-Niebla believes that the materials requested in request #42 will confirm his allegations that the United States has a policy of entering into agreements with individuals who they know are violent narcotics traffickers, so long as those persons are willing to provide information against other drug traffickers, and that they entered into such an agreement with the leadership of the Sinaloa Cartel. Such individuals have also been permitted to commit murders and other violent acts. Mr. Zambada-Niebla also believes that the materials requested confirm that as in the case before this Court, the United States government had a policy and a pattern of not sharing information with the Mexican government even if that meant that narcotics trafficking and death and destruction, would continue to take place.

CONCLUSION

Based on the above, it is respectfully submitted that Mr. Zambada-Niebla is entitled to the discovery requested in his motion.

Endnotes

---

[1] **US Customs and Border Protection** is not confined to operations in the United States. There are 327 officially designated ports of entry here and an additional 14 pre-clearance locations in Canada, Ireland and the Caribbean manned by the Border Patrol. CBP is also in charge of the Container Security Initiative, which identifies and inspects foreign cargo in its mother country before it is to be imported into the United States.

- More than 21,180 CBP Officers screen passengers and cargo at over 300 ports of entry.
- Over 2,200 CBP Agriculture Specialists work to curtail the spread of harmful pests and plant and animal diseases that may harm America's farms and food supply or cause bio- and agro-terrorism.
- Over 21,370 Border Patrol Agents protect 1,900 miles (3,100 km) of border with Mexico and 5,000 miles (8,000 km) of border with Canada.
- Nearly 1,050 Air and Marine Interdiction Agents prevent people, weapons, narcotics, and conveyances from illegal entry by air and water.
- Nearly 2,500 employees in CBP revenue positions collect over $30 billion annually in entry duties and taxes through the enforcement of trade and tariff laws. These collections provide the second largest revenue for the U.S. Government. In addition, these employees fulfill the agency's trade mission by appraising and classifying imported merchandise. These employees serve in positions such as import specialist, auditor, international trade specialist, and textile analyst.
- The CBP Canine Enforcement Program conducts the largest number of working dogs of any U.S. federal law enforcement agency. K-9 teams are assigned to 73 commercial ports and 74 Border Patrol stations throughout the nation.

CBP assess all passengers flying into the U.S. for terrorist risk via Joint Terrorism Task Force and systems such as Advance Passenger Information System (APIS), United States Visitor and Immigrant Status Indication Technology US-VISIT, and the Student and Exchange Visitor System SEVIS. CBP also works with the U.S. Food and Drug Administration to screen high-risk imported food shipments in order to prevent bio-terrorism/agro-terrorism.

Through the Container Security Initiative, CBP works jointly with host nation counterparts to identify and screen containers that pose a risk at the foreign port of departure before they are loaded on board vessels bound for the U.S. CSI is implemented in 20 of the largest ports in terms of container shipments to the U.S., and at a total of 58 ports worldwide.

The Secure Electronic Network for Travelers Rapid Inspection program allows pre-screened, low-risk travelers from Mexico to be processed through dedicated lanes. NEXUS is a similar program on the country's northern border with Canada. Along both borders, CBP has implemented the Free and Secure Trade, which utilizes transponder technology and pre-arrival shipment information to process participating trucks as they arrive at the border. An agreement with Canada allows CBP to target, screen, and examine rail shipments headed to the U.S.

[2] **Apprehensions by Southwest Border Patrol sectors for FY 2009:**

- San Diego Sector: 118,721
- El Centro Sector: 33,521
- Yuma Sector: 6,951
- Tucson Sector: 241,673
- El Paso Sector: 14,999
- Marfa Sector: 6,360
- Del Rio Sector:17,082
- Laredo Sector: 40,569
- Rio Grande Valley Sector: 60,989

[3] **American Embassy Cable**, April 14, 2009

SUBJECT: DHS SECRETARY NAPOLITANO AND ATTORNEY GENERAL HOLDER MEET WITH MEXICAN PRESIDENT CALDERON
202258
2009-04-14 16:02:00
09MEXICO1048
Embassy Mexico
CONFIDENTIAL
R 141602Z APR 09
FM AMEMBASSY MEXICO
TO SECSTATE WASHDC 6006
DEPT OF JUSTICE WASHINGTON DC
DEPT OF HOMELAND SECURITY WASHINGTON DC
INFO ALL US CONSULATES IN MEXICO COLLECTIVE
TAGS: PREL PTER ETRD MX
C O N F I D E N T I A L MEXICO 001048
E.O. 12958: DECL: 04/07/2019
TAGS: PREL PTER ETRD MX
Classified By: CDA Leslie Bassett for reasons 1.4 b,d

¶1. (C) Summary: DHS Secretary Janet Napolitano and Attorney General Eric Holder held a wide-ranging conversation with President Felipe Calderon April 3 which covered the range of security issues from border infrastructure to the rising price of cocaine in the U.S. DHS Secretary Napolitano laid out a number of specific measures she hoped the U.S. and Mexico could move forward on. Attorney General Holder discussed drug courts and rehabilitation efforts in the U.S. President Calderon reiterated his belief the U.S. should reinstitute the ban on assault weapons and consider a national weapons registry. The cordial conversation served as a good summary of the two U.S. cabinet members' separate but hectic rounds of meetings in Mexico including their participation in the April 1-3 binational arms trafficking conference. End Summary.

Arms Trafficking

¶2. (C) AG Holder opened the conversation by reviewing the very fruitful conversations held during the two-day arms trafficking conference between U.S. and Mexican subject matter experts. Secretary Napolitano suggested one way of dealing with arms trafficking would be increased inspections of travelers leaving the U.S. for Mexico. She had recently ordered additional resources to the border for increased southbound inspections, and offered to coordinate inspection points with Mexico so Mexican Customs could apply its inspection resources in complementary areas. She highlighted the utility of trained canine units to USG detection efforts. Secretary Napolitano also observed that as the U.S. and Mexico became more successful at controlling land crossings, smugglers would likely move to maritime routes, putting pressure on the Mexican Navy. Calderon acknowledged the utility of canines, noting that Mexico was working to develop its own canine training facility. The President also reiterated that Mexico believes the 2004 expiration of the U.S. ban on assault weapons directly affected the more aggressive posture by drug cartels today, and asked that the U.S. consider re-imposing the ban while acknowledging the political difficulties. The President also requested that the U.S. consider a national weapons registry to make tracing weapons more efficient, especially after re-sale. AG Holder noted that to support ongoing investigations of arms traffickers the U.S. needed to request ready access to weapons held by the Mexican army in warehouses, so those weapons could be traced.

Border Infrastructure

¶3. (C) President Calderon noted that he was very interested in a safer border and hoped that technology would advance so that every vehicle could pass through non-invasive inspection without inconvenience to legitimate travelers or shippers. He asked for USG assistance to expand Mexico's inventory of non-invasive inspection equipment (NIIE). Mexico would tighten border inspections and criminals would learn they can't use the border for crime. Secretary Napolitano noted the Obama Administration's March 20 announcements increased law enforcement presence at the border, a step Calderon said Mexico welcomed. Foreign Secretary Espinosa added that militarization of the border would be a difficult issue for

Mexico. Sec. Napolitano noted that the decision to move additional National Guard forces to the border was currently under review, but should it be favorable the National Guard would serve only in support roles to CBP. President Calderon then presented Secretary Napolitano with a list of six border crossing projects (Otay Mesa, Anzalduas, El Chapparal, Guadelupe-Tornillo, Colombia-Webb and San Jeronimo-San Teresa) which he hoped could be accelerated, perhaps in time for President Obama's visit. Secretary Napolitano noted that the stimulus bill included additional resources for ports of entry, and added that she and Secretary Espinosa had agreed to look at aligning our visions of the border over the longer term.

Cooperation Against Security Threats

¶4. (C) Mexican Secretary of Government Gomez Mont cited the recent successful collaboration between ICE and Mexican Customs to stop smuggling from the government oil company Pemex. This was an example of great cooperation, Secretary Gomez-Mont stressed. Mexico looked forward to launching very soon a fusion task force to detect and deter criminal activity across Mexico, and hoped it could link to U.S. intel centers like EPIC once it was up and running. President Calderon praised cooperation with both DOJ and DHS, then solicited Attorney General Holder's support regarding acquisition of some equipment the Mexican intelligence agency CISEN was hoping to purchase, but which had been held up due to reservations expressed by a DOJ agency. Calderon also highlighted excellent cooperation between the Mexican Navy and the U.S. Coast Guard.

¶5. (C) President Calderon acknowledged that Mexico had an increasing drug consumption problem, and solicited USG support in sharing successful techniques to rehabilitate serious addicts. AG Holder noted that the U.S. would engage more aggressively in demand reduction in the coming years, allocating significant resources to drug courts that would supervise mandatory treatment for addicts, or remand them to prison if they failed treatment. These programs were very successful, the Attorney General said. Prevention and rehabilitation programs would take markets away from the cartels. Calderon agreed, then added that as Mexico became more successful in interdicting drugs like cocaine, for example, the market price would rise higher in the U.S., providing a greater incentive to traffickers to stay in the business. He needed the benefit of U.S. expertise to understand how, working together, we might drive the price of drugs down so cartels would not longer see trafficking as a profitable enterprise. Secretary Napolitano took the opportunity to congratulate President Calderon on Mexico's success in clamping down on precursor chemicals for methamphetamine production.

¶6. (C) Calderon then turned to his efforts in Ciudad Juarez, noting that Mexico sees a success in Juarez as a benchmark for its security strategy. Since he had dispatched the military and federal police to Juarez, Calderon noted, crime had fallen 80 percent. Yesterday was the first time in years, he continued, that there had not been a single murder in Chihuahua. Calderon said he recognized the military did not pose a permanent solution, so would work to reform and equip local police, and insist on the support of local authorities. Both AG Holder and Secretary Napolitano said the U.S. applauds Calderon's efforts and appreciates the sacrifices of the agents and soldiers working toward a secure Mexico.

Migration

¶7. (C) President Calderon agreed that migration was a difficult issue in these economic times. He appreciated President Obama's commitment to comprehensive migration reform. For Mexico the near-term challenge was to work to change the image of Mexico so that any migration debate, when the time was appropriate, would not be colored by anti-Mexican sentiment. He also hoped there might be an opportunity to expand the temporary worker visa programs in sectors where labor shortages might still be a challenge. DHS Secretary Napolitano noted that she and Foreign Secretary Espinosa had discussed a high level group to discuss migration issues as they pertained under existing legislation, as there was certainly more we could do together on that front. She looked forward to working with colleagues at the Department of State and Justice on this idea.

Accessed at WikiLeaks website:
http://wikileaks.org/cable/2009/04/09MEXICO1048.html
[4] **American Embassy Cable** 2009-10-29 18:14:00
SUBJECT: MEXICO ARMS TRAFFICKING: ACCESS TO CONFISCATED WEAPONS, A NECESSARY STEP
232113 2009-10-29 18:14:0009 MEXICO3114, authored by John Feeley, the U.S. chargé d'affaires,
232113
09MEXICO3114
Embassy Mexico
CONFIDENTIAL
Classified By: Classified by Political Minister Counselor Gustavo Delga do: Reason: 1.4 (b),(d).
¶1. (SBU) Summary. Mexico is a awash with illegal firearms from unknown suppliers that arm organized crime groups and fuel escalating violence. Investigation and prosecution of illegal arms dealers is thwarted by in-fighting among Mexican institutions and legal restrictions that prevent the sharing of important information. Successful prosecution of illegal arms traffickers will depend on U.S. law enforcement agencies gaining access to confiscated weapons to form actionable intelligence and launch investigations. End Summary

A Recipe for Problems: Too Many Cooks, Too Little Love
¶2. (C) Currently, government warehouses throughout Mexico have approximately 140,000 weapons either confiscated from crime scenes or gathered from check points. Some of these weapons -- in storage for over 10 years -- are suspected to have little investigative value. The warehouses are the responsibility of the Mexican Army (SEDENA), which maintains a piece-meal list of information on at least 64,000 weapons collected since the start of the Calderon administration in December 2006. SEDENA's decision to share this information with us in July of this year prompted ICE and ATF to review the data in an effort to open criminal investigations against individuals suspected of knowingly selling weapons to individuals linked to drug trafficking

organizations (DTOs). DIA analysts initiated a separate effort to identify the origin of the weapons as well as trafficking patterns. Unfortunately, the information is incomplete and lacks source data, a reflection of the inconsistent and uneven collection methods employed by Mexican Federal Police (SSP), Mexican Attorney General (PGR), and SEDENA officials in their investigation of confiscated weapons. (Septel analyzes efforts to systematically collect and share weapons forensic information.)

¶3. (SBU) PGR assumes legal authority for confiscated weapons stored in warehouses that correspond to Mexican criminal investigations. Once the PGR completes its initial investigation, it turns over the actual weapon and all information it has gathered over to the Mexican judiciary, which retains jurisdiction over the weapon over the course of judicial proceedings. Upon termination of all investigative and judicial proceedings, SEDENA is assigned responsibility for disposition or destruction of the weapons -- a process that could take years.

¶4. (SBU) Besides the sheer magnitude of the weapons collected, the GOM's disjointed approach for managing the weapons it stores in its warehouses has fostered an ad-hoc system with many accountability gaps. On frequent occasions, GOM agencies -- with their conflicting priorities and competing responsibilities -- openly dispute who has the lead on key arms investigations. PGR holds tightly to its authority as the prosecutorial, investigative, and forensic arm of the GOM; while the SSP retains its position as the lead federal law enforcement agency, an investigative role recently expanded in new legislation. Both agencies have the authority to conduct crime scene investigation and collect forensic evidence, yet information sharing across bureaucratic lines is virtually nonexistent. SSP generally agrees to share information on cases only when the case is transferred to the prosecutor (PGR).

¶5. (SBU) U.S. law enforcement agencies have a strong interest in obtaining information from weapon seizures as this information forms the basis of intelligence, follow-on domestic investigations, and potential prosecutions. A February 2009 Mexican Supreme Court ruling, however, restricts any access to weapons that are involved in court cases. The USG has had limited success obtaining access to warehouses and weapons, with the exception of some high-level visits, affording rare opportunities to get a look inside the warehouses. Even though the GOM provided information on 64,000 confiscated arms, the incomplete information needs to be verified and experts need access to the actual weapons to obtain additional evidence -- source data, obliteration data and pictures -- to provide the basis for investigations and subsequent U.S. judicial cases. SEDENA insists it is willing to grant U.S. law enforcement agencies access to confiscated weapons and blames PGR for any denials. In mid-August, SEDENA reviewed with us twelve instances in which its approval of our official requests for access were overturned by the PGR, based on the February 2009 Supreme Court case.

¶6. (SBU) Comment. Claims by Mexican and U.S. officials that upwards of 90 percent of illegal recovered weapons can be traced back to the U.S. is based on an incomplete survey of confiscated weapons. In point of fact, without wider access to the weapons seized in Mexico, we really have no way of verifying these numbers. Joint efforts to develop intelligence that can serve the impetus for investigations and prosecutions of individuals or companies that market firearms to the cartels, will require Mexican and USG law enforcement agencies to share essential crime scene forensic information on a real time basis. Post law enforcement agencies will continue to work closely with their Mexican counterparts to break down institutional divisions and facilitate more information sharing on arms trafficking cases both among the Mexican agencies and with U.S. partners. End Comment

Accessed on July 2, 2011 at:

http://www.wikileaks.ch/cable/2009/10/09MEXICO3114.html

5 DOJ/OIG Report, November 2010:

"ATF stated that its common definition of a "successful trace" is a trace that provides any additional historical or identifying information concerning the firearm beyond the original information submitted in the trace request. However, ATF staff provided us different definitions of a successful trace, such as one that identifies *the first purchaser. We define a successful trace as one that identifies the gun dealer who originally sold the weapon because that is the minimum result that can provide ATF with usable intelligence information.*

According to ATF National Tracing Center data, an invalid serial number was the most common reason for unsuccessful traces from Mexico. However, crime gun traces can be unsuccessful for many other reasons. For example, the requester may not have provided a manufacturer or importer, or the gun may have been manufactured prior to 1968 when the Gun Control Act was enacted and thus no records were required."

[6] **Statute of limitations for straw purchasing-related crimes** is 5 years. See Title 18 U.S.C. § 3282. Notwithstanding the 5-year statute of limitations, we found that many Southwest border USAOs establish much shorter thresholds for the prosecution of these types of cases. For example, the Northern District of Texas (encompassing ATF's Dallas Field Division) typically will not accept ATF straw purchasing-related cases with a time-to-crime of more than 1 year, while the Southern District of Texas (encompassing the Houston Field Division) established a threshold of less than 3 years for these cases.

[7] **Sources of ATF data on firearms:**
- ATF Form 4473 over the counter firearms transfer information provided by all retail purchasers of firearms since 1968, Every time a gun store goes out of business they are required by law to turn over all firearms transaction records to the ATF; and this absolutely includes the make, model, serial number and caliber of the weapon/s you purchased combined with your full legal name, a complete physical description (eye and hair color, height and weight) physical street addresses, your Social Security number, birthplace and birth date, drivers license number, issue and expiration dates, etc.), and it may contain any other personal information the dealer adds such as your phone number, email address or photograph.

- 4473 e-Forms, an online version of the paper ATF form 4473 and delivered via the internet. It does not contain specific firearms data but it does capture the type weapon(s) in the sale (i.e. long gun, hand gun, both, etc.).
- ATF/FBI phone-in records of gun store initiated criminal background checks which access the computerized NICS criminal records system to clear or deny retail sales of firearms. Although this system does not capture the make/model/serial number data of the retail sale, it does capture all the same personal and private data on American citizens contained in the Form 4473 and captures as well information on the type weapon(s) in the sale (i.e. long gun, hand gun, both, etc.).
- ATF 5300.11, ongoing manufacturing, inventory and export sales records submitted by licensed OEM gun manufacturers. ATF 5320.2 similarly captures manufacturer importation data.
- ATF Form 3310.4 Report of Multiple Sale or Other Disposition of Pistols and Revolvers data: any retail customer who purchases more than one hand gun in a five day period must be reported by the dealer to the ATF within 24 hours. Notification may be by facsimile or mail. This form also contains the same Form 4473 personal information on the buyer as well as the serial numbered weapons data, including make, model and caliber(s) involved in the sale.

And a host of others including ATF Form 1370.2—Requisition for Firearms/Explosives Forms, ATF Form 3310.6—Interstate Firearms Shipment Theft/Loss Report, ATF Form 3310.11—Federal Firearms Licensee Theft/Loss Report, and ATF Form 3310.11A—Federal Firearms Licensee Theft/Loss Continuation Sheet.

[8] **American Embassy Cable:** DHS SECRETARY NAPOLITANO AND ATTORNEY GENERAL HOLDER MEET WITH MEXICAN PRESIDENT CALDERON
2009-04-14 16:02:00

09MEXICO1048
Embassy Mexico
CONFIDENTIAL
R 141602Z APR 09
FM AMEMBASSY MEXICO
TO SECSTATE WASHDC 6006
DEPT OF JUSTICE WASHINGTON DC
DEPT OF HOMELAND SECURITY WASHINGTON DC
INFO ALL US CONSULATES IN MEXICO COLLECTIVE

C O N F I D E N T I A L MEXICO 001048

E.O. 12958: DECL: 04/07/2019
TAGS: PREL PTER ETRD MX
SUBJECT: DHS SECRETARY NAPOLITANO AND ATTORNEY
GENERAL HOLDER MEET WITH MEXICAN PRESIDENT CALDERON
Classified By: CDA Leslie Bassett for reasons 1.4 b,d

¶1. (C) Summary: DHS Secretary Janet Napolitano and
Attorney General Eric Holder held a wide-ranging conversation
with President Felipe Calderon April 3 which covered the
range of security issues from border infrastructure to the
rising price of cocaine in the U.S. DHS Secretary Napolitano
laid out a number of specific measures she hoped the U.S. and
Mexico could move forward on. Attorney General Holder
discussed drug courts and rehabilitation efforts in the U.S.
President Calderon reiterated his belief the U.S. should
reinstitute the ban on assault weapons and consider a
national weapons registry. The cordial conversation served
as a good summary of the two U.S. cabinet members' separate
but hectic rounds of meetings in Mexico including their
participation in the April 1-3 binational arms trafficking
conference. End Summary.

Arms Trafficking

¶2. (C) AG Holder opened the conversation by reviewing the very fruitful conversations held during the two-day arms trafficking conference between U.S. and Mexican subject matter experts. Secretary Napolitano suggested one way of dealing with arms trafficking would be increased inspections of travelers leaving the U.S. for Mexico. She had recently ordered additional resources to the border for increased southbound inspections, and offered to coordinate inspection points with Mexico so Mexican Customs could apply its inspection resources in complementary areas. She highlighted the utility of trained canine units to USG detection efforts. Secretary Napolitano also observed that as the U.S. and Mexico became more successful at controlling land crossings, smugglers would likely move to maritime routes, putting pressure on the Mexican Navy. Calderon acknowledged the utility of canines, noting that Mexico was working to develop its own canine training facility. The President also reiterated that Mexico believes the 2004 expiration of the U.S. ban on assault weapons directly affected the more aggressive posture by drug cartels today, and asked that the U.S. consider re-imposing the ban while acknowledging the political difficulties. The President also requested that the U.S. consider a national weapons registry to make tracing weapons more efficient, especially after re-sale. AG Holder noted that to support ongoing investigations of arms traffickers the U.S. needed to request ready access to weapons held by the Mexican army in warehouses, so those weapons could be traced.

Border Infrastructure

¶3. (C) President Calderon noted that he was very interested in a safer border and hoped that technology would advance so that every vehicle could pass through non-invasive inspection without inconvenience to legitimate travelers or shippers. He asked for USG assistance to expand Mexico's inventory of non-invasive inspection equipment (NIIE). Mexico would tighten border inspections and criminals would learn they can't use the border for crime. Secretary Napolitano noted the Obama Administration's March 20 announcements increased law enforcement presence at the border, a step Calderon said Mexico welcomed. Foreign Secretary Espinosa added that militarization of the border would be a difficult issue for Mexico. Sec. Napolitano noted that the decision to move additional National Guard forces to the border was currently under review, but should it be favorable the National Guard would serve only in support roles to CBP. President Calderon then presented Secretary Napolitano with a list of six border crossing projects (Otay Mesa, Anzalduas, El Chapparal, Guadelupe-Tornillo, Colombia-Webb and San Jeronimo-San Teresa) which he hoped could be accelerated, perhaps in time for President Obama's visit. Secretary Napolitano noted that the stimulus bill included additional resources for ports of entry, and added that she and Secretary Espinosa had agreed to look at aligning our visions of the border over the longer term.

Cooperation Against Security Threats

¶4. (C) Mexican Secretary of Government Gomez Mont cited the recent successful collaboration between ICE and Mexican Customs to stop smuggling from the government oil company Pemex. This was an example of great cooperation, Secretary Gomez-Mont stressed. Mexico looked forward to launching very soon a fusion task force to detect and deter criminal activity across Mexico, and hoped it could link to U.S. intel centers like EPIC once it was up and running. President Calderon praised cooperation with both DOJ and DHS, then solicited Attorney General Holder's support regarding acquisition of some equipment the Mexican intelligence agency CISEN was hoping to purchase, but which had been held up due to reservations expressed by a DOJ agency. Calderon also highlighted excellent cooperation between the Mexican Navy and the U.S. Coast Guard.

¶5. (C) President Calderon acknowledged that Mexico had an increasing drug consumption problem, and solicited USG support in sharing successful techniques to rehabilitate serious addicts. AG Holder noted that the U.S. would engage more aggressively in demand reduction in the coming years, allocating significant resources to drug courts that would supervise mandatory treatment for addicts, or remand them to prison if they failed treatment. These programs were very successful, the Attorney General said. Prevention and rehabilitation programs would take markets away from the cartels. Calderon agreed, then added that as Mexico became more successful in interdicting drugs like cocaine, for example, the market price would rise higher in the U.S., providing a greater incentive to traffickers to stay in the business. He needed the benefit of U.S. expertise to understand how, working together, we might drive the price of drugs down so cartels would not longer see trafficking as a profitable enterprise. Secretary Napolitano took the opportunity to congratulate President Calderon on Mexico's success in clamping down on precursor chemicals for methamphetamine production.

¶6. (C) Calderon then turned to his efforts in Ciudad Juarez, noting that Mexico sees a success in Juarez as a benchmark for its security strategy. Since he had dispatched the military and federal police to Juarez, Calderon noted, crime had fallen 80 percent. Yesterday was the first time in years, he continued, that there had not been a single murder in Chihuahua. Calderon said he recognized the military did not pose a permanent solution, so would work to reform and equip local police, and insist on the support of local authorities. Both AG Holder and Secretary Napolitano said the U.S. applauds Calderon's efforts and appreciates the sacrifices of the agents and soldiers working toward a secure Mexico.

Migration

¶7. (C) President Calderon agreed that migration was a difficult issue in these economic times. He appreciated President Obama's commitment to comprehensive migration reform. For Mexico the near-term challenge was to work to change the image of Mexico so that any migration debate, when the time was appropriate, would not be colored by anti-Mexican sentiment. He also hoped there might be an opportunity to expand the temporary worker visa programs in sectors where labor shortages might still be a challenge. DHS Secretary Napolitano noted that she and Foreign Secretary Espinosa had discussed a high level group to discuss migration issues as they pertained under existing legislation, as there was certainly more we could do together on that front. She looked forward to working with colleagues at the Department of State and Justice on this idea.

[9] **American Embassy Cable to US Secretary of State**, Subject: ONDCP WALTERS MEETINGS WITH MEXICAN OFFICIALS 2007-04-13 22:28:00
07MEXICO1854
Embassy Mexico
CONFIDENTIAL
07MEXICO965|07MEXICO966
VZCZCXYZ0000
PP RUEHWEB

DE RUEHME #1854/01 1032228
ZNY CCCCC ZZH
P 132228Z APR 07
FM AMEMBASSY MEXICO
TO SECSTATE WASHDC PRIORITY 6452

C O N FI D E N T I A L MEXICO 001854

E.O. 12958: DECL: 04/13/2017
SUBJECT: ONDCP WALTERS MEETINGS WITH MEXICAN
OFFICIALS
REF: A. MEXICO 965
¶B. MEXICO 966

Classified By: NAS Director Scott Danaher for Reason 1.4 (B, D)

¶1. (C) SUMMARY: The February 27 visit by John Walters (ONDCP)
helped initiate coordination with the newly installed
Calderon Administration. In separate meetings with Attorney
General Medina Mora and Public Security Secretary Garcia
Luna, Director Walters emphasized the importance of
information sharing for interdiction and for attacking drug
trafficking organizations. Noting that the U.S. was awaiting
Mexican thoughts about a strategic counter-drug partnership,
he urged early operational cooperation, and discouraged
megaprograms as likely to be too ponderous to be effective.
He emphasized U.S. willingness to work in partnership with
Mexico at the Southwest Border, and on database and
information sharing, arms trafficking, specific law
enforcement operations, and training and equipment suited for
requirements identified by Mexico. While ONDCP Director
Walters pressed Mexican naval officials for progress on a
maritime agreement, they remained reticent on the subject
although generally open to better U.S.-Mexico cooperation.
END SUMMARY.

¶2. (SBU) On February 27, John Walters (Director of the White
House Office of National Drug Control Policy - ONDCP) and
staff visited Mexico City for meetings with leaders of the
newly installed Calderon Administration, including Eduardo
Medina Mora (Attorney General) and Genaro Garcia Luna

313

(Secretary for Public Security). Walters also met with the Army (SEDENA), the Navy and GOM health authorities.

¶3. (SBU) In Walters, meeting with Eduardo Medina Mora, the AG reemphasized many topics raised with recent USG visitors (reftels), including the GOM's priority on attacking the cartels, improving interdiction (with an emphasis on methamphetamines and a reorientation towards Mexico's southern border), improving eradication, improving anti-money laundering efforts, stemming the growth of small-scale drug dealing, promoting prevention and rehabilitation, improving intelligence gathering and assessing and countering arms trafficking. The AG emphasized the need for both governments to break down the partitions that artificially divide our respective anti-money laundering efforts, and to seek new means to pursue money launderers. The AG also focused in on the threat of Chinese exports of methamphetamine precursors, asking for USG help in urging the Chinese to better control their exports and in improving coordination of inspection of trade and interdiction of illicit goods transiting Long Beach destined for Mexico.

¶4. (C) Walters expressed his concern for ensuring that top-level people in the Mexican policy community have adequate personal protection to prevent traffickers from defeating significant reforms by intimidation and selective assassination. With respect to Mexican concerns about weapons entering from the United States, Walters told Medina that ATF was prepared to conduct serial number traces of all weapons referred by Mexican authorities, and that the U.S. would initiate proactive surveillance and investigation of gun shows and other sources in the Southwest Border area, particularly the sales of armor piercing munitions. Medina acknowledged the importance of serial number traces, but requested a level of information sharing that would provide Mexican access to information about purchasers of

military-style munitions and pro-actively put them in a
position to arrest and prosecute.

¶5. (C) With respect to cash movements, Walters said the U.S.
would be prepared to follow Mexico's lead, but suggested that
strengthening investigations and invocation of U.S. foreign
assets control legislation could effectively hit traffickers
cash supply and cause considerable disruption.

¶6. (C) Turning to methamphetamine, Walters reviewed
consultations with his German, Indian and Chinese
counterparts, as well as in international organizations,
noting U.S. interest in working to control precursor
chemicals at the source. He added that if the Attorney
General thought it would advance policy, the two of them
might approach the Chinese jointly -- a proposal Medina
accepted.

¶7. (C) Moving to legislation currently in the Mexican
Congress to expand the authority of state and local
jurisdictions to enforce drug laws, Walters suggested a
sustained dialogue as the legislation advanced.

¶8. (SBU) Walters discussed the pending reorganization of the
federal police forces into a single entity in his meeting
with Genaro Garcia Luna. GGL is ambitious, hoping to reverse
the endemic corruption that has afflicted the SSP personnel,
essentially by paying his staff better, introducing more
stringent selection criteria and vetting all 20,000 of them.
(In coming years, this staffing level will likely rise to
40,000.) Walters also emphasized the USG's desire to see
better coordination with ATF on arms trafficking.

¶9. (SBU) In meetings at SEDENA with Gen. Oliver Cen (Deputy
Chief of Staff for Operations) and Gen. Morafin
(Intelligence), the Army emphasized its need for help with

demand reduction amongst its own elements, as well as more broadly; this was especially true with regards to methamphetamine use in Mexico. Gen. Oliver also noted the shift of responsibility for all forms of eradication to the military, with the Office of the Attorney General (PGR) transferring to SEDENA the equipment (aircraft, parts and facilities) PGR had used previously for aerial fumigation of opium poppy. SEDENA planned to adopt a new standard operating procedure in its manual eradication activities, employing dozens of surge operations with a more focused approach for maximum impact, instead of permanently deploying the 20,000-30,000 troops that SEDENA and Marina have fielded in the past. They also discussed VIP security, which is the responsibility of SEDENA. Walters noted that ATF was willing to work with SEDENA to address the rampant arms smuggling that feeds into the violence associated with Mexico's drug trafficking organizations (DTOs).

¶10. (SBU) In a working lunch with the DCM and Navy (Marina) Admiral Enrique Henaro Galan (Chief of Staff, CNO), Admiral Roberto Gomez Caranza (Deputy Chief of Operations) and others, Walters pressed for Mexican consideration of a maritime agreement. While generally friendly, the Navy delegation indicated that cooperation could be improved outside the context of a formal agreement, and suggested that the Secretariat of Foreign Relations (SRE) was the better place to press the issue of an agreement. The luncheon made clear the excellent relationship that exists between the Navy and the U.S. Coast Guard representative at post, and highlighted the Navy's general interest in cooperating with the U.S.

¶11. (SBU) In a final meeting with Mauricio Hernandez Avila (Under Secretary of Health for Prevention and Promotion) and Dr. Carlos Rodriguez Ajenjo (Technical Secretary of National Council Against Addiction - CONADIC), Walters shared insights on the means by which ONDCP tracked real-time changes in drug usage in the United States. Hernandez recounted his hope that the past de facto policy of tolerance for illicit use of drugs and alcohol by minors at the individual level would be changed in the Calderon administration. There was a huge bulge in the population profile, with a youth cohort aging into adulthood, and with high levels of abuse of all drugs of concern, including tobacco. The powerful alcohol industry created demand in ads aimed at youths and young adults, complicating any message the GOM might put out. Hernandez also noted a desire to pair cities along the border in an attempt to address illicit consumption of drugs, alcohol and cigarettes among youth.

[10] **US Embassy Cable: TRACKING NARCO-GRENADES, March 2009**

194998
2009-03-03 17:19:00
09MONTERREY100
Consulate Monterrey
SECRET//NOFORN

VZCZCXRO7584
PP RUEHWEB
DE RUEHMC #0100/01 0771547
ZNY SSSSS ZZH
P R 031719Z MAR 09 ZDS
FM AMCONSUL MONTERREY
TO RUEHME/AMEMBASSY MEXICO 4622
RUEHC/SECSTATE WASHDC PRIORITY 3569
INFO RUEHXC/ALL US CONSULATES IN MEXICO COLLECTIVE
RUEHCD/AMCONSUL CIUDAD JUAREZ 0070
RHMFISS/DEPT OF JUSTICE WASHINGTON DC
RHMFISS/FBI WASHINGTON DC
RUEHGD/AMCONSUL GUADALAJARA 0114

RUEHGD/DTS GUADALAJARA
RUEHHO/AMCONSUL HERMOSILLO 0048
RUEHHO/DTS HERMOSILLO
RHMFISS/HQ USNORTHCOM
RUEHRS/AMCONSUL MATAMOROS 0260
RUEHRS/DTS MATAMOROS
RUEHRD/AMCONSUL MERIDA 0275
RUEHRD/DTS MERIDA
RUEHMC/AMCONSUL MONTERREY 9135
RUEHNG/AMCONSUL NOGALES 0012
RUEHNL/AMCONSUL NUEVO LAREDO 0221
RUEHNL/DTS NUEVO LAREDO
RUEHSN/AMEMBASSY SAN SALVADOR 0035
RUEHUL/AMEMBASSY SEOUL 0006
RUEHTM/AMCONSUL TIJUANA 0102
RUEHTM/DTS TIJUANA

S E C R E T SECTION 01 OF 02 MONTERREY 000100

C O R R E C T E D C O P Y - Classification

PM FOR DTCC FOR BALLARD, DS FOR IP/ITA, WHA FOR MEX AND CEN, EAP
FOR EAP/K
SIPDIS

E.O. 12958: DECL: 3/3/2034
TAGS: ETTC MASS SNAR PGOV KCRM CASC MX KS
SUBJECT: MEXICO: TRACKING NARCO-GRENADES

CLASSIFIED BY: Bruce Williamson, Principal Offficer, Consul General Monterrey, State.

REASON: 1.4 (a), (b), (d)
¶1. (SBU) During recent months Mexican narco-traffickers have directed a series of grenade attacks directed against, inter alia,

Mexican law enforcement and military facilities, civilian crowds, and U.S. consular installations. The escalation in the strength and power of the weapons used by the narco-traffickers has not only cost lives, but has taken its toll in terms of the damage done to local civil society.

¶2. (S) AmConsulate General Monterrey's ATF Office, the ATF Explosives Technology Branch, and AmEmbassy Mexico DAO have been working with Mexican law enforcement authorities to identify the origin of various grenades and other explosive devices recovered locally over the past few months, including the unexploded M26A2 fragmentation grenade hurled at the Consulate itself during the October 11, 2008 attack. Other ordnance recovered includes 21 grenades recovered by Mexican law enforcement on October 16, 2008 after a raid at a narco-warehouse in Guadalupe (a working class suburb of Monterrey), and twenty-five 40mm explosive projectiles, a U.S. M203 40mm grenade launcher, and three South Korean K400 fragmentation grenades recovered the same day in an abandoned armored vehicle that suspected narco-traffickers used to escape apprehension.

¶3. (S/NF) Local Mexican law enforcement has recovered a Grenade spoon and pull ring from an exploded hand grenade used in a January 6, 2009 attack on Televisa Monterrey, a Monterrey television station. Based upon ATF examination, it appears that the grenade used in the attack on the Consulate has the same lot number, and is of similar design and style, as the three of the grenades found at the narco-warehouse in Guadalupe. On January 7, 2009, the Mexican Army recovered 14 M-67 fragmentation grenades and 1 K400 fragmentation grenade in Durango City, Durango. Finally and perhaps most disturbing, on January 31, 2009 three men tossed a K-75 grenade into a night club near Pharr, Texas -- an East Texas border town --but the grenade did not explode. The attackers may have been targeting three off-duty police officers who were in the club at the time.

319

¶4. (S) The lot numbers of some of the grenades recovered, including the grenade used in the attack on Televisa, indicate that previously ordnance with these same lot numbers may have been sold by the USG to the El Salvadoran military in the early 1990s via the Foreign Military Sales program. We would like to thank AmEmbassy San Salvador for its ongoing efforts to query the Government of El Salvador as whether any of its stocks of grenades and other munitions have been diverted or are otherwise unaccounted for.

¶5. (SBU) AmConsulate Monterrey requests that Department instruct AmEmbassy Seoul to discreetly query the Korean government regarding the whereabouts, disposition, and the possibility of any missing stocks of South Korean-made:

--- 40mm High Explosives Cartridges K200, with Lot numbers HWB95L615-012; HWB95L615-014; EC-87E615-061; EC-88G615-071, EC-84D610-096, EC-83H615-012, and EC-83H815-012.

--- K400 Fragmentation Grenades, with Lot numbers EC-89E605-063, HEB96H605-033, HWB96H605-033, HWB96H-609-003, KG94DK400002-017, KG94D002-017, HWB89S605-063, ME183D, and HWB95K605-029.

--- K402 Fragmentation Grenades, with Lot numbers HWB96H605-063 and HWB96H605-033.

--- K75 Fragmentation Grenade, with Lot numbers EC-85E605-031 and EC89E605-073.

¶6. (SBU) Any information as to the destination of this ordnance and to whom it may have been sold would be most appreciated. This information will be used in an U.S. ongoing criminal investigation. WILLIAMSON

Illegal Immigration (OTM) and US Weapons Sales[11]--
Highlighted countries also received eTrace access

	Afghanistan	Argentina	Bahamas	Belize
OTM's FY07	2	82	15	53
OTM's FY08	6	66	21	71
OTM's FY09	4	77	13	64
OTM Total	12	225	49	188
Weapons Sales FY10	$75,834,983	$6,416,445	$164,211	$876,373
Total Authorized Sales	$2,774,094,786	$32,870,166	$202,762	$1,067,296

	Bolivia	Brazil	Chile	Colombia
OTM's FY07	92	1205	66	467
OTM's FY08	74	977	60	432
OTM's FY09	52	798	43	421
OTM Total	218	2980	169	1320
Weapons Sales FY10	$259,247	$37,134,259	$13,463,123	$30,518,245
Total Authorized Sales	$4,522,160	$209,601,160	$107,726,546	$82,634,238

	Costa Rica	Dom. Rep.	Ecuador	Egypt
OTM's FY07	192	562	958	9
OTM's FY08	181	819	1578	17
OTM's FY09	173	865	1313	14
OTM Total	546	2246	3849	40
Weapons Sales FY10	$2,691,278	$3,559,910	$8,061,054	$7,250,336
Total Authorized Sales	$21,267,275	$17,176,099	$14,196,292	$91,084,897

Cont'd...

	El Salvador	Guatemala	Honduras	Iraq
OTM's FY07	14118	17335	22914	16
OTM's FY08	12685	16394	19354	10
OTM's FY09	11693	15576	14631	16
OTM Total	38496	49305	56899	42
Weapons Sales FY10	$777,348	$2,147,316	$232,425	$46,009,990
Total Authorized Sales	$2,038,579	$5,265,671	$651,843	$1,217,960,133

	Jamaica	Lebanon	Nicaragua	Pakistan
OTM's FY07	117	14	1647	27
OTM's FY08	160	15	1467	42
OTM's FY09	174	9	976	41
OTM Total	451	38	4090	110
Weapons Sales FY10	$793,704	$177,580	$358,997	$11,938,866
Total Authorized Sales	$2,741,210	$5,350,307	$1,383,332	$77,811,072

	Panama	Paraguay	Peru	Venezuela
OTM's FY07	34	14	332	91
OTM's FY08	35	9	372	78
OTM's FY09	36	14	368	67
OTM Total	105	37	1072	236
Weapons Sales FY10	$1,484,994	$1,825,134	$7,271,126	
Total Authorized Sales	$11,513,738	$2,416,112	$29,741,163	

[12] Groups designated as Foreign Terrorist Organizations

List is current as of January 19, 2010, organized by region and country of origin:

Middle East
- Gaza and the West Bank
  Abu Nidal Organization (ANO) (International)
  Al-Aqsa Martyrs' Brigades
  HAMAS
  Palestine Liberation Front (PLF)
  Popular Front for the Liberation of Palestine (PFLP)
  PFLP-General Command (PFLP-GC)
- Iraq
  Ansar al-Islam (Iraqi Kurdistan)
  Kata'ib Hezbollah (Iraq)
  Kongra-Gel (formerly Kurdistan Workers' Party) (KGK, formerly PKK, KADEK, Kongra-Gel) (Turkey, Iraq, Iran, Syria)
  Tanzim Qa'idat al-Jihad (QJBR) (al-Qaida in Iraq) (formerly Jama'at al-Tawhid wa'al-Jihad, JTJ, al-Zarqawi Network)
- Lebanon
  Asbat an-Ansar
  Hezbollah
- Pakistan
  Harakat ul-Mujahidin (HUM)
  Jaish-e-Mohammed (Army of Mohammed) (JEM)
  Lashkar-e Tayyiba (Army of the Righteous) (LT) (Muridke, Pakistan)
  Lashkar i Jhangvi
  Tehrik-i-Taliban Pakistan (TTP)
- Uzbekistan
  Islamic (IMU) (Uzbekistan)

- Israel
  Kahane Chai (Kach)
- Iran
  Mujahedin-e Khalq Organization (MEK)

Jundallah (People's Resistance Movement of Iran, or PRMI)
- Saudi Arabia
    al-Qaida (Global)
    al-Qaida in the Arabian Peninsula (AQAP)
    al-Qaida in the Islamic (formerly GSPC) (The Maghreb)

Asia

- Japan
    Aum Shinrikyo (Japan)
- South East Asia
    Jemaah Islamiya organization (JI)
- Bangladesh
    Harkat-ul-Jihad (HUJI-B) (Bangladesh)
- Sri Lanka
    Liberation Tigers of Tamil Eelam (LTTE) (Sri Lanka)
- Philippines
    Abu Sayyaf Group (ASG) (Philippines)
    Communist Party of the Philippines/New People's Army (CPP/NPA) (Philippines)

Africa

- Somalia
    Al-Shabaab
- Algeria
    Armed Islamic (GIA)
- Egypt
    Gama'a al-Islamiyya
    Egyptian Islamic
- Libya
    Libyan Islamic (LIFG)
- Morocco
    Moroccan Islamic (GICM)

Europe

- United Kingdom of Great Britain and Northern Ireland

Continuity Irish Republican Army (CIRA) (Northern Ireland)
Real IRA (Northern Ireland)
- Greece
Revolutionary Organization 17 November
Revolutionary Struggle
- Turkey
Revolutionary People's Liberation Party/Front (DHKP/C)
- Spain
Euskadi Ta Askatasuna (Basque Fatherland and Liberty) (ETA) (Spain, France)

South America
- Colombia
National Liberation Army (ELN)
Revolutionary Armed Forces of Colombia (FARC)
United Self-Defense Forces of Colombia (AUC)
- Peru
Shining Path (Sendero Luminoso, SL)

[13] **An Explanatory Memorandum, confiscated on August 20, 2004, in Maryland detailing the Muslim Brotherhood plan for the overthrow of the United States**
On the General Strategic Goal for the Group In North America
5/22/1991
Contents:
1 - An introduction in explanation
2- The Concept of Settlement
3- The Process of Settlement
4- Comprehensive Settlement Organizations
In the name of God, the Beneficent, the Merciful Thanks be to God, Lord of the Two Worlds And Blessed are the Pious The beloved brother The General Masul, may God keep him The beloved brother secretary of the Shura Council, may God keep him The beloved brothers Members of the Shura Council, may God keep them God's peace, mercy and blessings be upon you. .. . To proceed,

I ask Almighty God that you, your families and those whom you love around you are in the best of conditions, pleasing to God, glorified His name be. I send this letter of mine to you hoping that it would seize your attention and receive your good care as you are the people of responsibility and those to whom trust is given.

Between your hands is an "Explanatory Memorandum" which I put effort in writing down so that it is not locked in the chest and the mind, and so that I can share with you a portion of the responsibility in leading the Group in this country.

What might have encouraged me to submit the memorandum in this time in particular is my feeling of a "glimpse of hope" and the beginning of good tidings which bring the good news that we have embarked on a new stage of Islamic activism stages in this continent. The papers which are between your hands are not abundant extravagance, imaginations or hallucinations which passed in the mind of one of your brothers, but they are rather hopes, ambitions and challenges that I hope that you share some or most of which with me. I do not claim their infallibility or absolute correctness, but they are an attempt which requires study, outlook, detailing and rooting from you.

My request to my brothers is to read the memorandum and to write what they wanted of comments and corrections, keeping in mind that what is between your hands is not strange or a new submission without a root, but rather an attempt to interpret and explain some of what came in the long-term plan which we approved and adopted in our council and our conference in the year (1987).

So, my honorable brother, do not rush to throw these papers away due to your many occupations and worries, All what I'm asking of you is to read them and to comment on them hoping that we might continue together the project of our plan and our Islamic work in this part of the world. Should you do that, I would be tha&il and grateful to you. I also ask my honorable brother, the Secretary of the Council, to add the subject of the memorandum on the Council agenda in its coming meeting. May God reward you good and keep you for His Daw'a.

Your brother Mohamed Akram

In the name of God, the Beneficent, the Merciful
Thanks be to God, Lord of the Two Worlds
And Blessed are the Pious
Subject: A project for an explanatory memorandum for the General Strategic goal for the Group in North America mentioned in the long-term plan

One: The Memorandum is derived from:
1 - The general strategic goal of the Group in America which was approved by the Shura Council and the Organizational Conference for the year is "Enablement of Islam in North America, meaning: establishing an effective and a stable Islamic Movement led by the Muslim Brotherhood which adopts Muslims' causes domestically and globally, and which works to expand the observant Muslim base, aims at unifying and directing Muslims' efforts, presents Islam as a civilization alternative, and supports the global Islamic State wherever it is".
2- The priority that is approved by the Shura Council for the work of the Group in its current and former session which is "Settlement".
3- The positive development with the brothers in the Islamic Circle in an attempt to reach a unity of merger.
4- The constant need for thinking and future planning, **an** attempt to read it and working to "shape" the present to comply and suit the needs and challenges of the future.
5- The paper of his eminence, the General Masul, may God keep him, which he recently sent to the members of the Council.
Two: An Introduction to the Explanatory Memorandum:
- In order to begin with the explanation, we must "summon" the following question and place it in front of our eyes as its relationship is important and necessary with the strategic goal and the explanation project we are embarking on. The question we are facing is: "How do you like to see the Islam Movement in North America in ten years?", or "taking along" the following sentence when planning and working, "Islamic Work in North America in the

year (2000): A Strategic Vision". Also, we must summon and take along "elements" of the general strategic goal of the Group in North America and I will intentionally repeat them in numbers. They are:

1- Establishing an effective and stable Islamic Movement led by the Muslim Brotherhood.

2- Adopting Muslims' causes domestically and globally.

3- Expanding the observant Muslim base.

4- Unifying and directing Muslims' efforts.

5- Presenting Islam as a civilization alternative

6- Supporting the establishment of the global Islamic State wherever it is.

- It must be stressed that it has become clear and emphatically known that all is in agreement that we must "settle" or "enable" Islam and its Movement in this part of the world. - Therefore, a joint understanding of the meaning of settlement or enablement must be adopted, through which and on whose basis we explain the general strategic goal with its six elements for the Group in North America.

Three: The Concept of Settlement:

This term was mentioned in the Group's "dictionary" and documents with various meanings in spite of the fact that everyone meant one thing with it. We believe that the understanding of the essence is the same and we will attempt here to give the word and its "meanings" a practical explanation with a practical Movement tone, and not a philosophical linguistic explanation, while stressing that this explanation of ours is not complete until our explanation of "the process" of settlement itself is understood which is mentioned in the following paragraph. We briefly say the following:

Settlement: "That Islam and its Movement become a part of the homeland it lives in".

Establishment: "That Islam turns into firmly-rooted organizations on whose bases civilization, structure and testimony are built".

Stability: "That Islam is stable in the land on which its people move".

Enablement: "That Islam is enabled within the souls, minds and the lives of the people of the country in which it moves".

Rooting: "That Islam is resident and not a passing thing, or rooted "entrenched" in the soil of the spot where it moves and not a strange plant to it".

Four: The Process of Settlement:

- In order for Islam and its Movement to become "a part of the homeland" in which it lives, "stable" in its land, "rooted" in the spirits and minds of its people, "enabled" in the life of its society and has firmly-established "organizations" on which the Islamic structure is built and with which the testimony of civilization is achieved, the Movement must plan and struggle to obtain "the keys" and the tools of this process in carry out this grand mission as a "Civilization Jihadist" responsibility which lies on the shoulders of Muslims and - on top of them - the Muslim Brotherhood in this country. Among these keys and tools are the following:

1- Adopting the concept of settlement and understanding its practical meanings:

The Explanatory Memorandum focused on the Movement and the realistic dimension of the process of settlement and its practical meanings without paying attention to the difference in understanding between the resident and the non-resident, or who is the settled and the non-settled understanding between the resident and the non-resident, or who is the settled and the non-settled and we believe that what was mentioned in the long-term plan in that regards suffices.

2- Making a fundamental shift in our thinking and mentality in order to suit the challenges of the settlement mission.

What is meant with the shift - which is a positive expression - is responding to the grand challenges of the settlement issues. We believe that any transforming response begins with the method of thinking and its center, the brain, first. In order to clarify what is meant with the shift as a key to qualify us to enter the field of settlement, we say very briefly that the following must be accomplished: - A shift from the partial thinking mentality to the comprehensive thinking mentality, - A shift from the "amputated" partial thinking mentality to the "continuous" comprehensive mentality. - A shift from the mentality of caution and reservation to the mentality of risk and controlled liberation.

- A shift from the mentality of the elite Movement to the mentality of the popular Movement.

- A shift from the mentality of preaching and guidance to the mentality of building and testimony

- A shift from the single opinion mentality to the multiple opinion mentality.

- A shift from the collision mentality to the absorption mentality. - A shift from the individual mentality to the team mentality. - A shift from the anticipation mentality to the initiative mentality. - A shift from the hesitation mentality to the decisiveness mentality. - A shift from the principles mentality to the programs mentality. - A shift from the abstract ideas mentality the true organizations mentality. This is the core point and the essence of the memorandum.

3- Understanding the historical stages in which the Islamic Ikhwani activism went through in this country:

The writer of the memorandum believes that understanding and comprehending the historical stages of the Islamic activism which was led and being led by the Muslim Brotherhood in this continent is a very important key in working towards settlement, through which the Group observes its march, the direction of its movement and the curves and turns of its road. We will suffice here with mentioning the title for each of these stages [The title expresses the prevalent characteristic of the stage] [Details maybe mentioned in another future study]. Most likely, the stages are:

A- The stage of searching for self and determining the identity.

B- The stage of inner build-up and tightening the organization.

C- The stage of mosques and the Islamic centers.

D- The stage of building the Islamic organizations - the first phase.

E- The stage of building the Islamic schools - the first phase.

F- The stage of thinking about the overt Islamic Movement - the first phase.

G- The stage of openness to the other Islamic movements and attempting to reach a formula for dealing with them - the first phase.

H- The stage of reviving and establishing the Islamic organizations - the second phase.

We believe that the Group is embarking on this stage in its second phase as it has to open the door and enter as it did the first time.

4- Understanding the role of the Muslim Brother in North America:

The process of settlement is a "Civilization-Jihadist Process" with all the word means. The Ikhwan must understand that their work in America is a kind of grand Jihad in eliminating and destroying the Western civilization from within and "sabotaging" its miserable house by their hands and the hands of the believers so that it is eliminated and God's religion is made victorious over all other religions. Without this level of understanding, we are not up to this challenge and have not prepared ourselves for Jihad yet. It is a Muslim's destiny to perform Jihad and work wherever he is and wherever he lands until the final hour comes, and there is no escape from that destiny except for those who chose to slack. But, would the slackers and the Mujahedeen be equal.

5- Understanding that we cannot perform the settlement mission by ourselves or away from people:

A mission as significant and as huge as the settlement mission needs magnificent and exhausting efforts. With their capabilities, human, financial and scientific resources, the Ikhwan will not be able to carry out this mission alone or away from people and he who believes that is wrong, and God knows best. As for the role of the Ikhwan, it is the initiative, pioneering, leadership, raising the banner and pushing people in that direction. They are then to work to employ, direct and unify Muslims' efforts and powers for this process. In order to do that, we must possess a mastery of the art of "coalitions", the art of "absorption" and the principles of "cooperation".

6- The necessity of achieving a union and balanced gradual merger between private work and public work:

We believe that what was written about this subject is many and is enough. But, it needs a time and a practical frame so that what is needed is achieved in a gradual and a balanced way that is compatible with the process of settlement.

7- The conviction that the success of the settlement of Islam and its Movement in this country is a success to the global Islamic Movement and a true support for the sought-after state, God willing:

There is a conviction - with which this memorandum disagrees - that our focus in attempting to settle Islam in this country will lead to negligence in our duty towards the global Islamic Movement in supporting its project to establish the state. We believe that the reply is in two segments: One - The success of the Movement in America in establishing an observant Islamic base with power and effectiveness will be the best support and aid to the global Movement project. And the second - is the global Movement has not succeeded yet in "distributing roles" to its branches, stating what is the needed from them as one of the participants or contributors to the project to establish the global Islamic state. The day this happens, the children of the American Ikhwani branch will have far-reaching impact and positions that make the ancestors proud.

8- Absorbing Muslims and winning them with all of their factions and colors in America and Canada for the settlement project, and making it their cause, future and the basis of their Islamic life in this part of the world:

This issues requires from us to learn "the art of dealing with the others", as people are different and people in many colors. We need to adopt the principle which says, "Take from people ... the best they have", their best specializations, experiences, arts, energies and abilities. By people here we mean those within or without the ranks of individuals and organizations. The policy of "taking" should be with what achieves the strategic goal and the settlement process. But the big challenge in front of us is: how to connect them all in "the orbit" of our plan and "the circle" of our Movement in order to achieve "the core" of our interest. To me, there is no choice for us other than alliance and mutual understanding of those who desire from our religion and those who agree from our belief in work. And the U.S. Islamic arena is full of those waiting ...., the pioneers. What matters is bringing people to the level of comprehension of the challenge that is facing us as Muslims in this country, conviction of our settlement project, and understanding the benefit of agreement, cooperation and alliance. At that time, if we ask for money, a lot of it would come, and if we ask for men, they would come in lines, What matters is that our plan is "the criterion and the balance" in our relationship with others.

Here, two points must be noted; the first one: we need to comprehend and understand the balance of the Islamic powers in the U.S. arena [and this might be the subject of a future study]. The second point: what we reached with the brothers in "ICNA" is considered a step in the right direction, the beginning of good and the first drop that requires growing and guidance.

9- Re-examining our organizational and administrative bodies, the type of leadership and the method of selecting it with what suits the challenges of the settlement mission:
The memorandum will be silent about details regarding this item even though it is logical and there is a lot to be said about it.

10- Growing and developing our resources and capabilities, our financial and human resources with what suits the magnitude of the grand mission:
If we examined the human and the financial resources the Ikhwan alone own in this country, we and others would feel proud and glorious. And if we add to them the resources of our friends and allies, those who circle in our orbit and those waiting on our banner, we would realize that we are able to open the door to settlement and walk through it seeking to make highest.

11- Utilizing the scientific method in planning, thinking and preparation of studies needed for the process of settlement:
Yes, we need this method, and we need many studies which aid in this civilization Jihadist operation. We will mention some of them briefly:
- The history of the Islamic presence in America.

- The history of the Islamic Ikhwani presence in America.
- Islamic movements, organizations and organizations: analysis and criticism.
- The phenomenon of the Islamic centers and schools: challenges, needs and statistics.
- Islamic minorities.
- Muslim and Arab communities.
- The U.S. society: make-up and politics.
- The U.S. society's view of Islam and Muslims ... And many other studies which we can direct our brothers and allies to prepare, either through their academic studies or through their educational centers or organizational tasking. What is important is that we start.

12- Agreeing on a flexible, balanced and a clear "mechanism" to implement the process of settlement within a specific, gradual and balanced "time frame" that is in-line with the demands and challenges of the process of settlement.

13- Understanding the U.S. society from its different aspects an understanding that "qualifies" us to perform the mission of settling our Dawa' in its country "and growing it" on its land.

14- Adopting a written "jurisprudence" that includes legal and movement bases, principles, policies and interpretations which are suitable for the needs and challenges of the process of settlement.

15- Agreeing on "criteria" and balances to be a sort of "antennas" or "the watch tower" in order to make sure that all of our priorities, plans, programs, bodies, leadership, monies and activities march towards the process of the settlement.

16- Adopting a practical, flexible formula through which our central work complements our domestic work.

17- Understanding the role and the nature of work of "The Islamic Center" in every city with what achieves the goal of the process of settlement:

The center we seek is the one which constitutes the "axis" of our Movement, the "perimeter" of the circle of our work, our "balance center", the "base" for our rise and our "Dar al-Arqam" to educate us, prepare us and supply our battalions in addition to being the "niche" of our prayers.

This is in order for the Islamic center to turn - in action not in words - into a seed "for a small Islamic society" which is a reflection and a mirror to our central organizations. The center ought to turn into a "beehive" which produces sweet honey. Thus, the Islamic center would turn into a place for study, family, battalion, course, seminar, visit, sport, school, social club, women gathering, kindergarten for male and female youngsters, the office of the domestic political resolution, and the center for distributing our newspapers, magazines, books and our audio and visual tapes.

In brief we say: we would like for the Islamic center to become "The House of Dawa'" and "the general center" in deeds first before name. As much as we own and direct these centers at the continent level, we can say we are marching successfully towards the settlement of Dawa' in this country. Meaning that the "center's" role should be the same as the "mosque's" role during the time of God's prophet, God's prayers and peace be upon him, when he marched to "settle" the Dawa' in its first generation in Madina. from the mosque, he drew the Islamic life and provided to the world the most magnificent and fabulous civilization humanity knew.

This mandates that, eventually, the region, the branch and the Usra turn into "operations rooms" for planning, direction, monitoring and leadership for the Islamic center in order to be a role model to be followed.

18- Adopting a system that is based on "selecting" workers, "role distribution" and "assigning" positions and responsibilities is based on specialization, desire and need with what achieves the process of settlement and contributes to its success.

19- Turning the principle of dedication for the Masuls of main positions within the Group into a rule, a basis and a policy in work. Without it, the process of settlement might be stalled [Talking about this point requires more details and discussion].

20- Understanding the importance of the "Organizational" shift in our Movement work, and doing Jihad in order to achieve it in the real world with what serves the process of settlement and expedites its results, God Almighty's willing:

The reason this paragraph was delayed is to stress its utmost importance as it constitutes the heart and the core of this memorandum. It also constitutes the practical aspect and the true measure of our success or failure in our march towards settlement.

The talk about the organizations and the "organizational" mentality or phenomenon does not require much details. It suffices to say that the first pioneer of this phenomenon was our prophet Mohamed, God's peace, mercy and blessings be upon him, as he placed the foundation for the first civilized organization which is the mosque, which truly became "the comprehensive organization". And this was done by the pioneer of the contemporary Islamic Dawa', Imam martyr Hasan al-Banna, may God have mercy on him, when he and his brothers felt the need to "re-establish" Islam and its movement anew, leading him to establish organizations with all their kinds: economic, social, media, scouting, professional and even the military ones. We must say that we are in a country which understands no language other than the language of the organizations, and one which does not respect or give weight to any group without effective, functional and strong organizations.

It is good fortune that there are brothers among us who have this "trend", mentality or inclination to build the organizations who have beat us by action and words which leads us to dare say honestly what Sadat in Egypt once said, "We want to build a country of organizations" - a word of right he meant wrong with. I say to my brothers, let us raise the banner of truth to establish right "We want to establish the Group of organizations", as without it we will not able to put our feet on the true path.

- And in order for the process of settlement to be completed, we must plan and work from now to equip and prepare ourselves, our brothers, our apparatuses, our sections and our committees in order to turn into comprehensive organizations in a gradual and balanced way that is suitable with the need and the reality. What encourages us to do that - in addition to the aforementioned - is that we possess "seeds" for each organization from the organization we call for.

- All we need is to tweak them, coordinate their work, collect their elements and merge their efforts with others and then connect them with the comprehensive plan we seek. For instance, We have a seed for a "comprehensive media and art" organization: we own a print and advanced typesetting machine, audio and visual center and art production office, magazines in Arabic and English [The Horizons, The Hope, The Politicians, Ila Falastine, Press Clips, al-Zaytouna, Palestine Monitor, Social Sciences Magazines.,.], art band, photographers, producers, programs anchor, journalists in addition to other media and art experiences".

Another example:

We have a seed for a "comprehensive Dawa' educational" organization: We have the Daw'a section in ISNA + Dr. Jamal Badawi Foundation + the center run by brother Harned al-Ghazali + the Dawa' center the Dawa' Committee and brother Shaker al-Sayyed are seeking to establish now + in addition to other Daw'a efforts here and there...".

And this applies to all the organizations we call on establishing.

- The big challenge that is ahead of us is how to turn these seeds or "scattered" elements into comprehensive, stable, "settled" organizations that are connected with our Movement and which fly in our orbit and take orders from our guidance. This does not prevent - but calls for – each central organization to have its local branches but its connection with the Islamic center in the city is a must.

- What is needed is to seek to prepare the atmosphere and the means to achieve "the merger" so that the sections, the committees, the regions, the branches and the Usras are eventually the heart and the core of these organizations.

Or, for the shift and the change to occur as follows:

1 - The Movement Department + The Secretariat Department - The Organizational & Administrative Organization - The General Center

2- Education Department + Dawa'a Com. - Dawa' and Educational Organization

3- Sisters Department- The Women's Organization

4- The Financial Department + Investment Committee + The Endowment- The Economic Organization

5- Youth Department + Youths Organizations Department- Youth Organizations

6- The Social Committee + Matrimony Committee + Mercy Foundation- The Social Organization

7- The Security Committee- The Security Organization

8- The Political Depart. + Palestine Com. - The Political Organization

9- The Group's Court + The Legal Com. - The Judicial Organization

10- Domestic Work Department- Its work is to be distributed to the rest of the organizations

11 - Our magazines + the print + our art band- The Media and Art Organization

12- The Studies Association + The Publication House + Dar al-Kitab - The Intellectual & Cultural Organization

13- Scientific and Medical societies - Scientific, Educational & Professional Organization

14- The Organizational Conference- The Islamic-American Founding Conference

15- The Shura Council + Planning Corn. - The Shura Council for the Islamic-American Movement

16- The Executive Office- Chairman of the Islamic Movement and its official

17- The General Masul- The Executive Office of the Islamic-American Movement Spokesman

18- The regions, branches & Usras - Field leaders of organizations & Islamic centers

Five: Comprehensive Settlement Organization:

- We would then seek and struggle in order to make each one of these above-mentioned organizations a "comprehensive organization" throughout the days and the years, and as long as we are destined to be in this country. What is important is that we put the foundation and we will be followed by peoples and generations that would finish the march and the road but with a clearly-defined guidance. And, in order for us to clarify what we mean with the comprehensive, specialized organization, we mention here the characteristics and traits of each organization of the "promising" organizations.

1- From The Dawa' and Educational Organization to include:
- The Organization to spread the Dawa' (Central and local branches).
- An institute to graduate Callers and Educators.
- Scholars, Callers, Educators, Preachers and Program Anchors,
- Art and communication technology, Conveyance and Dawa'.
- A television station.
- A specialized Dawa' magazine.
- A radio station.
- The Higher Islamic Council for Callers and Educators.
- The Higher Council for Mosques and Islamic Centers.
- Friendship Societies with the other religions ... and things like that.

2- The Political Organization to include:
- A central political party.
- Local political offices.
- Political symbols.
- Relationships and alliances.
- The American Organization for Islamic Political Action
- Advanced Information Centers.. . .and things like that.

3- Media [The Media and Art Organization] to include:
- A daily newspaper.
- Weekly, monthly and seasonal magazines.
- Radio stations.
- Television programs.
- Audio and visual centers.
- A magazine for the Muslim child.
- A magazine for the Muslim woman.
- A print and typesetting machines.
- A production office.

- A photography and recording studio
- *Art* bands for acting, chanting and theater.
- A marketing and art production office ... and things like that,

4- Economically [The Economic Organization] to include:
- An Islamic Central bank.
- Islamic endowments.
- Investment projects.
- An organization for interest-free loans .... and things like that.

5- Scientifically and Professionally [The Scientific, Educational and Professional Organization] to include:
- Scientific research centers.
- Technical organizations and vocational training.
- An Islamic university.
- Islamic schools.
- A council for education and scientific research.
- Centers to train teachers.
- Scientific societies in schools.
- An office for academic guidance.
- A body for authorship and Islamic curricula...and things like that.

6- Culturally and Intellectually [The Cultural and Intellectual Organization] to include:
- A center for studies and research.
- Cultural and intellectual foundations such as [The Social Scientists Society - Scientists and Engineers Society
- An organization for Islamic thought and culture.
- A publication, translation and distribution house for Islamic books.
- An office for archiving, history and authentication
- The project to translate the Noble Quran, the Noble Sayings .... and things like that.

7- Socially [The Social-Charitable Organization] to include:
- Social clubs for the youths and the community's sons and daughters
- Local societies for social welfare and the services are tied to the Islamic centers

- The Islamic Organization to Combat the Social Ills of the U.S. Society
- Islamic houses project
- Matrimony and family cases office .... and things like that.

8- Youths [The Youth Organization] to include:
- Central and local youth foundations.
- Sports teams and clubs
- Scouting teams .... and things like that.

9- Women [The Women Organization]: to include:
- Central and local women societies.
- Organizations of training, vocational and housekeeping.
- An organization to train female preachers.
- Islamic kindergartens ... and things like that.

10- Organizationally and Administratively [The Administrative and Organization] to include:
- An institute for training, growth, development and planning
- Prominent experts in this field
- Work systems, bylaws and charters fit for running the most complicated bodies and organizations
- A periodic magazine in Islamic development and administration.
- Owning camps and halls for the various activities.
- A data, polling and census bank.
- An advanced communication network.
- An advanced archive for our heritage and production .... and things like that.

11- Security [The Security Organization] to include:
- Clubs for training and learning self-defense techniques.
- A center which is concerned with the security issues [Technical, intellectual, technological and human]. .. .and things like that.

12- Legally [The Legal Organization] to include:
- A Central Jurisprudence Council.
- A Central Islamic Court.
- Muslim Attorneys Society.
- The Islamic Foundation for Defense of Muslims' Rights ... and things like that.

And success is by God.

A list of our organizations and the organizations of our friends
[Imagine if t they all march according to one plan! ! !]
1- ISNA = ISLAMIC SOCIETY OF NORTH AMERICA
2- MSA = MUSLIM STUDENTS' ASSOCIATION
3- MCA = THE MUSLIM COMMUNITIES ASSOCIATION
4- AMSS = THE ASSOCIATION OF MUSLIM SOCIAL SCIENTISTS
5- AMSE = THE ASSOCIATION OF MUSLIM SCIENTISTS AND ENGINEERS
6- IMA = ISLAMIC MEDICAL ASSOCIATION
7- ITC = ISLAMIC TEACHING CENTER
8- NAIT= NORTH AMERICAN ISLAMIC TRUST
9- FID= FOUNDATION FOR INTERNATIONAL DEVELOPMENT
10- IHC= ISLAMIC HOUSING COOPERATIVE
11- ICD= ISLAMIC CENTERS DIVISION
12- ATP= AMERICAN TRUST PUBLICATIONS
13- AVC= AUDIO-VISUAL CENTER
14- IBS= ISLAMIC BOOK SERVICE
15- MBA= MUSLIM BUSINESSMEN ASSOCIATION
16- MYNA= MUSLIM YOUTH OF NORTH AMERICA
17- IFC= ISNA FIQH COMMITTEE
18- IPAC= ISNA POLITICAL AWARENESS COMMITTEE
19- IED= ISLAMIC EDUCATION DEPARTMENT
20- MAYA = MUSLIM ARAB YOUTH ASSOCIATION
21- MISG = MALASIAN [sic] ISLAMIC STUDY GROUP
22- IAP = ISLAMIC ASSOCIATION FOR PALESTINE
23- UASR = UNITED ASSOCIATION FOR STUDIES AND RESEARCH
24- OLF = OCCUPIED LAND FUND
25- MIA = MERCY INTERNATIONAL ASSOCIATION
26- ISNA = ISLAMIC CIRCLE OF NORTH AMERICA
27- BMI = BAITUL MAL INC
28- IIIT = INTERNATIONAL INSTITUTE FOR ISLAMIC THOUGHT
29- IIC = ISLAMIC INFORMATION CENTER

[14] **Shia Islam** is the second largest denomination of Islam, after Sunni Islam. The followers of Shia Islam are called **Shi'ites** or **Shias**. "Shia" is the short form of an Islamic phrase "the followers of

Ali", "faction of Ali", or "party of Ali". Like other schools of thought in Islam, Shia Islam is based on the teachings of the Islamic holy book, the Quran and the message of the final prophet of Islam, Muhammad. In contrast to other schools of thought, Shias believe that only Allah has the right to choose a representative to safeguard Islam, the Quran and Shariah (based upon verses in the Quran which stipulate this according to Shia belief). Shias believe that these Quranic verses make it clear that only Allah chooses a vice-regent on Earth, therefore, unlike Sunni Islamic sects, Shias believe leaders must be direct descendents of Mohammad and/or his family. This means that God's representatives like Prophets and Imams cannot be elected by common Muslims, which is why Shias disown the 7th century election and selection of Abu Bakr, Umar and Uthman by the people, preferentially recognizing only twelve Imams descended from Mohammad. Thus Shias do not consider Mohammad's son in law Ali to be the fourth Caliph, rather the first certified "Imam". Shias believe that there are numerous narrations in the elements of Sharia Law where the prophet selected Ali as his successor.

Shias believe that Mohammad's family, the Ahl al-Bayt ("the People of the House"), and certain individuals among his descendants, who are known as infallible Imams, have special spiritual and political authority over the community and they acquired this authority since God gave it to them in the same way God chose Adam, Noah, Abraham, Moses, David, Jesus and other prophets and Imams such as the offspring of Abraham and from amongst the Children of Israel as well as kings, such as King Saul. Shia Muslims further believe that Ali, Mohammad's cousin and son-in-law, was the first of The Twelve Imams and was the rightful successor to Mohammad and thus reject the legitimacy of the first three caliphs. According to this view, Ali as the successor of Mohammad not only ruled over the community in justice, but also interpreted the Shariah Law and its esoteric meaning. Hence he was regarded as being free from error and sin (infallible), and appointed by God by divine decree to be the first Imam.

As a result, Shi'ites favor narratives called Hadiths attributed to Mohammad and successive Imams, and credited to the Prophet's family and close associates, in contrast to the Sunni traditions where the Sunnah is largely narrated by the Prophet Mohammad's companions, whom Sunnis hold to all be trustworthy. Thus the Quran and Hadith interpretation and differences in Hadith narrators are the main distinction of the Shia and Sunni Islamic traditions.

The most radical of the Shia Muslims are known as the Twelvers, referring to the recognized Imams descending from Mohammad. As the last of these twelve died without offspring, the Shia were technically without spiritual direction from a hereditary leader. In the end, they concocted a story that the twelfth Imam was "occultated" (meaning Allah had placed him into a sort of spiritual limbo) awaiting the moment when the last Imam would return to establish Islam and Allah as the one and only authority on earth. Approximately 90% of all Shiites reside in Iran.

[15] **Sunni historical origins**: With Mohammad's death in 632, disagreement broke out over who would succeed him as defactor leader of the Muslim community. *Umar ibn al-Khattab*, a prominent companion of Muhammad, nominated *Abu Bakr*, who was Mohammad's companion and close friend. Others added their support and Abu Bakr was made the first caliph. Abu Bakr's immediate task was to avenge a recent defeat by Byzantine (or Eastern Roman Empire) forces, although he first had to put down a rebellion by Arab tribes in an episode known as the Ridda wars, or "Wars of Apostasy". Abu Bakr's death in 634 resulted in the succession of Umar as the caliph, followed by Uthman ibn al-Affan and Ali ibn Abi Talib. These four are known as *al-khulafā' ar-rāshidūn* ("Rightly Guided Caliphs"). Under them, the territory under Muslim rule expanded deeply into Persian and Byzantine territories. When Umar was assassinated in 644, the election of Uthman as successor was met with increasing opposition. In 656, Uthman was also killed, and Ali assumed the position of caliph. After fighting off opposition in the first civil war (the "First Fitna"), Ali was assassinated by Kharijites in 661. Following this,

Mu'awiyah, who was governor of Levant, seized power and began the Umayyad dynasty.

These disputes over religious and political leadership would give rise to schism in the Muslim community. The majority accepted the legitimacy of the three rulers prior to Ali, and became known as Sunnis. A minority disagreed, and believed that Ali was the only rightful successor; they became known as the Shi'a.

[16]   **Department   of   Justice   NDIC   Accomplishments, Fiscal Year 2007**

The National Drug Intelligence Center's mission is to support national policymakers and law enforcement decision makers with strategic domestic drug intelligence; to facilitate information sharing and liaison between intelligence and law enforcement agencies; to provide timely support to law enforcement authorities by conducting document and computer exploitation of materials collected in connection with federal, state, and local law enforcement activity; and, finally, to provide training in support of the above efforts. All of these functions support our nation's counternarcotics program and support the U.S. Department of Justice (DOJ) Strategic Plan. The following report is a summary of NDIC mission accomplishments during fiscal year (FY) 2007.

In FY2007, the intelligence analysis staff of the NDIC produced 37 major recurring assessments and 3 major topical drug assessments. Earlier this year, NDIC published and disseminated the *National Drug Threat Assessment 2007*, our signature product that presents a comprehensive account of the threat to the United States posed by the trafficking and abuse of illicit and pharmaceutical drugs. Since then, we completed 27 planned drug market analyses for the High Intensity Drug Trafficking Area (HIDTA) program and 9 regional drug threat assessments for the Organized Crime and Drug Enforcement Task Force (OCDETF) program of the DOJ. These reports provide a strategic overview of the illicit drug situation in each respective market or region by highlighting significant trends and law enforcement concerns and are frequently used by the requestors when developing their annual strategies or allocating assets and resources. In addition to the recurring assessments, NDIC produced three major assessments on particular drug threats: the *National Methamphetamine Threat Assessment 2007*, the *Domestic Cannabis Cultivation Assessment 2007*, and the *Southwest Asian Heroin Assessment*. These strategic reports assist national-level decision makers by offering analysis on the current status and future outlook of these complex drug threats.

In FY2007, NDIC continued to produce intelligence products for and provide analytical support to other federal agencies and significant nonfederal entities enjoined in the fight against drug trafficking and related criminal activities. For the Anti-Drug Intelligence Community Team (ADICT), NDIC prepared the domestic portion of the *Mexican Methamphetamine Assessment*, an analysis of methamphetamine production by Mexican criminal organizations and the subsequent distribution of the drug in the United States. For the Federal Bureau of Investigation (FBI)-led National Gang Intelligence Center (NGIC), we produced a report entitled Gangs: Toward a 2007 National Threat Assessment, which will serve as the foundation for NGIC's 2007 National Gang Threat Assessment.

Additional collaborative efforts include publication of a report on the Black Market Peso Exchange in coordination with the Department of Defense (DoD), which was disseminated to all DEA domestic field offices and three international field offices. For DoD's Counter Narcotics Analysis Cell, NDIC participated on a project regarding Lebanese drug traffickers and authored a portion of the published classified report. Further, NDIC contributed information towards development of the National Security Council's *National Southwest Border Counternarcotics Strategy* and associated *Implementation Plan*. In collaboration with interagency working group partners, NDIC made significant contributions to the development of the *2007 National Money Laundering Strategy*. Additionally, in close collaboration with the Office of the Director of National Intelligence, DoD, Department of Homeland Security (DHS), FBI, and others, NDIC is serving a key role in the launching of Intellipedia, a web-based system designed to enhance the collection and sharing of information among counterdrug and other intelligence agencies. Finally, NDIC once again chaired discussion groups at the 2007 Major City Drug Commanders Conference and prepared an annual report summarizing the drug information gleaned from these forums for the Major City Chiefs Association.

Among our partner agencies, the Office of National Drug Control Policy (ONDCP) continues to be a frequent and highly-valued customer. At the request of ONDCP, NDIC prepared the *U.S.-Canada Drug Threat Assessment 2007.* This assessment provides analysis regarding the drug threat posed to the United States from Canada and covers trafficking, money laundering, and drug policy issues. Earlier this year, we also produced two situation reports for ONDCP that examined recent cocaine and methamphetamine shortages reported in several U.S. markets and identified the possible causes. These reports demonstrated our ability to collect the most current drug information through our Field Program Specialists (FPSs) and quickly produce intelligence products to meet our customers' needs. The FPSs were also instrumental in collecting information that enabled NDIC to support ONDCP's Drug Market Model Initiative by reporting on drug market fluctuations, criminal activities of addicts, and the operations of retail-level drug organizations. Finally, NDIC has partnered with ONDCP's Office of State and Local Affairs to coordinate the testing and application of a data analysis tool developed by Carnegie Mellon University that may prove adept at performing network analysis of drug trafficking organizations.

Throughout FY2007, NDIC's Document Exploitation (Doc Ex) and Computer Exploitation (Comp Ex) programs made significant contributions to ongoing high-level investigations targeting drug trafficking, money laundering, terrorism, and other criminal activities that impact U.S. national security. In FY2007, the Doc Ex Branch completed 71 missions, half of which were in support of OCDETF investigations. Eighty-eight percent of Doc Ex missions were at the request of DEA or FBI, while other Doc Ex missions were conducted on behalf of U.S. Immigration and Customs

Enforcement (ICE), the Internal Revenue Service (IRS), the U.S. Attorneys Office (USAO), and DoD. The success of NDIC's Doc Ex program and the increased demand for foreign language missions encouraged NDIC to establish a satellite Doc Ex unit at the Utah National Guard Joint Language Training Center, which contributed 12 foreign language missions to the 68 total Doc Ex missions in FY2007.

During FY2007, NDIC's Doc Ex program provided invaluable support to law enforcement and prosecuting authorities in the investigation and prosecution of illicit drug trafficking. In early FY2007, NDIC provided Doc Ex support to a DEA diversion case that resulted in a federal grand jury indicting four individuals working in a Baltimore pharmacy for diverting 8 million dosage units of hydrocodone and conspiring to launder the proceeds. In what has been called the largest criminal pharmaceutical drug investigation in DEA Baltimore history, prosecutors are seeking forfeiture of $20 million.

Earlier this year, NDIC's Doc Ex Branch supported the DEA Bogotá Country Office's investigation that targeted a designated Consolidated Priority Organization Target (CPOT) and a high-level leader of the North Valley Cartel. This investigation was initiated in December 2003 in conjunction with the Colombian National Police, DEA's New York Field Division, USAO Eastern District of New York, DEA's Special Operations Division, and the DOJ Criminal Division's Narcotics and Dangerous Drugs Section. This CPOT and high-level leader of the North Valley Cartel was indicted in the Eastern District of New York for conspiracy to import cocaine, money laundering, and conspiracy to commit murder. He was also indicted in the District of Columbia under the North Valley Cartel Racketeer Influenced and Corrupt Organizations Conspiracy Indictment. Both indictments allege his leadership status in the North Valley Cartel and his numerous acts of violence, corruption of government officials, and use of maritime and aviation smuggling routes to move multiton quantities of cocaine to the United States and Europe as well as the subsequent laundering of proceeds back to Colombia. In January 2007, the Bogotá Country Office in conjunction with the Colombian National Police seized four money caches in Cali containing over $80 million in cash and gold bullion. More recently, NDIC was credited with playing a key role in the largest steroid enforcement action in U.S. history. Operation Raw Deal, a multijurisdictional OCDETF investigation, targeted the global underground trade of anabolic steroids, human growth hormones, and insulin growth factor. More than 140 federal search warrants were executed on targets throughout the United States, resulting in 124 arrests and the seizure of 56 steroid labs. In total, 11.4 million dosage units of steroids were seized as well as 242 kilograms of raw steroid powder of Chinese origin. In addition, $6.5 million, 25 vehicles, 3 boats, 27 pill presses, and 71 weapons were seized in U.S. raids. The operation spanned the United States, Mexico, Canada, China, Belgium, Australia, Germany, Denmark, Sweden, and Thailand.

Although Doc Ex missions are predominantly conducted in support of drug trafficking investigations, they have frequently been conducted to confirm suspected links or reveal unknown links between drug trafficking and terrorism. In FY2007, the Doc Ex Branch supported several drug-terrorism investigations including a Doc Ex mission that identified links between southern Philippines drug traffickers and elements of designated foreign terrorist organizations, namely the Abu Sayyaf Group and Jamayah Islamiyah.

Doc Ex Branch has supported another drug-terror investigation aimed at disrupting and dismantling five Arab Tri-Border Area (TBA) drug trafficking organizations (DTOs) that operate in Argentina, Brazil, and Paraguay as well as in surrounding areas and in Europe and the Middle East. All five groups have been linked to Islamic Radical Groups.

NDIC's Doc Ex Branch supported DEA's Special Operations Division by analyzing information on a high-level drug trafficker, money launderer, arms dealer, and terrorist who is documented in 74 DEA investigations dating back to the 1970's. Historical evidence indicated that this individual and his associates have trafficked multiton quantities of hashish and heroin and laundered tens of millions of dollars in drug proceeds. In addition, this individual had also brokered international multimillion dollar arms deals for Yemen, Kuwait, Syria, Argentina, Brazil, Bulgaria, and Colombia and has supported several Middle Eastern terrorist groups including the Palestine Liberation Front, the Palestine Liberation Organization, and the Popular Front for the Liberation of Palestine.

NDIC's Comp Ex program continued to provide critical and timely assistance to the intelligence and law enforcement communities during FY2007 by exploiting various electronic media. In support of 61 cases conducted by DEA; FBI; ICE; Health and Human Services; DoD; Bureau of Alcohol, Tobacco, Firearms and Explosives; IRS; and the Johnstown Police Department in Johnstown, Pennsylvania, personnel assigned to NDIC's Comp Ex Branch examined 535 computer hard disk drives and 303 mobile phones totaling approximately 20 terabytes (20 thousand billion bytes) of data. To put this into perspective, it is estimated that the Library of Congress contains 20 terabytes of data.

FY2007 also marked significant milestones in the demand and use of NDIC-developed software. First, NDIC began a groundbreaking program to provide Interpol the Real-time Analytical Intelligence Database (RAID), NDIC's main Doc Ex analytical software. With NDIC's assistance, Interpol distributed and provided training on NDIC's RAID application to various member countries in West Africa for use in combating drug trafficking and money laundering. This collaborative effort has resulted in the successful deployment of RAID to law enforcement personnel in Cote-d'Ivoire and Nigeria. Most recently, this effort was expanded to include cooperation from the United Nations Office of Drugs and Crime with the installation and training of RAID to Cape Verde law enforcement and judicial officials. Second, NDIC furnished its in-house developed software to the U.S. military and DoD. In July 2007, NDIC furnished a U.S. Army Document Exploitation Unit Multinational Forces Iraq, with our computer forensics software, HashKeeper.

This past fiscal year, NDIC became a charter member of the Defense Intelligence Agency's FORUM collection system. FORUM is a web-based tool for DoD and law enforcement agencies to collaborate and share counterdrug intelligence requirements and information via a secure communications network (ADNET-S). Currently, there are 320 registered FORUM users including collection managers representing DEA, EPIC, DHS, JIATF-West, JIATF-South, JTF-North, BORFIC, and several HIDTAs. NDIC's participation on FORUM streamlines the submission and management of Requests for Information (RFIs) and assists in the identification of intelligence gaps/shortfalls, reducing duplication of effort. On September 27, 2007, NDIC hosted the FORUM Primary Member Group (PMG) Quarterly Meeting in Johnstown, PA. The chief purpose of the meeting was to discuss information sharing initiatives, future funding issues and validate the PMG Charter.

In FY2007, NDIC continued to provide library and training services to the intelligence and law enforcement communities. NDIC produces and disseminates the *Counternarcotics Publications Quarterly (CPQ)*, an annotated and indexed bibliography of reports, intelligence memoranda, papers, and target studies submitted by federal, state, and local agencies. For each quarter of FY2007, more than 270 copies of the classified *CPQ* were distributed to federal officials at the headquarters of the Defense Intelligence Agency, DEA, FBI, U.S. Customs and Border Protection (CBP), Central Intelligence Agency, National Security Agency (NSA), and ONDCP; and more than 1,100 copies of the sensitive *CPQ* were distributed to FBI and DEA field offices as well as USAO district offices, state police headquarters, and sheriffs' offices.

In FY2007, NDIC trained 4,703 federal, state, and local law enforcement personnel in 66 training sessions on topics related to basic drug intelligence analysis. NDIC trained 1,004 law enforcement professionals in 16 DEA-sponsored sessions and 586 law enforcement professionals in 10 sessions sponsored by the HIDTA offices. NDIC also conducted four iterations of the Multiagency Course, an intensive 1- week, video tele-training, entry-level drug intelligence analysis course. Taught by instructors from NDIC and other federal agencies, these four iterations were attended by 216 professionals. These training sessions afforded students the opportunity to meet fellow law enforcement professionals and develop relationships that ultimately bring the law enforcement community together in an atmosphere of trust, which is critical to advancing information sharing.

In addition to conducting training for counterdrug professionals, NDIC also hosted two significant training seminars during FY2007. Specifically, NDIC hosted over 65 money laundering investigators and analysts from the intelligence and law enforcement communities for a 2-day training course and networking session covering the Black Market Peso Exchange. During the week of the anniversary of 9/11, NDIC also hosted representatives from DoD, DHS, FBI, Financial Crimes Enforcement Network (FinCEN), NSA, and other agencies for a 5-day course on combating terrorism. This course provided lectures from a dozen top-level terrorism experts from the Intelligence Community and academia.

Also in FY2007, NDIC enhanced the automated tools and systems used by our analytical staff and completed plans to ensure the continued operability of the NDIC computer network. In May, NDIC's Human Resources (HR) function was audited by DOJ HR officials. While NDIC has not yet received the final results, DOJ officials communicated their intent to recommend that NDIC remain "Green" with regards to its HR Human Capital effort.

As the above accomplishments clearly demonstrate, NDIC continues to focus its resources on providing federal policymakers and the intelligence and law enforcement communities with timely intelligence products, services, and support in our collective battle against drug trafficking and related threats. Our management and staff are energized by the knowledge that our accomplishments contribute to the counterdrug community's successes and look forward to providing an even higher level of support in the future.

[17] **Letter from Senator Charles Grassley and Rep. Darrell Issa to Attorney General Eric Holder**: July 5,2011

Congress of the United States
Washington, DC 20510

The Honorable Eric H. Holder, Jr.
Attorney General
U.S. Department of Justice
950 Pennsylvania Avenue, NW
Washington, DC 20530
Dear Attorney General Holder:

Yesterday, Acting ATF Director Kenneth Melson participated in a transcribed interview regarding Operation Fast and Furious and related matters with both Republican and Democratic staff. He appeared with his personal counsel, Richard Cullen of McGuire Woods LLP. His interview had originally been scheduled through the Justice Department to occur on July 13 in the presence of DOJ and ATF counsel. As you know, however, under our agreement Department witnesses who choose to attend a voluntary interview with their own lawyer are free to exercise that right rather than participate with counsel representing the Department's interests.

After being made aware of that provision of our agreement, Acting Director Melson chose to exercise that right and appeared with his own lawyer. We are disappointed that no one had previously informed him of that provision of the agreement. Instead, Justice Department officials sought to limit and control his communications with Congress. This is yet another example of why direct communications with Congress are so important and are protected by law.

Acting Director Melson's cooperation was extremely helpful to our investigation. He was candid in admitting mistakes that his agency made and described various ways he says that he tried to remedy the problems. According to Mr. Melson, it was not until after the public controversy that he personally reviewed hundreds of documents relating to the case, including wiretap applications and Reports of Investigation (ROIs). By his account, he was sick to his stomach when he obtained those documents and learned the full story. Mr. Melson said that he told the Office of the Deputy Attorney General (ODAG) at the end of March that the Department needed to reexamine how it was responding to the requests for information from Congress.

According to Mr. Melson, he and ATF's senior leadership team moved to reassign every manager involved in Fast and Furious, from the Deputy Assistant Director for Field Operations down to the Group Supervisor, after learning the facts in those documents. Mr. Melson also said he was not allowed to communicate to Congress the reasons for the reassignments. He claimed that ATF's senior leadership would have preferred to be more cooperative with our inquiry much earlier in the process.

However, he said that Justice Department officials directed them not to respond and took full control of replying to briefing and document requests from Congress. The result is that Congress only got the parts of the story that the Department wanted us to hear. If his account is accurate, then ATF leadership appears to have been effectively muzzled while the DOJ sent over false denials and buried its head in the sand. That approach distorted the truth and obstructed our investigation. The Department's inability or unwillingness to be more forthcoming served to conceal critical information that we are now learning about the involvement of other agencies, including the DEA and the FBI.

The Role of DEA, FBI, and Other Agencies

When confronted with information about serious issues involving lack of information sharing by other agencies, which Committee staff had originally learned from other witnesses, Mr. Melson's responses tended to corroborate what others had said. Specifically, we have very real indications from several sources that some of the gun trafficking "higher-ups" that the ATF sought to identify were *already known* to other agencies and may even have been paid as informants. The Acting Director said that ATF was kept in the dark about certain activities of other agencies, including DEA and FBI. Mr. Melson said that he learned from ATF agents in the field that information obtained by these agencies could have had a material impact on the Fast and Furious investigation as far back as late 2009 or early 2010. After learning about the possible role of DEA and FBI, he testified that he reported this information in April 2011 to the Acting Inspector General and directly to then-Acting Deputy Attorney General James Cole on June 16, 2011.

The evidence we have gathered raises the disturbing possibility that the Justice Department not only allowed criminals to smuggle weapons but that taxpayer dollars from other agencies may have financed those engaging in such activities. While this is preliminary information, we must find out if there is any truth to it. According to Acting Director Melson, he became aware of this startling possibility only after the murder of Border Patrol Agent Brian Terry and the indictments of the straw purchasers, which we now know were substantially delayed by the u.s. Attorney's Office and Main Justice. Mr. Melson provided documents months ago supporting his concerns to the official in the ODAG responsible for document production to the Committees, but those documents have not been provided to us.

It is one thing to argue that the ends justify the means in an attempt to defend a policy that puts building a big case ahead of stopping known criminals from getting guns. Yet it is a much more serious matter to conceal from Congress the possible involvement of other agencies in identifying and maybe even working with the same criminals that Operation Fast and Furious was trying to identify. If this information is accurate, then the whole misguided operation might have been cut short if not for catastrophic failures to share key information. If agencies within the same Department, co-located at the same facilities, had simply communicated with one another, then ATF might have known that gun trafficking "higher-ups" had been already identified. This raises new and serious questions about the role of DEA, FBI, the United States Attorney's Office in Arizona, and Main Justice in coordinating this effort. Nearly a decade after the September 11th attacks, the stovepipes of information within our government may still be causing tragic mistakes long after they should have been broken down.

Efforts to Oust Melson

In the last few weeks, unnamed administration officials have indicated to the press that Acting Director Melson would be forced to resign. According to Mr. Melson, those initial reports were untrue. Regardless of what we might have thought before about how he should handle a request to resign, we now know he has not been asked to resign. We also now have the benefit of hearing his side of the story and will have a chance to examine what he said and compare it to the other evidence we are gathering. However, that will take some time.

Mr. Melson served as the First Assistant to the U.S. Attorney in the Eastern District of Virginia for 21 years, from 1986 to 2007. That is a career position. After the controversy over the firing of the U.S. Attorneys, he took over the Executive Office for U.S. Attorneys (EOUSA). He indicated that he was asked to convert to a non-career Senior Executive Service (SES), a politically appointed position, in order to speed the hiring process, and he agreed. However, his former position at EOUSA is currently filled by a career SES employee, Marshall Jarrett. As you know, for civil servants, the distinction between career and non-career status is significant.

In 2009, he said he was asked to take over as Acting Director of the ATF. Acting Director of the ATF is by its nature a temporary job. According to Mr. Melson, he was willing to serve the Department with the understanding that after a short tenure as Acting Director, he would return to a position as a career senior executive elsewhere within the Department.

However, two days after he told Acting Deputy Attorney General Cole about serious issues involving lack of information sharing, the *Wall Street Journal* reported that unnamed sources said that Melson was about to be ousted. The revelations about Operation Fast and Furious have focused intense scrutiny on the ATF. It has no doubt taken a toll on the agency and the good people who work there. Much of that damage has occurred because the Department prevented ATF from being more forthcoming and responsive to questions from Congress. This is the context in which Mr. Melson decided to submit to an on-the-record interview with private counsel, pursuant to our agreement with the Department.

Technically, Mr. Melson no longer enjoys the due process protections afforded to career officials. Given his testimony, unless a permanent director is confirmed, it would be inappropriate for the Justice Department to take action against him that could have the effect of intimidating others who might want to provide additional information to the Committees.

We hope that the Department will take a much more candid and forthcoming approach in addressing these very serious matters with the Committees. If other important fact witnesses like Mr. Melson have a desire to communicate directly with the Committees they should be informed that they are free to do so. They should also be notified that if they are represented by personal counsel, they may appear with personal counsel rather than with Department lawyers.

Any decision about Mr. Melson's future with the Department would need to be justified solely on the basis of the facts and the needs of the agency, rather than on his decision to speak to us. We encourage you to communicate to us any additional significant information about any such decision so that we can work together to ensure that it would not impede our investigation. For now, the Office of Inspector General is still conducting its review, and we are still conducting ours. Knowing what we know so far, we believe it would be inappropriate to make Mr. Melson the fall guy in an attempt to prevent further congressional oversight.

Sincerely,

Darrell Issa, Chair Committee on Oversight & Government Reform
U.S. House of Representatives
Charles E. Grassley, Ranking Member Committee on the Judiciary
United States Senate
cc:
The Honorable Elijah E. Cummings, Ranking Member
U.S. House of Representatives, Committee on Oversight & Government Reform
The Honorable Patrick Leahy, Chairman
U.S. Senate, Committee on the Judiciary

[18] **Bloody Sunday**: On March 7, 1965, 525 to 600 civil rights marchers headed east out of Selma on U.S. Highway 80. The march was led by John Lewis of SNCC and the Reverend Hosea Williams of SCLC, followed by Bob Mants of SNCC and Albert Turner of SCLC.

When archers crossed the Edmund Pettus Bridge they found a wall of state troopers waiting for them on the other side. Sheriff Jim Clark had issued an order for all white males in Dallas County over the age of twenty-one to report to the courthouse that morning to be deputized. Commanding officer John Cloud told the demonstrators to disband at once and go home. Williams tried to speak to the officer, but Cloud curtly informed him there was nothing to discuss. Seconds later, the troopers began shoving the demonstrators. Many were knocked to the ground and beaten with nightsticks. Another detachment of troopers fired tear gas. Mounted troopers charged the crowd on horseback.

Brutal televised images of the attack, which presented people with horrifying images of marchers left bloodied and severely injured, roused support for the U.S. civil rights movement. Amelia Boynton was beaten and gassed nearly to death; her photo appeared on the front page of newspapers and news magazines around the world. Seventeen marchers were hospitalized, leading to the naming of the day "Bloody Sunday".

[19] **Marquette Park Civil Rights Protests 1966:** Martin Luther King decided to take his protests north in 1966. He led a group of marchers (protesters) into the all-white housing areas near Marquette Park in Chicago. The protesters had bottles, bricks and rocks thrown at them - one of the bricks hit King but he was not severely hurt and continued with the march. The incident at Marquette Park was part of the protests led by the Chicago Freedom Movement (of which King was co-chairman). It was a year-long campaign for open housing. It started in January 1966 when King and his wife Coretta moved into a North Lawndale slum (on the west side of Chicago). King and the movement wanted to make Chicago a racially open city. They wanted it to be a place where everyone could live without fear of racial attacks. The march was not as successful as King and the Southern Christian Leadership Conference (SCLC) had hoped. A rather vague agreement was created with Richard J. Daley (the Mayor of Chicago) containing failed promises of open housing legislation and improving living conditions. This march was part of a series of

marches coordinated by the Chicago Freedom Movement the marriage of King's SCLC and the CCCO (Coordinating Council of Chicago Organizations) led by King's co-leader in Chicago Al Raby. [20] Library of Congress reply to Thomas Dodd regarding translation of the 1938 German Gun Control Law:

THE LIBRARY OF CONGRESS,
Washington, D.C., July 12, 1968.

Hon. THOMAS J. DODD,
Chairman, Special Subcommittee To Investigate Juvenile Delinquency, U.S. Senate, Washington, D.C.

DEAR SENATOR DODD: Your request of July 2, 1968, addressed to the Legislative Reference Service, for the translation of several German laws has been referred to the Law Library for attention.

In compliance with your request and with reference to several telephone conversations between Miss Frank of your Office and Mr. Fred Karpf, European Law Division, we are enclosing herewith a translation of the Law on Weapons of March 18, 1938, prepared by Dr. William Sólyom-Fekete of that Division, as well as the Xerox copy of the original German text which you supplied.

The translation of the Decree implementing the Law on Weapons of March 19, 1938, and the pertinent provisions of the Federal Hunting Law of March 30, 1961, is in preparation and will be sent to you as soon as completed.

Sincerely yours,

LEWIS C. COFFIN,
Law Librarian.

[21] DEPARTMENT OF JUSTICE

Bureau of Alcohol, Tobacco, Firearms and Explosives

[OMB Number 1140-NEW]

Agency Information Collection

Activities: Proposed Collection;

Comments Requested

ACTION: 60-Day Emergency Notice of Information Collection Under Review: Report of Multiple Sale or Other Disposition of Certain Rifles. The Department of Justice, Office of Justice Programs, will submit the following information collection request to the Office of Management and Budget (OMB) for review and clearance in accordance with emergency review procedures of the Paperwork Reduction Act of 1995. OMB approval has been requested by January 5, 2011. This notice requests comments from the public and affected agencies concerning the proposed information collection. If granted, the emergency approval is only valid for 180 days. Comments should be directed to OMB, Office of Information and Regulation Affairs, Attention: Department of Justice Desk Officer (202) 395-6466, Washington, DC 20503.

During the first 60 days of this same review period, a regular review of this information collection is also being undertaken. All comments and suggestions, or questions regarding additional information, to include obtaining a copy of the proposed information collection instrument with instructions, should be directed to Barbara A. Terrell, *Barbara.Terrell@atf.gov* Firearms Industry Programs Branch, Fax (202) 648–9640, Bureau of Alcohol, Tobacco, Firearms and Explosives, 99 New York Avenue, NE., Washington DC 20226. Written comments and suggestions from the public and affected agencies concerning the proposed collection of information. Your comments should address one or more of the following four points:

—Evaluate whether the proposed collection of information is necessary for the proper performance of the functions of the agency, including whether the information will have practical utility;

—Evaluate the accuracy of the agencies estimate of the burden of the proposed collection of information, including the validity of the methodology and assumptions used;

—Enhance the quality, utility, and clarity of the information to be collected; and

—Minimize the burden of the collection of information on those who are to respond, including through the use of appropriate automated, electronic, mechanical, or other technological collection techniques or other forms of information technology, *e.g.,* permitting electronic submission of responses.

Summary of Collection:

(1) *Type of information collection:* New.

(2) *The title of the form/collection:* Report of Multiple Sale or Other Disposition of Certain Rifles.

(3) *The agency form number, if any, and the applicable component of the department sponsoring the collection:* Form Number: ATF F 3310.12. Bureau of Alcohol, Tobacco, Firearms and Explosives.

(4) *Affected public who will be asked or required to respond, as well as a brief abstract:* Primary: Business or For-Profit Other: None.

Need for Collection

The purpose of the information is to require Federal Firearms Licensees to report multiple sales or other dispositions whenever the licensee sells or otherwise disposes of two or more rifles within any five consecutive business days with the following characteristics: (a) Semi automatic; (b) a caliber greater than .22; and (c) the ability to accept a detachable magazine.

(5) An estimate of the total number of respondents and the amount of time estimated for an average respondent to respond/reply: It is estimated that 8,479 respondents will complete a 12 minute form.

(6) An estimate of the total public burden (in hours) associaed with the collection: The estimated total public burden associated with this information collection is 1,696 hours. If additional information is required contact: Lynn Murray, Department Clearance Officer, Policy and Planning Staff, Justice Management Division, United States Department of Justice, 145 N Street, NE., Two Constitution Square, Room 2E–502, Washington, DC 20530.

Dated: December 14, 2010.

Lynn Murray, *Department Clearance Officer, PRA, United States Department of Justice.* [FR Doc. 2010–31761 Filed 12–16–10; 8:45 am]

[22] NRA/NSSF Lawsuit against ATF

IN THE UNITED STATES DISTRICT COURT FOR THE DISTRICT OF COLUMBIA

J & G SALES, LTD. 440 Miller Valley Road Prescott, AZ 86301
and FOOTHILLS FIREARMS, LLC 11792 South Foothills Blvd. Yuma, AZ 85367
Plaintiffs
v.

KENNETH MELSON Acting Director Bureau of Alcohol, Tobacco, Firearms & Explosives 99 New York Avenue, N.E. Washington, D.C. 20226
Defendant

COMPLAINT (For Declaratory Judgment and Injunctive Relief)

1) This is an action to secure the statutory right of licensedfirearm dealers not to submit reports and information with respect

torecords maintained as required by statute, and to secure the privacy rights of lawful purchasers of firearms, by preventing the Bureau of Alcohol, Tobacco, Firearms & Explosives ("BATFE") from unlawfully requiring licensed firearm dealers to submit a report of sale or other disposition to unlicensed persons of two or more semi-automatic rifles of greater than .22 caliber (including .223/5.56) capable of accepting a detachable magazine within five (5) consecutive business days.

Parties

2) Plaintiff J&G Sales, Ltd. (hereinafter "J&G") is a federally licensed dealer in firearms pursuant to 18 U.S.C. § 923, which is incorporated under the laws of Arizona and has its principal place of business in Prescott, Arizona.

3) Plaintiff Foothills Firearms, LLC (hereinafter "Foothills") is a federally-licensed dealer in firearms pursuant to 18 U.S.C. § 923, which is incorporated under the laws of Arizona and has its principal place of business in Yuma, Arizona.

4) Defendant Kenneth Melson is Acting Director, BATFE, a bureau of the United States Department of Justice, and has his principal place of business in Washington, D.C., and is being sued in his official capacity as such. The Attorney General has delegated the administration and enforcement of Chapter 44 of Title 18, U.S.C. to the BATFE.

Jurisdiction

5) Jurisdiction is founded on 28 U.S.C. § 1331 in that this case arises under the laws of the United States, and is a controversy to which the United States is a party. Plaintiff seeks review pursuant to 5 U.S.C. § 702 and 28 U.S.C. § 2201.

Applicable Statutes And Regulations

6) 18 U.S.C. § 923(g)(1)(A) provides:

Each licensed importer, licensed manufacturer, and licensed dealer shall maintain such records of importation, production, shipment, receipt, sale, or other disposition of firearms at his place of business for such period, and in such form, as the Attorney General may by regulations prescribe. Such importers, manufacturers, and dealers shall not be required to submit to the Secretary reports and information with respect to such records and the contents thereof, *except as expressly required by this section.* (Emphasis added).

7) Pursuant to 18 U.S.C. § 923(g)(1)(A), 27 C.F.R. § 478.125(e) provides that a licensed dealer shall maintain firearm acquisition and disposition records which include, *inter alia*, the date of sale or other disposition, the name and address of the buyer, the name of the manufacturer and importer (if any), the model, serial number, type, and the caliber or gauge of the firearm.

8) 18 U.S.C. § 923(g)(3)(A) provides: Each licensee shall prepare a report of multiple sales or other dispositions whenever the licensee sells or otherwise disposes of, at one time or during any five consecutive business days, two or more pistols, or revolvers, or any combination of pistols and revolvers totalling [sic] two or more, to an unlicensed person. The report shall be prepared on a form specified by the Attorney General and forwarded to the office specified thereon and to the department of State police or State law enforcement agency of the State or local law enforcement agency of the local jurisdiction in which the sale or other disposition took place, not later than the close of business on the day that the multiple sale or other disposition occurs.

9) Reports of multiple sales of rifles within any given period are not expressly required by § 923. 10) 18 U.S.C. § 923(g)(5)(A) provides: Each licensee shall, when required by letter issued by the Attorney General, and until notified to the contrary in writing by the Attorney General, submit on a form specified by the Attorney General, for periods and at the times specified in such letter, all record information required to be kept by this chapter or such lesser record information as the Attorney General in such letter may specify.

11) 18 U.S.C. § 923(g)(7) provides: Each licensee shall respond immediately to, and in no event later than 24 hours after the receipt of, a request by the Attorney General for information contained in the records required to be kept by this chapter as may be required for determining the disposition of 1 or more firearms in the course of a bona fide criminal investigation.

12) 18 U.S.C. § 923(g)(1)(B) provides: The Attorney General may inspect or examine the inventory and records of a licensed importer, licensed manufacturer, or licensed dealer without such reasonable cause or warrant –
(i) in the course of a reasonable inquiry during the course of a criminal investigation of a person or persons other than the licensee;
(ii) for ensuring compliance with the record keeping requirements of this chapter –
(I) not more than once during any 12-month period; or
(II) at any time with respect to records relating to a firearm involved in a criminal investigation that is traced to the licensee.
(iii) when such inspection or examination may be required for determining the disposition of one or more particular firearms in the course of a bona fide criminal investigation.
13) 18 U.S.C. § 926(a) provides: The Attorney General may prescribe only such rules and regulations as are necessary to carry out the provisions of this chapter [Chapter 44 of 18 U.S.C.] . . . No such rule or regulation prescribed after the date of the enactment of the Firearms Owners' Protection Act [P.L. 99-308, 100 Stat. 449 (1986)] may require that records required to be maintained under this chapter or any portion of the contents of such records, be recorded at or transferred to a facility owned, managed, or controlled by the United States or any State or any political subdivision thereof, nor that any system of registration of firearms, firearms owners, or firearms transactions or dispositions be established. Nothing in this section expands or restricts the Attorney General's authority to inquire into the disposition of any firearm in the course of a criminal investigation.
14) The Consolidated Appropriations Act, 2010, Pub.L. 111-117, div. B, tit. 2, 123 Stat. 3034, 3128 (2009), provides appropriations for necessary expenses of the BATFE, with the following proviso: Provided, That no funds appropriated herein shall be available for salaries or administrative expenses in connection with consolidating or centralizing, within the Department of Justice, the

records, or any portion thereof, of acquisition and disposition of firearms maintained by Federal firearms licensees . . . .

15) The Department of Defense and Full-Year Continuing Appropriations Act for the 2011 fiscal year, Pub.L. 112-10, div. B., tit. 1, § 1101(a)(6), 125 Stat. 38, 102-03 (2011), continued the Consolidated Appropriations Act, 2010, in effect until September 30, 2011.

Facts

16) J&G and Foothills each received a letter addressed to "Dear Federal Firearms Licensee" and dated July 12, 2011, from Charles Houser, Chief, National Tracing Center (hereafter "the letter"). In the letter, Houser states that Melson has delegated his authority as Acting Director to issue the letter to Houser. A copy of the letter is attached herewith and incorporated herein by reference. 17) The letter purports to demand portions of records pursuant to the BATFE's authority under 18 U.S.C. § 923(g)(5). Specifically, the letter directs J&G and Foothills to submit information from the acquisition and disposition records of J&G and Foothills concerning the sale or other disposition to an unlicensed person of two or more semiautomatic rifles capable of accepting a detachable magazine and with a caliber greater than .22 (including .223/5.56) within five (5) consecutive business days.

18) The letter enclosed ATF Form 3310.12 (Report of Multiple Sale Or Other Disposition of Certain Rifles), which requires J&G and Foothills to report the following information about the purchaser and the firearms purchased: name, residence address, sex, race, identification number, identification type, identification State, date and place of birth, and the serial numbers, manufacturers, importers, models, and calibers of the rifles.

19) The letter requires that the reports be provided to the BATFE beginning with sales made on August 14, 2011 and until BATFE provides written notice to stop.

20) The reports are required to be sent to the National Tracing Center.

21) A similar letter has been, or will be, sent to all federal firearms licensees in Texas, New Mexico, Arizona, and California. The BATFE

has estimated that 8,479 licensees are subject to the requirements of the letter, or 13.3% of the approximately 63,535 licensees nationwide.

22) J&G and Foothills have sold two or more semi-automatic rifles capable of accepting a detachable magazine and with a caliber greater than .22 (including .223/5.56) to the same persons within five (5) consecutive business days, and will continue to sell such rifles to the same persons within five (5) consecutive business days.

23) The information was not requested in relation to any criminal investigation.

24) The information requested did not concern the sale of pistols or revolvers.

25) Upon information and belief, when the National Tracing Center receives the forms, it retains the information from J&G's and Foothills' records permanently in a consolidated and centralized database within the Department of Justice.

26) Upon information and belief, the letter sent to J&G and Foothills was authorized, caused, and approved by Melson.

27) J&G and Foothills have been, and will continue to be, threatened with, and subjected to, irreparable harm, and have no adequate remedy at law.

28) The irreparable harm inflicted on J&G and Foothills includes economic loss as a result of having to devote employee time to preparing the reports and the loss of business from both in-state and out-of-state potential purchasers of semi-automatic rifles capable of accepting a detachable magazine and with a caliber greater than .22 (including .223/5.56) who would have bought such rifles but have been dissuaded from doing so because they wish to protect their privacy rights. J&G and Foothills face civil and criminal sanctions, including revocation of their licenses, should they fail to comply.

29) There is also irreparable harm to the privacy rights of J&G's and Foothills' customers, an injury which J&G and Foothills may assert as the customers' privacy rights are inextricably bound up with J&G's and Foothills' statutory rights and J&G and Foothills are

fully as effective proponents of their customers' rights as the customers. Further, there is a genuine obstacle to the customers' assertion of their privacy rights in that assertion of those rights in litigation results in nullification of the right.

COUNT ONE

(Unlawful Demand For Records Not Expressly Required by Law and Not For a Bona Fide Criminal Investigation)

30) Paragraphs 1 through 29 are realleged [sic] and incorporated herein by reference.

31) The letter requires the submission of records and contents thereof which are not expressly required by 18 U.S.C. § 923, in violation of § 923(g)(1)(A).

32) The authority of the BATFE to require the reporting of information contained in licensee records with respect to the multiple sale or other disposition of semi-automatic rifles capable of accepting a detachable magazine and with a caliber greater than .22 (including .223/5.56) is limited by 18 U.S.C. § 923(g)(1)(B), § 923(g)(3)(A), § 923(g)(7), and § 926(a).

33) The letter exceeds Melson's authority.

COUNT TWO

(Violation on Prohibition of Consolidation of Records)

34) Paragraphs 1 through 33 are realleged [sic] and incorporated herein by reference.

35) The BATFE is an entity within the Department of Justice.

36) The letter requires reporting of "the records, or any portion thereof, of acquisition and disposition of firearms maintained by Federal firearms licensees."

37) By receiving and retaining such records or portions thereof within the National Tracing Center, including the name and address of the purchaser, BATFE is "consolidating or centralizing," and will continue to consolidate or centralize, such records in violation of Pub.L. 111-117 and Pub.L. 112-10.

WHEREFORE, J&G and Foothills pray that the court:

1) Enter a declaratory judgment that the letter and the Form3310.12: (a)are beyond the scope of Melson's authority under 18 U.S.C. § 923(g)(1)(B), § 923(g)(3)(A), § 923(g)(5)(A), §

923(g)(7), and § 926(a), and contrary to the Consolidated Appropriations Act, 2010, Pub.L. 111-117, 123 Stat. 3034 (2010).

2) Issue preliminary and permanent injunctions requiring, or otherwise compelling, Melson and his officers, agents, and employees, to refrain from initiating any administrative, civil, or criminal actions or proceedings against J&G and Foothills for not submitting information required by the letter to the BATFE, and forthwith to destroy any and all such information already submitted to the BATFE and kept there or disseminated to any other office or agency.

3) Award J&G and Foothills costs, including attorney's fees, pursuant to, *inter alia*, 18 U.S.C. § 924(d) and 28 U.S.C. § 2412.

4) Grant such other and further relief as may be proper.

Respectfully submitted,

J & G SALES, LTD.

FOOTHILLS FIREARMS, LLC

By Counsel

/s/

Richard E. Gardiner

D.C. Bar # 385916

Suite 403

3925 Chain Bridge Road

Fairfax, VA 22030

(703) 352-7276

(703) 359-0938 (fax)

/s/

Stephen P. Halbrook

D.C. Bar # 379799

Suite 403

3925 Chain Bridge Road

Fairfax, VA 22030

(703) 352-7276

(703) 359-0938 (fax)

[23] **The Barbary War**: The war stemmed from the Barbary pirates' attacks upon American merchant shipping in an attempt to extort

ransom for the lives of captured sailors, and ultimately blood money from the United States to avoid further attacks. Before the Treaty of Paris, which granted America's independence from Great Britain, American shipping was protected by France during the Revolutionary years under the Treaty of Alliance (1778–83). Although the treaty does not mention the Barbary States in name, it refers to common enemies between both the U.S. and France, which would include the Barbary States and pirates in general. As such, piracy against American shipping only began to occur after the end of the American Revolution, when the U.S. government lost its protection under the Treaty of Alliance.

INDEX

propaganda, 10, 19, 33, 63, 71, 72, 94, 106, 139, 140

Q

Qur'an, 94, 96, 97, 98, 99, 106, 117, 118, 119, 120, 121

R

Rahman
, Sheik Omar Abdel, 98
recovery act funds, 37
Reliance of the Traveler, 118, 119, 120, 121
Reno
, Janet, 39
Richard Mack, 153
Rio Rico, 15, 17
rip crews, 157
rip-crews, 27
Roll
, John, 46
rule of law, 20, 151

S

Scott Wilson, 30
semi-automatic, 13, 29, 68, 72, 73, 75, 78, 134
serial numbers, 32, 46, 58, 65, 88
Sharia, 94, 95, 96, 97, 106, 117, 118, 120
Sierra La Esmeralda, 17
Sierra Madre Occidental, 17
Sinaloa, 1, 49, 56, 77
Sipsey Street Irregulars, 6, 56, 125
smuggling, 15, 23, 24, 25, 27, 48, 89, 117, 121, 301, 310, 316, 348

socialist, 1, 8, 10, 42, 72, 75, 94, 100, 151
socialists, 134, 136, 137, 141, 154
Southwest Border Initiative, 2, 32, 36, 39, 42, 56, 58, 123
sovereignty, 1, 5, 24, 28, 47, 48, 49, 107, 118, 122
Soviet Union, 9, 71, 79, 80, 83, 88, 100
Spanish, 17, 18, 21, 42, 58, 62, 63, 82
State Department, 78, 83, 87, 115
Stephen Halbrook, 153
STRATFOR.com, 34
Straw Sale, 6
Sunna ahadith, 117
Suspect Gun Database, 55, 59, 60, 62

T

Tampa, 56, 87
tax evasion, 121
TBR
, Tri-Border Region, 114, 115, 116
Tea Party, 25, 26
terror, 89, 94, 105, 107, 108, 116, 120, 154, 349
terrorism, 3, 4, 5, 10, 13, 20, 21, 23, 27, 47, 94, 100, 107, 122, 131, 136, 297, 298, 347, 349, 352
terrorist, 5, 10, 14, 15, 22, 48, 82, 90, 93, 95, 97, 98, 100, 108, 114, 115, 116, 117, 121, 136, 298, 349
terrorists, 1, 9, 15, 16, 25, 27, 80, 88, 90, 101, 106, 107, 120, 121

About the Author...

 Charly was originally trained as a photo-journalist by the US Army Defense Information School during the Viet Nam era in 1971. He spent most of his career as an engineer specializing in robotics, artificial intelligence and analog computer design. He retired (the first time) in 1996 as a Senior Technical Author for Intel Corporation's Microcontroller Division.

Charly has been involved in firearms activism for over two decades, has won numerous awards as a competitive shooter, is a graduate of Gunsite Ranch during the Cooper era and is a member of the first group of twenty instructors to be certified in Arizona as concealed weapons trainers. In the early 1990's he served as the Public Information Officer for the Arizona State Rifle and Pistol association during the Clinton administration's anti-rights assault on firearms owners. Now retired (again) he has also been a gunsmith, a federally licensed Class III firearms dealer and has been a long time Endowment Life Member of the National Rifle Association.

He has authored books and magazine articles on a wide range of diverse subjects including pre-historic archaeology, conservative activism, civil disobedience, computer technology, competitive shooting, antique firearms, ammunition reloading and ballistics.

This is his sixth book in the Warfield Activist series.

WARFIELD PRESS

PRESCOTT, ARIZONA